From a *Whisper* to a RIOT

The Gay Writers Who Crafted an American Literary Tradition

by

Adam W. Burgess, Ph.D.

ACKNOWLEDGEMENTS

Many individuals have contributed their time, resources, and expertise to various areas of this project. I would first like to thank Dr. Ibis Gómez-Vega, from whom I have learned so much, and who has helped me shape and focus every aspect of this project. By sharing with me her exceptional knowledge of queer and minority American literature, I have gained a unique understanding of this period that will continue to inform my future research. Next, I am indebted to Dr. Scott Balcerzak, who helped me begin the process of engaging with complicated theoretical arguments in queer, feminist, and masculinity studies, and whose guidance and encouragement were important in my decision to embrace this project. I am grateful to Dr. Bradley Peters, who offered invaluable feedback in the early stages of this project and who made helpful suggestions for obscure readings and necessary resources. I would also like to thank Dr. Nancy Wingfield, expert in the history of gender and sexuality, who became an inspiration as well as an invaluable resource as I completed a graduate certificate in LGBT Studies. These professors introduced me to a wealth of applicable information both inside and outside of my research area that helped to broaden my perspectives and ultimately produce a stronger and more thorough investigation. Finally, thank you to my spouse, family, friends, and colleagues for their support, as well as those who contributed by reading early (and later) drafts.

DEDICATION

For Jesse

"Love is the right to say: I do and I do and I do..." –Richard Blanco

TABLE OF CONTENTS

CHAPTER 1

THE GENESIS OF A GAY AMERICAN TRADITION

"In the bright light of day their eyes burned with a tenderness against each other, as if to say: now it is done; we have reached the just-beyond; there is no going back to something less; there is no ending. But they knew the time had been too much, that all the time to come would be too much, not for themselves, but for others—for the living and the dead." –Thomas Hal Phillips, *The Bitterweed Path*, p. 312.

In *The History of Sexuality* (1976), Michel Foucault argues that the contemporary

understanding of homosexuality as a distinctive identity rooted in a "quality of sexual

sensibility" was first articulated just before the turn of the twentieth-century (43). Indeed,

nineteenth-century developments in "psychology, jurisprudence, and literature" motivated not

only social and political "controls" of nontraditional sexualities, but also for the creation of a

discourse environment wherein "homosexuality began to speak in its own behalf, to demand that

its legitimacy or 'naturality' be acknowledged" (101). The nineteenth-century, then, created the

language and definitions that twentieth-century writers would begin to use in order to self-

identify, to question, to expand upon, and to redefine sexual identity. This engagement with the

new homosexual "species" would create, in literature, a unique and diverse field. If this new

understanding of homosexuality has its genesis in the nineteenth-century, then why does the

majority of criticism pertaining to gay American literature ignore the first half of the twentieth-century[1]? In the following, I examine the relatively omitted history of gay American literature from 1903 to 1968[2].

In their introduction to *Pages Passed from Hand to Hand* (1997), Mark Mitchell and David Leavitt imagine a nineteenth century homosexual customer urgently searching a bookstore's shelves for stories about love involving same-sex partners. Despite the probable difficulties for readers hoping to find these books on public display, the editors claim that "the surprise . . . is that the books were there all along, if only you had known where to look" (xvii). A similar "surprise" occurs in gay American literature. The overwhelming evidence in criticism pertaining to gay literature would lead readers to believe that the only major works to come out of this tradition began appearing as late as the 1940s, with Truman Capote and Gore Vidal. In fact, there were a number of writers shaping and contributing to the tradition as early as 1903[3]. Gay literature, according to Gregory Woods, "offers . . . a broad range of interest, both in terms of identifiably shared emotions and as a documentary glimpse of 'our' sexual history" (2).

---

[1] Even groundbreaking works of queer theory and literary studies, such as Eve Kosofsky Sedgwick's *Epistemology of the Closet* (1990) and Mark Lilly's *Gay Men's Literature in the Twentieth Century* (1993) focus primarily on European writers, "major writers" (e.g. Henry James, Oscar Wilde) and the *potentially* gay masters (e.g. Herman Melville). In these texts and in similar scholarship, there also tends to be a wide gap between the works of Wilde and Christopher Isherwood, for example.

[2] A notable exception is James Levin's *The Gay Novel in America* (1991) which includes a chapter on early twentieth-century gay American pulp fiction as well as sections devoted to gay writing in the 1950s and 1960s, but even this work ignores the period between 1900 and 1920 and merely glosses the 1920s and 1930s, with Forman Brown's *Better Angel* being the only non-pulp piece mentioned.

[3] Robert Drake's *The Gay Canon: Great Books Every Gay Man Should Read* (Anchor 1998) does an admirable job of presenting a chronological history of gay literature (broadly defined), beginning with 1 Samuel and ending with contemporary texts; however, inclusion of American writers is minimal and often not explicitly homosexual (e.g. Henry David Thoreau and Anne Rice).

Accepting this argument, it is then incumbent upon scholars to acknowledge and examine the full range of that history, particularly those periods, such as the early-twentieth century, which have been neglected but which can and will greatly inform scholarship in the field.

As Mark Lilly argues, "in comparison with the established success, especially in the United States, of studies based on women and race, gay studies are in their infancy" (xii). This makes inquiry into gay literature a pressing concern, and examination of those overlooked but foundational texts, such as Charles Warren Stoddard's *For the Pleasure of His Company* (1903), Edward I. Prime-Stevenson's *Imre: A Memorandum* (1906), Henry Blake Fuller's *Bertram Cope's Year* (1919) and Forman Brown's *Better Angel* (1933) all the more urgent. In addition to identifying influential texts, I will employ methods of historiography and literary studies to distinguish features of early gay literature in America in a way that demonstrates consistency and shared concerns throughout, thus helping to create and define a distinct literary community or tradition.

Gay American literature, as a field of study distinct from queer theory and LGBT studies, is both a simple and complex concept. On its surface, the term indicates any literature written by gay (male) American writers. This inclusive definition is complicated by the question of what it means to be gay, a question that can be asked not only of writers but also of texts[4]. The field has been defined in criticism of poetry, drama, and narrative fiction, as well as literary criticism in

---

[4] As David M. Halperin notes, it is sexual identity that "endows each of us . . . with a personal essence defined (at least in part) in specifically sexual terms; it implies that human beings are individuated at the level of their sexuality, that they . . . belong to different types or kinds of being by virtue of their sexuality" (259). Crucial to my study of early-twentieth-century gay American literature is the fact that each of these narratives has a male protagonist who identifies as homosexual, recognizes himself as an "other," and exists within a text that actively communicates with other gay texts.

general. For example, Ellen Bosman and John P. Bradford argue that "GLBT literature exhibits the same characteristics that all other literature does, but what distinguishes it are sexual and gender orientation or identity and voice" (7). They add that "this identity is so central to the literature that it qualifies these works as a genre." This sentiment is echoed in Robert K. Martin's *The Homosexual Tradition in American Poetry* (1979), in which Martin "considers the extent to which an author's awareness of himself as a homosexual has affected how and what he wrote" (xv). Here he notes a specifically gay identity in literature. In establishing criteria for examining gay poets, such as Walt Whitman, Hart Crane, Allen Ginsberg, and James Merrill, Martin argues that "the sense of a shared sexuality has led many gay writers to develop a particular tradition, involving references to earlier gay writers" and posits that the tradition "formed partly out of a need for communication . . . and partly out of a feeling of exclusion from the traditions of male heterosexual writing" (ibid).

Martin's argument is accurate, but what is important to note in these examples is the distinct distance between the work of Walt Whitman in the mid-nineteenth century and Ginsberg and Merrill in the mid-twentieth[5]. There is significant scholarship devoted to the works of Hart Crane, the only identified gay writer between this significant gap in time; this book aims to advance the discussion by incorporating critical interpretation of a number of significant gay writers publishing gay texts at that time.

Gregory Woods, in his 1990 chapter "Absurd! Ridiculous! Disgusting! Paradox in Poetry by Gay Men," agrees with Bosman and Bradford when he notes that "there is an enormous

---

[5] Other scholarship devoted specifically to American poetry is similarly limited. In his book, *Articulate Flesh: Male Homo-Eroticism & Modern Poetry* (1987), for example, Gregory Woods chooses to focus specifically on five writers, many of whom (Hart Crane, W.H. Auden, and Allen Ginsberg) appear in a significant amount of scholarship.

common space of themes shared by the literatures of gay and straight men" (qtd. in Lilly 176-77); but, he finds something "peculiar" about the gay male's social status: "As with women, blacks, Jews, the working class, so too with gay men: not only are the disadvantaged defined as the Other, but they are forced into the defensive cultural position of having to define *themselves* as such" (184). Once again, the criticism has signified identity as a key to the homosexual literary tradition, though, for Woods, poetry in particular "is the ideal medium for a creativity that liberates." Significantly, however, the book in which this article appears focuses much attention on later gay writers, such as John Rechy and Andrew Holleran, and on European writers, such as Jean Genet and Ronald Firbanks. There is limited discussion of early-twentieth-century gay Americans.

It is not only in poetry that critics have found common strands supporting a gay American literary tradition; a similar case has been made for drama. In an article on Terrence McNally's *Love! Valour! Compassion!* (1994), Ray Schultz begins by discussing Tony Kushner's *Angels in America* (1991) and by questioning the primary concerns of "gay dramatic literature" (96). Schultz is not here coining a term, but instead assuming that gay dramatic literature is an established genre in its own right. While the essay's primary goal is to evaluate issues of class and socioeconomic status in the play, Schultz's analysis posits that in McNally, as in Kushner, "white, straight America is often pitted in opposition to . . . white, gay America" (96). Furthermore, this occurs in the context of a world where heterosexuals are "exerting, arguably, unconscious influence over how these men may classify themselves and each other"

(103)[6]. The gay presence in drama is again presented in opposition to the heterosexual

normative, and identifying as "gay" becomes both a necessity and a problem.

Mark Lilly, in his criticism of Tennessee Williams' *The Glass Menagerie* (1945) and *A Streetcar Named Desire* (1947), argues a similar point. He claims that in both plays Williams is attempting to "subvert the heterosexist culture" by appealing to readers who will have "experienced the same group victimization, social rejection and legal oppression" (153). Lilly aligns himself with previously mentioned literary critics when he identifies that Williams "insists on the possibility of refusing the prevailing norms of society and creating alternative realities" (154); thus, what Woods finds in gay poetry and what Schultz and Lilly see in gay drama, is, first, an awareness of self as homosexual other and, second, a willingness to "use that awareness as part of the subject matter" (Martin 165) of their works, even when that awareness is expressed only through allusion or coded reference (xv)[7].

In addition to American poetry and drama, we also find a gay tradition rooted in the early twentieth-century novels. As Gregory Woods argues, "towards the end of the nineteenth-century, at very roughly the same time that the existence of 'the homosexual' as a distinct type of individual was being definitively established, the novel started to take over from poetry as the best place in which accessibly to express the quotidian realities of homosexual lives" (136).

---

[6] I will comment more on the relationship between race and sexuality as well as masculinity and sexuality later in this book.

[7] In gay fiction, this is commonly expressed through the theme of isolation and loneliness. The narrator of *Imre*, for example, recalls his own moments of "darkness" and "sadness" (29) and remembers being "horrified" and "filled with suicidal guilt and shame" when first realizing his desires for other men. Later, when Oswald and Imre tell each other their personal stories, the narrator juxtaposes the "most brilliant minds and gifts, of intensest [sic] energies . . . scores of pure spirits, deep philosophers, bravest soldiers, highest poets and artists" against "the Race-Homosexual" which "apparently ever would be . . . ignoble, trivial, loathe-some, feeble-souled and feeble-bodied creatures! . . . the very weaklings and rubbish of humanity!" (112).

Woods finds in the fictional narrative that the homosexual is often represented as the negative other. He claims "a man's homosexuality amounts to a tragic flaw . . . from the moment of his rise, he is fated to fall" (275). This may be true for much of the gay pulp fiction of the time, but it is not necessarily the case for all of gay literature. Indeed, gay novelists in the twentieth-century began to "transform the 'mainstream' itself" by coming out and self-asserting, or self-identifying (289). They "ensured that there was an increasing amount of work for the censors to do" as they "began to explore ways of reintegrating the homosexual character into social fictions" (ibid).

Christopher Bram seems to agree, as he posits that "the gay revolution began as a literary revolution" led by figures such as Gore Vidal, Allen Ginsberg, and James Baldwin (ix) who "boldly used their personal experience in their work." Both of these studies, however, demonstrate the same troubling practice of overlooking early-twentieth-century writers and texts. Woods organizes his text by theme, and he notably and appropriately encourages a study of the long-history of a gay literary tradition, beginning with the Geeks and Romans; excluded, however, is discussion of the most influential early gay American works. Prime-Stevenson earns brief mention, but Charles Warren Stoddard, Forman Brown, Henry Blake Fuller, and André Tellier, among others, are completely absent. Similarly, Christopher Bram's *Eminent Outlaws* (2012) is exceptional in its coverage of later twentieth-century gay American literature, but the study essentially reinforces the flawed notion that the gay literary tradition in America began in the 1950s. My work aims to correct this misunderstanding by evaluating gay American literature written and published between 1903 and 1968. My research investigates and explicates upon gay novels, primarily, but I do include Mark Crowley's *The Boys in the Band* (1968) in chapter five as an example of drama written and performed immediately before Stonewall that exhibits the tensions of the period. The play is significantly placed on the cusp of what many refer to as the "gay revolution" and, as such, creates a unique opportunity for historiographic inquiry.

While "there is no consensus at the moment as to [the] scope" of gay men's literature (Lilly xv), the fact is that gay American literature responds to, challenges, avoids, subverts, and sometimes embraces the public definitions of homosexuality at any given time, including what it means to be masculine and male. Whether in poetry, drama, or the novel, the gay American literary tradition is marked by common themes of self-identification, awareness of self-as-other, and a willingness to communicate, openly or in code, about same-sex desire, oftentimes while making reference to earlier gay writers[8]. This is especially true of the foundational texts which, despite their reputation, are not universally tragic or stereotypical in their portrayal of gay men.

A persistent theme in early Gay American novels, for example, is the ability to discover and act upon one's true sexuality while living or traveling abroad. This theme works in much the same way as it does in American Regionalism, which is to say that readers may accept the bizarre or unfamiliar nature of an American work that functions, in this case, not in a particularly peculiar region *inside* the country but, instead, outside of the United States altogether. Although the characters may be American, the perceived threat is neutralized because they act upon their instincts and desires when abroad. This is the case in some of the early texts, such as *Imre* and James Baldwin's *Giovanni's Room* (1956), which may seem surprisingly explicit in their

---

[8] George Chauncey notes, significantly, that "several gay scholars working at the turn of the [twentieth] century sought to construct a gay historical tradition" (283). He refers specifically to a writer, Edward Carpenter, who included exhaustive lists of presumed homosexual writers in his own works as a means for communicating to his gay readers that a history did exist (though Carpenter often used writers such as Melville, whose sexuality is not certain). I will demonstrate a similar practice in the works evaluated for this book.

homosexual themes until one takes into consideration that they are less dangerous to American audiences by virtue of their exotic externality.

Although the accepted contemporary trend has been to study lesbian, gay, bisexual and transgender (LGBT) texts together, this work is more specific in its scope: gay male literature. As such, it is restricted to known homosexual male writers, which eliminates "probable" gay writers who are often studied elsewhere and from a queer theory perspective[9]. It is further limited to the early twentieth-century, specifically works published between 1903 and 1968. The rationale for this timespan begins with an acknowledgment that the first openly gay novel written and published by an openly gay man is Stoddard's *For the Pleasure of His Company*; the closing date, 1968, is selected because it is the year preceding one of the defining moments in queer American history, the Stonewall Riots, after which the landscape of gay studies changes drastically. The two dominant areas of study for gay literature in America are, first, the period that includes and immediately follows the Stonewall Riots and second, the period that deals with and immediately follows the AIDS crisis. These examinations are critical and understandably exhaustive; however, the abundance of attention paid to studies within them further explains why less attention has been given to literature published before these momentous events. I must also stress the necessity of similar scholarship for lesbian, bisexual, and transgender literary studies, although those studies are beyond the scope of this work.

"LGBT" has become a self-assumed umbrella term for the sexual groups who have found it necessary to collaborate and cooperate for political, economic, and social reasons. In the 1950s and 1960s, for instance, gay groups such as the Mattachine Society, and lesbian groups such as

---

[9] Examples of this include Robert Drake's *The Gay Canon* and Jeffrey Meyers's *Homosexuality & Literature 1890-1930* (Athlone 1977).

the Daughters of Bilitis, developed independently to address the concerns of, and advance the causes of, their particular populations (gay men and lesbian women, respectively); however, they also created publications, such as the *Mattachine Review* and *The Ladder*, which not only broadened and made more accessible these conversations, but also encouraged cross-community awareness and paved the way for writers such as James Baldwin, Ann Bannon, Alma Routsong, Jane Rule, John Rechy, and Valerie Taylor to publicly criticize sexual prejudice and to offer "strikingly explicit and appealing representations of same-sex sex, love, and intimacy" (Stein 64). This type of cooperation and synchronistic influence, which would later include "trans activism" and "bisexual activism," helped in the formation of the contemporary "LGBT movement" which supplanted what had previously been highly independent and exclusionary "gay" and "lesbian" movements (186).

Still, a common anti-heteronormativity and a need to cooperate as minority classes does not necessarily signify that each group's history, culture, and goals coincide with those of the other groups. David M. Halperin, in *How to Be Gay* (2012), re-emphasizes the problems that arise from "clustering" LGBT studies when he notes that this approach often results in viewing "the spectrum of minority identities" as simply "a smorgasbord of delectable but insignificant and meaningless variations" (72). There are, in fact, very real differences, and by studying the gay identity in American literature, we avoid problems associated with the "umbrella approach" and we give due and equal attention to each literary tradition in its own right. In other fields, such as history, these movements are underway[10]. In the conclusion to this project, I briefly

---

[10] Excellent examples of historical investigations of gender and sexuality in specific terms include Joanne Meyerowitz's *How Sex Changed* (Harvard 2004), which explores transgender history, as well as Stephen Angelides's *A History of Bisexuality* (U Chicago 2001).

revisit this discussion and offer additional thoughts and suggestions for potential studies in literature.

The second chapter is titled "Convenient (Dis)placement: The Importance of Time and Place." In it, I explore how a text's setting, both temporal and physical, provides potential opportunities for gay men's sexual freedom in early American literature. This theme is effectively located in such works as Prime-Stevenson's *Imre: A Memorandum* (1906), Forman Brown's *Better Angel*, Thomas Hal Phillips's *The Bitterweed Path* (1949), and James Baldwin's *Giovanni's Room*. In Baldwin's work, for example, Richard Tomlinson argues that "the homosexual and expatriate experiences" are intricately related (142). This argument can be applied more broadly as a feature of these early twentieth-century gay texts. Although the writers are American, the exotic and distant settings allow reasonable distance from the "real world," enough to tolerate what would not be accepted in an American setting[11]. With such similarities, one must wonder why some writers, such as James Baldwin for example, have received the critical attention they deserve, while others, such as Phillips and Brown, have not. As Anthony Slide correctly explains, *Better Angel* "is a first-rate, firsthand account that can stand against any contemporary novel dealing with the maturation of any small-town American boy, gay or straight" (33). In analyzing these works together, I hope to demonstrate the necessity of advancing scholarship of the period in general and of the overlooked texts in particular.

In chapter three, "The Power of Pulp Fiction: Constructing & Perpetuating Stereotypes," I explore what is arguably the most popular and, even now, the most influential of gay texts, the pulp novel. As Michael Bronski notes, "gay pulp is not an exact term, and it is used somewhat

---

[11] *Imre* takes place in Hungary and *Giovanni's Room* in Paris. *Better Angel* begins in the United States, but the protagonist's major awakening and formative same-sex sexual experiences happen while he is in Europe.

loosely to refer to a variety of books that had very different origins and markets" (*Pulp Friction* 2). For the purposes of this book, I explore the "dime store novel," or cheap paperback versions of gay pulp fiction, which originated circa 1930. These are the sensation novels that dealt with supposedly "unsavory" topics in a manner that would be deemed unprintable by the major presses and potentially criminal by the U.S. government. Specifically, I will discuss André Tellier's *Twilight Men* (1931), Charles Henri Ford and Parker Tyler's *The Young and Evil* (1933), Charles Jackson's *The Fall of Valor* (1946), and George Sylvester Viereck's *Men into Beasts* (1952). These novels, along with psychoanalytical interpretations of divergent sexualities[12], are largely responsible for the persistent depiction of gay male characters as sick, feminine, and suicidal[13].

These texts also operated as a type of subversive media that created a new language for gay men, one which translated into the culturally-specific as well as the popular discourses, and resulted in a strong, rebellious cultural community. Some locations, like New York City, were particularly receptive to gay pulp novels of this period. As George Chauncey notes, "the early thirties . . . saw book publishers race to satisfy the public's growing interest in the gay scene, for a flurry of gay-themed novels appeared between 1931 and 1934. Several of them depicted New York's gay world" (324). While many of these novels may not merit "high literary" status, they

---

[12]In her critical historiography, *How Sex Changed* (Harvard 2002), Joanne Meyerowitz provides comprehensive historical context for the role that psychology and psychotherapy played in reinforcing negative depictions of non-traditional sexualities. Additionally, Margot Canaday's *The Straight State* (Princeton 2009) advances this discussion by examining how the psychological field significantly influenced politics and the legal (mis)treatment of homosexuals in America during the twentieth century.

[13] In his analysis of *Twilight Men*, for example, Anthony Slide calls the work "tragic and melodramatic" (1), common descriptors for gay pulp fiction.

are significant in that they helped to shape and promulgate popular culture's conversations about homosexuality and homosexual spaces.

In chapter four, "Intertextuality: The Self, The Other, and Coded Community," I explore another topic mentioned previously, communication. Beginning in the 1940s, with the advent of McCarthyism and the "Lavender Scare," gay American writers were placed in a precarious position as the United States government began to fear that the abuses of communism abroad were taking hold domestically, and they began to actively search for someone to blame. Homosexuals, rather than communists, became prime targets because they were supposedly easier to identify and could be scapegoated as "security threats." This environment created a backlash in cultural communities which had been almost shockingly accepting of homosexual literature, art, and lifestyles during the interwar periods (Johnson 53-55). Soon, many gay writers, such as Gore Vidal and Truman Capote, would find it necessary to downplay the homosexual themes in their works. Fortunately, gay writers before them had already established a willingness to communicate with other gay readers and writers by addressing gay themes through a system of codes and references[14].

In *For the Pleasure of His Company*, for example, Charles Warren Stoddard avoids communicating homosexual themes overtly, but he certainly uses codes to get his point across. Take for example the scene where Paul Clitheroe admits to Miss Juno that most girls have no "form nor features, nor tint nor texture, nor anything that appeals to a fellow of taste and sentiment" (92) and concludes with the declaration that "they are not [his girls], and not one of

---

[14] David Bergman, in *Gaiety Transfigured* (1991), posits two strategies gay writers use for representing homosexuality in their works: the first is a process of normalizing as found in Radclyffe Hall's *The Well of Loneliness* (1928); the second is a strategy of radical subversion, as found in the works of Oscar Wilde (26-27).

them ever will be" if he can help it. This is one of the more obvious codes, but others include descriptive words that are applied to Clitheroe throughout the book, such as "pretty," "dainty," and "very feminine" (130), all of which signify to the reader if not homosexuality, at least femininity. Both coded language and a willingness to communicate with a self-aware discourse community of gay writers are also demonstrated in *Imre* and *Bertram Cope's Year* (1919), and would be further developed in later works such as Forman Brown's *Better Angel*.

The fifth chapter, "Resistance and Acquiescence: Problems of Gender and Sexuality" will act as counterbalance to chapter three. In it, I investigate Edward Prime-Stevenson's *Imre*, Robert Scully's *A Scarlet Pansy* (1932), Sanford Friedman's *Totempole* (1965) and Mart Crowley's *The Boys in the Band* (1968), to argue that in the gay literary tradition, concepts of gender and sexuality, including masculinity, are complicated, fluid, and considerably more complex than they are made to appear in the popular pulp novels.

Despite obvious inaccuracies, there is historical precedent for stereotyping gay men as essentially feminine. In Robert Aldrich's important European historiography[15], he explains how imperialists and colonizers often depicted the colonized culture's men as effeminate in order to justify their dominance over, and sexual relations with, indigenous men[16]. Additionally, Aldrich incorporates the letters and journals of gay writers, such as André Gide and E.M. Forster, to support the claim that white European males felt a sense of masculine superiority to native males

---

[15] *Colonialism and Homosexuality.* London: Routledge, 2003. Print.

[16] Eve Kosofsky Sedgwick helpfully advances this discussion in "Queer and Now" when she emphasizes the relationship between "race, ethnicity, postcolonial nationality . . . and other identity-constituting, identity-fracturing discourses" (8).

in Africa, Asia, Australia and the Middle East[17]. This practice of feminizing homosexual men,

especially the passive/receptive or submissive partner, ever-present in political, imperial, and

social discourse[18], has become a persistent theme in early American gay literature, as will be

made clearer in chapter three outlined above. My analysis of the literature, however, will reveal

that there is in fact a surprising range of masculinity represented in the fictive male-male

relationships.

Rather than simply reinforcing the categorization of gay men as feminine or demanding

that male-male relationships require one male/active and one female/passive partner, thereby

reinforcing socially-constructed gender roles, these texts present a wide range of possibilities for

same-sex sexual and romantic relationships. Whereas popular pulp fiction often reinforces

cultural expectations of what it means to be gay, the less popular and typically more literary of

these early gay texts seem to anticipate later feminist and gay rights movements by making the

personal political. In this case, that means crafting queer representations that are more realistic

than sensational[19]. Thus, early twentieth-century gay American literature is in many ways

"subverting and displacing those naturalized and reified notions of gender that support masculine

hegemony and heterosexist power" (Butler 46) by refusing to conform to gender expectations.

---

[17] Victor J. Seidler also discusses masculine "control as domination" in his book, *Rediscovering Masculinity: Reason, Language and Sexuality* (Routledge 1989).

[18] We can find further examples in other European and American cultural phenomena, such as the "Pink Triangle" that gay men were forced to wear while under Nazi occupation, or the "Lavender Scare" element of the McCarthy era. These stereotypically soft colors are applied to gay men in public spheres as a way of "sissifying" and feminizing them.

[19] Rafael Perez-Torres explores this further in his piece, "The Ambiguous Outlaw: John Rechy and Complicitous Homotextuality" (Murphy 1994). Torres finds that Rechy learned lessons from the feminist movement. In this chapter, I explore how many early texts anticipated liberation through use of realistic personalities, relationships, etc.

Lastly, in chapter six I conclude with a general summary of the project and its findings. In addition, I address pending questions, including those which arose over the course of the project. I briefly mention and contextualize the changes that began to occur in the decade before Stonewall in order to offer a final argument that it was the first half of the twentieth-century which established the cultural and creative precedent for the revolutionary works that would come out of the late 1950s. Essentially, this project is an attempt to demonstrates that the history and tradition of gay literature in America is much longer and much richer than has been accepted to date. As Morris B. Kaplan writes in *Sodom on the Thames: Sex, Love, and Scandal in Wilde Times* (2005):

> Some recent queer theory and feminist thought have insisted on the importance of the intersection between sexuality and gender and of both with other social forms such as race, class, religion, ethnicity, and nationality. Storytelling allows us to go beyond listing these categories to show how they mutually inflect each other in specific situations. (265)

Kaplan is justifying his decision to write history in narrative episodes; however, this justification can be applied effectively to the study of literature (storytelling) rather than the crafting of it. This book hopes to fulfill Kaplan's promise by acting as a literary historiography, one which investigates texts in a certain context and identifies the shared features that act as foundation for a gay tradition within the larger American literary period in which these texts are found.

There are many works that examine gay American writing in the twentieth-century; however, there is limited scholarship dealing with the early examples explored in the following chapters. The output of texts by gay American writers begins before the twentieth-century, certainly, but grows rapidly in scale and clarity of purpose after the Whitman years, beginning especially with Edward I. Stevenson's *Imre: A Memorandum* (1906) and *The Intersexes* (1910). Travel-writer Charles Warren Stoddard also published gay fiction, such as *For the Pleasure of*

His Company with smaller presses, and these early novels were soon followed by those of Henry Blake Fuller and Forman Brown. These formative texts ultimately gave rise to a homosexual literary renaissance in the 1940-1960s, led by Gore Vidal, Truman Capote, and Tennessee Williams. The earlier texts, which were certainly known to mid-century writers, have been largely neglected in scholarship. To discuss the tradition of gay male writing in twentieth-century America, it is necessary to reclaim these earliest examples[20].

---

[20] Again, it should be noted that certain works, such as *The Columbia Anthology of Gay Literature* (Fone 1998), do include and recognize the works of writers I intend to discuss (e.g. Edward I. Prime-Stevenson and Charles Warren Stoddard); however meaningful and comprehensive scholarship on these writers and texts is lacking.

CHAPTER 2

CONVENIENT (DIS)PLACEMENT: THE IMPORTANCE OF TIME AND PLACE

"I met with a mass of serious studies, German, Italian, French, English, from the chief European specialists and theorists on the . . . topic: many of them with quite other views than those of my well-meaning but far too conclusive Yankee doctor." –E. I. Prime-Stevenson, *Imre*, p. 96

In the early twentieth-century, if an American writer, homosexual or otherwise, wanted to

publish a "homosexual novel," there were few avenues for doing so in an open and legal fashion.

The first option might have been to ensure that the story was a didactic one that ultimately

"taught" the reader homosexuality was wrong, dangerous, or demented; hence the many

examples of gay novels whose homosexual characters are either reformed or killed. The other

option was to distance the story from the recognizable United States, to make the "homosexual

problem" something outlandish and external, a thing which might happen, but not here. In most

cases, this meant setting the story in another country; or, in rarer circumstances, it meant

distancing the story from the contemporary audience's place in time[1]. These geographic and

temporal distances allowed American readers to feel safe, if not comfortable, reading typically

taboo subjects because of the psychological buffer created between the fictive setting and most

---

[1] In some cases, authors have done both to great acclaim. We might consider the overwhelming popularity of certain gay historical fiction, such as Mary Renault's novels about ancient Greece. As Norman W. Jones writes, "the novels focus on Alexander's romances with men" and "they continue to be popular among lesbian and gay readers" (72), despite the fact that Renault's first gay-themed novel was published in 1956, more than a half-century ago.

readers' actual worlds and life experiences. It should be noted that many of the texts to be discussed in this chapter were written and published during the modernist period, and one of the main themes in American modernism is the expatriate. Daniel Katz (2007) argues that "the association of modernism with expatriation and exile is venerable to the point of being a cliché" (1); nevertheless, the rationale for gay writers to expatriate, or describe their sense of exile, should be understood on two levels: first, in fitting with the American modernist movement of the period; and second, as a *necessary* function rather than an aesthetic one, such as might be the case for writers like Ernest Hemingway and F. Scott Fitzgerald.

We might compare this phenomenon to what science-fiction or fantasy writers achieve; their stories explore some of the most debated and contested ideas successfully because they need not rely on a recognizable reality nor an identifiable cultural experience. In American literature, we might also consider works such as Charlotte Perkins Gilman's *Herland* (1915), for example, which offers a close examination and critique of traditional gender roles by removing American male characters to a distant, unidentifiable community where only women live and rule. Kate Chopin also succeeded in publishing literature with provocative and taboo themes, such as female sexuality and suicide, by virtue of her "Creoleness." She set her stories in a region that seemed distant and exotic to the majority of readers and were therefore fantastical enough to avoid being perceived as a direct threat to contemporary mores.

In early twentieth-century gay American literature, this distancing became a common practice. Indeed, Mae G. Henderson, paraphrasing Jacob Stockinger, notes that "voyage and travel are clearly important structuring tropes in the expatriation novel, but . . . these same tropes are also classic topoi in what [Stockinger] describes as 'homotextuality,' that is to say, the homosexual text" (316). Indeed, these tropes allowed writers such as Edward Prime-Stevenson,

Forman Brown, James Baldwin, and Thomas Hal Phillips to discuss homosexuality much more openly and honestly than had been previously allowed, and oftentimes in positive terms. This treatment was blatantly opposed to what was acceptable of gay-themed narratives being published at the time. In *Playing the Game* (1977), Roger Austen compares two novels, James Baldwin's *Giovanni's Room* (1956) and William Talsman's *The Gaudy Image* (1958); the first of these is set in France while the second is set in the United States. Although "both Talsman and Baldwin have a gift for lyrical evocation" (153), writes Austen, Talsman disrupts conventions in two important and unacceptable ways: first, the novel is "dreamy" and positive, as opposed to Baldwin's more acceptable moody, self-conscious tone; second, it takes place in the United States. The second slight is, I argue, the more critical because, as will become clearer throughout this chapter, although Baldwin's novel is not necessarily the most hopeful or uplifting, others in this tradition, such as *Imre* and *Better Angel,* manage to conclude with some degree of happiness and satisfaction for the main character(s). To begin this discussion of American homosexuality distanced by time or space, I turn to Edward Irenaeus Prime-Stevenson's *Imre.*

Prime-Stevenson sets *Imre* in Crimea. This location creates an automatic geographic distance[1] from the American audience, which is in itself important to the success and reception of the piece. This also allows for two additional factors to be incorporated into the story: first, an element of exoticism that heightens the otherwise abrupt and hyper-masculine[2] romance between the two main characters; and second, a proximity to the more progressive psychological and

---

[1] In *Colonialism and Homosexuality* (2003), Robert Aldrich notes that "homosexually inclined writers . . . were drawn overseas, and traces of their experiences (or fantasies) appear in both their lives and works" (106).

[2] Chapter five is devoted to depictions and interpretations of masculinity in these early-twentieth century gay American texts, and *Imre* is a primary example.

philosophical European opinions about homosexuality at the time, examples of which are given throughout the story in a style that verges on Platonic dialogue. Interestingly, the complexity of the distance Prime-Stevenson creates is not limited purely to the fictive world but extends into meta-fictive and actual realities as well. As James J. Gifford remarks in his introduction to the Broadview edition, "[*Imre*] is ostensibly written by Oswald, who sends the book to Xavier Mayne to edit, who in turn is the cover for Edward Prime-Stevenson—an intriguing subterfuge" (Prime-Stevenson 20). Ingenious, indeed, and it sets the expectation of distance-as-safety for these foundational texts in an emerging tradition. The first factor created by the extra-American setting, exoticism, functions in two ways: first, in its purest form as a location that is other, distant, and unrecognizable for most American readers; second, in its being set during wartime. One of the two main characters, a military officer, necessarily interacts with other soldiers both in martial and civilian settings; this amplifies the general distance with a secondary component.

As Gifford notes, "the choice of Budapest as the setting for *Imre* is inspired" (18). He elaborates to explain that Prime-Stevenson had been to the region many times and was thus intimately familiar with it. Verisimilitude may be of some importance to the success of a literary work, but the brilliant choice of setting is not limited to the fact that Prime-Stevenson selected a place with which he was familiar; this is, after all, a creative work, and most of his readers would not know, or need to know, too many facts about the city itself. Indeed, Prime-Stevenson, though describing the city landscape in excellent and accurate detail, still attempts to disguise it by changing the names of places. Budapest, for example, is called Szent-Istvánhely. Distancing the setting is a type of mask that Prime-Stevenson places on this work, just as Prime-Stevenson masked his own name under a pseudonym (Xavier Mayne) and then again under the narrator's name, Oswald. It should come as no surprise, then, that the names of people and places within the narrative are also masked. Indeed, "the mask" is a common trope in gay fiction, and one

which is explored thoroughly in *Imre*, beginning with the first chapter, titled, appropriately,

"Masks." The mask not only acts as a rhetorical shield, but it also aids in perpetuating the idea of

the exotic.

An excellent example of Prime-Stevenson's efforts to create distance by establishing and

elevating the exotic nature of his masked setting comes at the very beginning of the first chapter,

when Oswald meets Imre. The young soldier is described as beautiful, but of the type that is

somehow characteristic of this particular region. He is "out of the ordinary" only to someone

who is unfamiliar with the people of this area:

> I remember that I had a swift, general impression that my neighbor was of no ordinary
> beauty of physique and elegance of bearing, even in a land where such matters are normal
> details of personality. And somehow it was also borne in upon me promptly that his
> mood was rather like mine [. . .] a face that was withal strikingly a temperamental face,
> as ever is bent toward friend or stranger. And it was a Magyar voice, that
> characteristically seductive thing in the seductive race. (36)

In this passage, Prime-Stevenson establishes three important themes: first, that the Magyar race

itself is idealized; second, that Imre, a Magyar, is even more strikingly attractive than the

stereotypically beautiful race of which he is a member; and third, that there is some unspoken

similarity between the two men, which Oswald describes here only as a "mood."

To the first point, Prime-Stevenson is reinforcing, or perhaps relying on, a longstanding

tradition of romanticizing the exotic other. Oswald, as the displaced American, sees in Imre a

beauty that is only partly physical; the principal attraction is actually the result of Oswald's

romanticizing Hungarian men in general. Robert Aldrich, in his study of nineteenth-century

colonialist writers, notes that "the world overseas, with latitude provided by travel and the

tolerant mores of 'native' populations, afforded opportunities for portrayals of sexual desires and behaviors considered reprobate in Europe" (106), or, in this case, the even more Victorian-

minded United States. This initial description of Imre reveals an attitude that, perhaps

unconsciously, reflects the "other as exotic" mentality. This perception is reinforced throughout

the novel, as when Oswald later describes listening to Imre speak in such a way as to equate

Imre's common vernacular with the masterful poems and dramas of some of history's greatest

writers and orators:

> Imre was a Magyar, one of a race in which sentimental eloquence is always lurking in the
> blood, even to a poetic passion in verbal utterance that is often out of all measure with the
> mere formal education of a man or a woman. He was a Hungarian: which means among
> other things that a cowherd who cannot write his name, and who does not know where
> London is, can be overheard making love to his sweetheart, or lamenting the loss of his
> mother, in language that is almost of Homeric beauty [. . .] Imre had his full share of
> Magyarism of temperament, and of its impromptu eloquence, taking the place of much of
> a literal acquaintance with Dante, Shakespeare, Goethe, and all the rhetorical and literary
> Parnassus in general. (55)

Thus, Prime-Stevenson again elevates a particular race to heightened proportions and then

situates the love-interest, Imre, at the pinnacle of that romantic apex. The motive is to persuade

the reader that Imre is a worthy love-interest for the protagonist; however, Prime-Stevenson,

through Oswald, relies on exoticism and distance, the American romanticizing the other, to

create a space which allows for this kind of love, a homosexual one, to exist. What Henry James

or Herman Melville[3] might allude to, Prime-Stevenson makes explicit.

There are two other instances of language being used to demonstrate distance while also

advancing the romance between Oswald and Imre. The first occurs near the end of the first

section, just after the two protagonists have come close to discovering the truth about the other,

---

[3] Indeed, in *Glances Backward* (2007) James Gifford draws a comparison between Melville's
"fraternity of feeling" and Prime-Stevenson's "friendship which is love, love which is
friendship" (359), with an important distinction that Melville's feelings for Hawthorne, or any
other man, may never truly be known because they were so carefully concealed.

then retreat. Oswald and Imre share a joke which the reader can only witness without comprehending because, as Oswald puts it, "there is no need of my writing out here a piece of humor not transferable with the least *espirit* into English, though mighty funny in Magyar" (68). This scene satisfies two important goals: it reinforces, just before the section break, the significant distance between the fictive world and the English-readers' own; and, it creates a bond between Oswald and Imre, a language they may share that is secret and untranslatable. Although the result of the conversation creates some suspicion and tension between the two men, the subject of their homosexuality having come close to being broached, this shared joke in a shared language reminds them, and the reader, of their communal "mood" which Oswald first noticed in Imre at the start of the narrative.

The second example comes much later, in the third and final section, and is important in similar ways, which is to say that it is located at an opportune moment in the narrative and it romanticizes the possibilities to be found in foreign languages, elevating once again the exotic non-American and reinforcing the importance of an expatriate setting. In this example, which follows Oswald's coming out story but precedes Imre's, the language difference is expressed in epistolary form, explained to the reader by Oswald as follows: "I have neglected to mention that the second person of intimate Magyar address, the "thou" and "thee," was used in these epistles of Imre, in my answers, with the same instinctiveness that had brought it to our lips on that evening in the Z. park" (108). Oswald reveals that he and Imre are addressing each other informally, or intimately, a possibility not available in the English language, as the English "you" does not differentiate in the same way. Oswald notes that there is "a kind of serious symbolism" in their choice of address, "as well as intimate sweetness" (ibid).

Thus, by setting the story in another country and by exploring the unique attributes of that country, such as its language, Prime-Stevenson, through his narrator, fulfills the promise laid out early in the narrative and in that first description of Imre: to romanticize the other, to advance Imre as the symbol of that romanticized other, and to explore a shared understanding between the two homosexual men which comes to fruition only after much discourse and, especially, two lengthy monologues from each character to the other, expressing their coming out stories. The displaced setting, then, not only acts as a mask that provides opportunity for honesty, but it also allows for Oswald and Imre's relationship to develop naturally from the expected or acceptable "homosocial" type that we find amply represented in literature of the period, to the fully romantic type, *because* of an exoticism which they share. I use the term homosocial as informed by Eve Kosofsky Sedgwick's treatment of it in her important study, *Between Men: English Literature and Male Homosocial Desire* (1985); specifically, I mean it as a point on a continuum of sexuality which allows for or perhaps even leads to homosexuality, but which for various reasons, primarily homophobia, many authors limited to the realm of "male bonding" (1). Said homophobia is located in Oswald's and Imre's deep fear of revealing their sexual/romantic interests to the other because of their past experiences which have been negative. Considering that "male bonding" or "manly love" were essential crutches in male homosexual literature, it becomes clear that Prime-Stevenson understood, at least implicitly, this continuum (which Sedgwick would eventually identify and problematize eighty years later) and used it to subvert expectations and provide to his readers a "happy" alternative.

The location also allows for the second major feature, the didactic treatment of homosexuality as a concept and identity, to be explored. As James Gifford aptly argues, Prime-Stevenson "writes two stories" within *Imre*, "one for the heterosexual reader, and one for the homosexual" (115). For both sets, he delivers a positive depiction of a romantic homosexual relationship, one which ends happily, as well as a discourse on scientific, religious, and moral theories pertaining to homosexuality. Mathew J. Livesey expresses the importance of this dual-function, as well as *Imre*'s role as model for this strategy, when he writes:

> Prime-Stevenson presents a special case, or rather represents a particular class of writers who were engaged in creating the theory of homosexuality as they practiced the narrative of the homosexual experience. Thus, the narrative possibilities afforded homosexual experience through the agency of the theoretical models being advanced at the time were of primary importance to early gay writers, for in the pages of the medical treatise were to be found the elements of representation of the gay experience. (76)

For readers "in the know," much of the sexological information would doubtless be familiar; nevertheless, interwoven as it is into an otherwise literary romance, the significance of Prime-Stevenson's arguments become both more palatable and more effective. James Wilper notes that "for constructing affirmative identities and mapping out relations between men, sexology proves to be insufficient" (52). *Imre* is an excellent example of a narrative that does "turn to history and the arts . . . to self-confidently historicize love between men, argue its cultural legitimacy, and thus the authenticity of this love" (ibid). Prime-Stevenson demonstrates his ethos through an awareness of the important sexological positions on homosexuality, but the true achievement is in his passionate rebuttal to any indication that homosexuality might be a disease, an evil, a disorder or the like. Most importantly, the setting again allows for Prime-Stevenson, through Oswald, to explore the latest and most relevant information about homosexuality, comparing views from sexologists in America and Europe, with the United States always playing the part of antagonist: outdated, backward, and old-fashioned.

An excellent example of this function, which combines sexology's tendency to classify with the author's desire to create a work of art, occurs in the first section, "Masks." Oswald and

Imre are discussing clothes and physical beauty when Oswald compliments Imre on his extraordinary physical appearance. Imre, somehow unaware of his attractiveness, or at least feigning such, asks Oswald to confirm that he, Imre, is "specially [sic] good-looking" (60). Oswald, rather than simply responding in the affirmative, tells Imre that he can "draft . . . a kind of technical schedule . . . stating how and why you are – not repulsive" (ibid) and adds to this a "diagnosis" or "memorandum and guidebook of Imre's emotional topography" (61). Thus, if the title of the book were not enough to reveal the secondary motive for the novel, it is surely made clear by the narrator's explanation: the story that is to follow is indeed a case study, such as sexologists had been performing on the homosexual. In this instance, the study is of one particular man, Imre. Prime-Stevenson is adapting the method of popular scientific writing used to "explain" the homosexual condition in order to advance his own theory, which is that a homosexual man is "simply what [he is] born! – a complete human being" (95).

These two moments are essential to, first, establishing the general structure of the book's narrative argument and, second, clarifying the narrator's stance about homosexuality, which is more progressive and accepting than even the more progressive European sexologists' theories at the time[4]. Neither would work in an American setting, however, as the reception of popular and academic/medical audiences would likely be confused at best, and at worst, contemptable.

---

[4] Alfred Kinsey's *Sexual Behavior in the Human Male* would not be published in America until 1948. After that, the arguments that "a wide variation in sexual behaviors was normal" and that advancing the rights of sexual minorities would also benefit the majority, began to gain support (Herzog 149). In Europe, however, prominent nineteenth-century sexologists, such as Richard von Krafft-Ebing, Havelock Ellis, and Edward Carpenter had already begun to "carefully assemble" what Michel Foucault calls "a great archive of the pleasures of sex" (63). These European pioneers, "thus began to keep an indefinite record of . . . people's pleasures" (64) and were well-ahead of their American contemporaries in attempts to understand homosexual individuals.

Prime-Stevenson makes this point clear when his narrator places heavy censure on an American psychologist who "spoke of [homosexuals] as simply – diseased. 'Curable,' absolutely 'curable'" (91). He compares this American doctor to the "serious studies" of European specialists "with quite other views than those of my well-meaning but far too conclusive Yankee doctor" (96) and later adds that one Viennese doctor in particular, whom Imre had consulted, "was much wiser . . . than [the] American theorist" (118). The American doctor, we learn, had suggested that Oswald marry a woman and be cured, whereas the Viennese doctor, possibly a fictive stand-in for von Krafft-Ebing, "warn[ed] him away from despising himself: from thinking himself alone, and a sexual pariah; from over-morbid sufferings; from that bitterness and despair which year by year all over the world can explain, in hundreds of cases, the depressed lives, the lonely existences" of homosexual men (118-119).

Clearly, setting the story in Europe, and especially in a place like Budapest which, Gifford notes, was "a popular gay cruising site" (35), satisfies the first necessity for a gay American novel in the early twentieth-century: distance. It also satisfies the second function of this particular text, which is to advance a theory-based argument for understanding and treating homosexuality as naturally occurring and with a potential for satisfying romantic outcomes. As will be discussed in a later chapter, however, the ability to achieve "normalcy" as a homosexual man and lover, according to Prime-Stevenson, came with certain caveats of masculinity[5]. Interestingly, while other novels of this period also find avenues for allowing their characters to achieve self-acceptance and happiness in homosexual relationships, they do not do so in the same way, nor with the same stipulations of conforming to one particular gender role.

---

[5] Masculinities in gay fiction will be explored in more detail in chapter five.

As with most of the texts explored in this book, critical study for *Better Angel* is severely lacking. One notable entry, however, is found in Anthony Slide's guide, *Lost Gay Novels* (2003). Slide writes that "*Better Angel* is one of the most enlightened gay novels of the first half of the twentieth century" (126), a sentiment with which I agree and aim to elaborate on in this and later chapters. *Better Angel* was originally published by Forman Brown in 1933, under the pseudonym Richard Meeker. Although there are significant differences between the publication histories of these two texts (*Imre* was published by a small, private press in France and *Better Angel* was published in the United States with a larger but traditionally pulp-oriented press), the narratives' similarities are striking. Brown's novel is similar to *Imre* in three important ways: first, its protagonist and other main characters are homosexual; second, these homosexual characters are for all intents and purposes healthy, even happy, at the end; and third, an essential portion of the novel, the true coming-of-age segment, takes place outside of the United States, with various other displacements, less distant, occurring throughout. According to Hubert Kennedy, the book was successful enough to receive two hardback printings in the 1930s, followed by a paperback in the 1950s, which was printed under a different title (*Torment*) but still pseudonymously. It was that edition which received its first major review, written by Richard Meyer and printed in the iconic *Mattachine Review* (Kennedy par. 2).

In that review, Meyer critiques the book with somewhat of a double-edged compliment. He states, first, that the narrative's protagonist, Kurt Gray, is "perhaps the healthiest homosexual in print" (ibid); this praise is undercut, however, with a common and prejudiced response to gay fiction that predestines gay characters to doomed fates. Meyer writes of the two lovers' outcome, "I wouldn't bet that they lived happily ever after" (ibid); this pessimistic verdict comes despite the fact that, by all narrative accounts, the two men are indeed happy and on a path toward permanent, mutually-desired monogamy and openly expressed love at the end of the tale. This calls attention to another similarity between *Imre* and *Better Angel*, which is that both titles received generally fair criticism, even, surprisingly, some praise; and yet they also suffered the same judgments that became almost cliché in criticism of gay fiction during the early twentieth-century. In his contemporary review of *Imre*, published just a year after the release of the book, Marc-André Raffalovich writes in *Chronique de l'unisexualité* that readers should come to the book with an open mind and, if the reader is "not a dark and ignorant persecutor of his nonconformist brothers" then he may find much value in the book (qtd in *Imre* 187); yet, following further praise about the virtues of the two main characters, Raffalovich cannot help but add, "even in allowing the truth of the confessions . . . even allowing that their liaison will be lasting and happy, the reader without prejudices . . . asks himself if it's not a perversion of celestial love to find the supreme friend in a man, a deviation from the love of man for God" (ibid).

These texts' positive characteristics were beyond simply unexpected for most audiences, gay and straight alike. Indeed, they were so far beyond the expected that they may have created some degree of cognitive dissonance in the reader. It is this dissonance to which James Levin is referring when he suggests, "perhaps it is this very wholesomeness which caused [*Better Angel*] to be seen as less than realistic in a period when few gays thought well of themselves" (47). After all, the homosexual, in science, government, and religion, was being perpetually described as, at best, a biological victim and, at worst, a dangerous criminal. *Better Angel*, like *Imre*, attempts to subvert these stereotypes and, despite partisan criticisms borne of a prejudicial culture, it succeeds.

We find this success, for example, in the fact that the main character is open about his homosexuality. He is able to identify, describe, and eventually accept it. Another way in which *Better Angel* successfully subverts cultural assumptions of the time period is in the physical and mental health and, especially, the "wholesome" decorum of its main character Kurt Gray. Each of these factors is made possible, however, through the narrative technique of displacement. Without Kurt's leaving home for college, graduate school, and Europe, respectively, he would not have had the opportunities or life experiences that ultimately allow him to define himself and make the important final choice as to how he would live his life: behind the mask (a reoccurring symbol in the book) or openly.

These successes come not without valid concerns, however. As noted in *The Gay and Lesbian Literary Heritage* (1995), "*Better Angel* can nonetheless allow Kurt and David no more than a 'secret' relationship, and one achieved only in opposition to any homosexual subculture, which it sees as a 'flayed and slightly nauseous society of *les hommes-femmes*'" (Summers 33). So, while Brown's characters find love and happiness within the fictive world the narrator creates, stereotypes about homosexuals are perpetuated for the sake of breaking them.

Better Angel functions as a bildungsroman in which the main character comes-of-age over the course of the narrative. In this case, the text allows readers, possibly for the first time, to witness a slow but full "coming out" process for its main character. Kurt Gray is a child when he is first introduced to the reader. He is described as "thirteen years old, but . . . he seemed still a little boy" (3). This observation is followed by a description that adds credence to the idea that Kurt is an innocent, a trope that will be revisited throughout the narrative. It is this innocence which supports the idea that Kurt is wholesome, even as he becomes a man, studies abroad, and ultimately finds a career. His personality, his opinion of an "ideal" love, and his lifestyle are often contrasted against the lives of more promiscuous characters, including his two primary

homosexual love interests, his bisexual European companion, and his best childhood friend who

becomes divorced soon after she marries. These comparisons are crucial to the success of the

story because they encourage readers to reassess their opinions of what it means to be

homosexual and to encourage the idea that there is, in fact, more than one type.

These comparisons are made possible by the fact that Kurt leaves the United States, after

college, to embark on a European art tour where he will study the great masters and complete his

own graduate portfolio. Taking Kurt out of the immediate setting of 1930s New York City,

where his friends remain, allows the contrasts to become even clearer. In addition, the

impression of Europe is that it is more progressive, a place where young men can acceptably

explore and come-of-age. In the United States, for example, Kurt is taught by his religious

leaders and his father that one must be ashamed of one's body and avoid all sexual sins, such as

masturbation. After his first experiences with masturbation, Kurt is mainly confused and perhaps

a bit afraid; however, he soon learns that his religion considers the action an "insidious vice . . .

fatal to the body and mind" (46). His father adds misplaced praise to this interpretation when he

tells Kurt, "playing with yourself is bad business. I'm glad you're a clean boy" (ibid). The body

shaming and sexual confusion begin when he is just a teenager, soon after Kurt admits to himself

that "all his life he had been pretending to things he was not, in order to simplify the task of

living" (58). This pretending[6] and Kurt's inability, or unwillingness, to maintain it, assist in his

---

[6] The idea of pretending is immediately followed by a symbol of the mask, which Prime-Stevenson and others also utilize, and which Forman Brown will employ throughout the narrative. Judith Butler writes insightfully on Jacques Lacan's interpretation of the female masquerade as it pertains to the concept of "lack"; however, the masquerade can be aptly applied to the gay man. Butler states, "masquerade suggests that there is a 'being' or ontological specification of femininity prior to the masquerade, a feminine desire or demand that is masked and capable of disclosure" (64). This explanation is steeped in gender theory; however, I will

decision[7] to first leave home for college, then leave the country for freer opportunity. He is not like his friend and love-interest Derry, in whom Kurt admires the "something certain" (65) which he himself, before traveling abroad, lacks.

The first time that Kurt expresses his desire to leave the United States is after he moves from Michigan to New York and begins a correspondence with David, the man who will eventually become his life partner. Ironically, Kurt muses about "how little difference place seemed to make" (108) while he and his friends are separated. After all, in letters to his friends back home, nothing seems to have changed. However, David hints at fantasies of taking Kurt away "to some distant and exotic rendezvous," which Kurt receives happily, like "a fictional heroine" (109). The seeds of travel, escape, and, ultimately, growth, which had been hindered by his remaining in the United States, even at a distance from his former life, are planted. It is not until after Kurt fulfills his desire to leave that he will begin to truly understand himself and his ideal place in the world. The promise of this happiness-in-travel arrives with the spring, when Kurt discovers that he has received a scholarship to Europe and thus an offer for "freedom such as he had never known" (133).

---

consider masquerade as it pertains to male-male sexual desire, which we must separate from gender (note: gender will be explored in a later chapter on gay masculinities). It suffices to say, for now, that the mask in gay men's literature functions in a similar fashion as explained by Butler vis-à-vis Lacan. In this case, a gay man feels he must appear as (perform) something he is not in order to function as "normal." This is one of the most important symbols in gay literature.

[7] The decision is also aided by Kurt's extensive reading of European sexology. The narrator explains that Kurt "had read for the first time the new psychology – Brill, Jung, Freud, Ellis, Carpenter; he had discovered Wedekind. From them he learned that his sin and Derry's was not the unique sort he had believed it to be. There were others, it seemed (at least in Europe there were) of his sort" (84-85). Like the symbol of the mask, many early-twentieth-century gay American texts explicitly referenced European psychology, as will be further discussed in the next chapter.

Before breaking away and discovering this freedom, Kurt must face a most difficult

challenge: "coming out" to Chloe, the woman who has been his best friend and who is in love

with him. Just days before Kurt is to leave for Europe, Chloe divorces her husband, telling him

that she loves Kurt instead. Chloe then visits Kurt and offers "to do something" for him, by

which she means, take his virginity (140). After the attempt, which is unsuccessful, Kurt's

reaction seems to set the stage for a necessary exit from the life he had been living:

> [Her lips] fastened upon his own, and something in him went cold and rigid. What was this?
> A kiss? This shame—this burning shame? Would it never end? . . . What did she think of
> him now? He could have possessed her completely, and he had felt only helpless dismay and
> a shriveling disgust. This was nature, raw and living. He did not want it. He walked to the
> mirror and stared at his image. 'Kurt Gray, Kurt Gray, what are you? What will all this mean
> to you?'" (141)

Kurt's reaction, here, and in particular the questions he asks himself, are indicative of

homosexual paranoia in which "self-consciousness equals cynicism" (Muñoz 420). The idea of

racial paranoia is explored comprehensively in "Feeling Brown, Feeling Down" (2013), and

offers much insight into how we can understand gay paranoia, too, as "not something that can be

wished away" (ibid), as Kurt is discovering for himself. While this scene may be melodramatic,

it is the final necessary impetus for Kurt's literal and psychological journey. As he leaves the

United States and settles in Europe, he is able to think fondly of his friends and family while

maintaining a safe distance to discover himself, which he does with the help of his art and the

persistence of a new acquaintance, an actor named Tony McGauran.

The relationship that builds between Tony and Kurt is reminiscent of a Gatsby-Carraway[8]

friendship. Consider Tony's arrival at the train station, as narrated by Kurt: "He descended from

---

[8] Nick Carraway's likely homosexuality has become clearer in critical readings in the last few
decades, especially in and following the argument made by Edward Wasiolek (1992). Wasiolek
writes, "Nick favors Gatsby because he favors what Gatsby is, feels so intensely for Gatsby
because he feels what Gatsby feels. Put bluntly we are confronted with the sympathy of one

his carriage in an aura of correct arriving—the handsome young adventurer doing Europe. A West End topcoat was flung over his shoulders, and he was surrounded by a mound of gleaming baggage" (165). Tony's arrival coordinates with the arrival of a letter from Chloe, which warns Kurt that he is being deceived by both Derry and David. She writes, "I'm pretty certain you don't know how utterly you are being fooled . . . I like you too well to see you deluded" (160). The combination of these two events, Chloe's warning and Tony's dazzling appearance in France, conspire to encourage Kurt's growth. He realizes, painfully, that he must be true to himself and understands that he finally has the opportunity to do so, now that he is away from the dangers and restrictions of his personal life. Chloe's letter also serves as a reminder that we are meant to view Kurt as the "ideal" homosexual man, uncorrupted, in contrast to his friends who are "artificial and weak" (160). The idea is reinforced later in the narrative when Kurt is confronted for the first time with sexual promiscuity (Tony's and, eventually, Derry's), a practice he cannot seem to understand.

During Kurt and Tony's stay together in France, a number of significant events occur which justify Europe as the place for Kurt's coming to terms with his sexuality. The first is the recognition he receives from Tony, which he must ultimately accept for himself, that he is "homosexual." The moment is an important one not just for this narrative but for the tradition of gay men's literature, as it is perhaps one of the earliest instances of a character being described as "homosexual" rather than an "invert," "Uranian," "pederast" or other such descriptor. As Vern

---

homosexual for another" (18). In addition, Kurt Gray, like Nick Carraway, is a supposed "innocent" who has left small-town United States to pursue adventure. McGauran, like Gatsby, is larger than life, inexplicably rich, and prone to gratuitous and elaborate demonstrations of wealth. Finally, there is an immediate attraction between the two men, and it will be McGauran who leads Gray, as Gatsby led Carraway, into manhood.

Bullough (2002) notes, "Karoly Maria Benkert coined the term homosexuality to describe [same-sex] relationships" in the late 1800s, and the defense of this definition and those who ascribed to it was taken up by Richard von Krafft-Ebing and Magnus Hirschfeld (2). The terminology was debated as late as the 1980s, when "homophile" was preferred in many cases (101), so it is all the more striking to find such usage in a novel from the 1930s. Kurt acknowledges and eventually accepts Tony's classification, though he ultimately rejects Tony's explanation of homosexuality, which he [Tony] believes can be cured by sleeping with women (175). This recalls the "solution" that Oswald's American doctor provided to him in *Imre*. Kurt rebels at this, thinking, "here was the old, old argument again, the one he had fought over so often, so futilely, and at last, he thought, to a successful finish" (177). For Kurt, mistresses and wives are no cure; instead, he is determined to seek "the perfection of love" (180), a love to be found only with another man.

Another important moment in Kurt's development comes near the end of his stay in Europe, when he and Tony are at a small café and, coincidentally, confronted by the presence of their former landlords, the Rubins, an American couple who upon discovering that Kurt and Tony are homosexual, evict them. In their presence, the normally staid Kurt makes his most impassioned and elegant speech about love and sexuality:

> Each kind of passion—man-and-woman passion, man-and-man passion—has all degrees of love; from love that is pure and high and fine, down the scale to lust that is ugly and despicable and beastly. Each kind has its prostitutes, its procurers and pimps and 'houses,' and each kind has its ideal lovers. It's Paola and Francesca, and Dante and Beatrice, on the one hand; and its David and Jonathan, and its Shakespeare and Willy, on the other. The only difference is—the only damned difference is that for us there's no way of getting social sanction—so we go around the world like a lot of sorry ghosts, being forever ashamed of a thing we've no reason to be ashamed of. (206-207)

The monologue is one of the most significant moments in the narrative for three reasons: first, it clarifies Kurt's previously vague concept of the "ideal" love; he is now explicit about what he means, a spiritual love that can exist between two same-sex individuals as well as the opposite; second, it demonstrates that Kurt no longer finds unfairness in the fact that he is homosexual, but in the fact that others treat him differently because of it; and finally, it prepares Kurt for the journey home. When he ends by saying "we go around the world like a lot of sorry ghosts," we understand that Kurt had been that ghost, grasping at Europe as a lifeline.

The final pages of this section, similarly to the first, place Kurt in an uncomfortable position with women. In the days leading up to his leaving the United States for Europe, Kurt nearly sacrificed his ideal by engaging in sexual intercourse with Chloe. In his last days in Europe, Kurt considers paying for a female prostitute to discover "this knowledge Tony was so anxious for him to achieve, this mystery that hides between a woman's thighs" (216); yet, though the opportunity is at hand, Kurt realizes, "no, this was not for him" (ibid). Now that he has come to understand and accept himself, he is ready to go home. Physical displacement is an important factor in creating an acceptable "queer space" in gay American narratives; however, other authors from this period have relied successfully on temporal displacement to create the same effect.

The first two texts in this study are similar in many ways, but especially in the fact that they physically displace their American narrator in order to advance his queer story. In *Imre*, this means a total escape for the narrator, Oswald, from America; in *Better Angel*, on the other hand, the narrator spends enough time in Europe to develop as an individual, separate from his friends and family back home in Michigan so that he can return to the United States a more confident and essentially "out" gay man. In the next example, Thomas Hal Phillips's *The Bitterweed Path* (1949), the entire story takes place in the United States but is displaced by the fact that it is set near the turn of the century, not long after the American Civil War[9]. While we can learn much

about a period by examining its literature in retrospect, as a kind of primary source document,

historical fiction also plays an important critical role. As Norman W. Jones argues, "historical

fiction helps illuminate gay and lesbian histories and the debates that question their very

existence" (3). Placing *The Bitterweed Path* into conversation with other early twentieth-century

gay texts whose narrative time periods reflected the time in which they were published

encourages us to view homosexual literature as complex and historically engaged, just as we

might view other American texts which treat history similarly as a means for understanding

contemporary issues. This is evident, for example, in works such as Nathaniel Hawthorne's *The

Scarlet Letter* (1850) and Arthur Miller's *The Crucible* (1953).

The Bitterweed Path also distinguishes itself from other early works in that it received

modest critical attention, including contemporary reviews from such publications as the *New

York Times* and *The New Yorker,* among others. John Howard argues that "it is the very subtlety

of Phillips's novel that accounts for publishers' initial interest, the critics' warm reception, and

the book's eventual fall into obscurity" (Phillips xiv). I would argue, however, that the narrative

is not as subtle in its treatment of sexuality as Howard and others might claim. Nor is this

subtlety the only reason for the book's success. Instead, it is the honest portrayal of a different

kind of love, composed in a masterful way, which encouraged early readership. In addition, the

narrative's displacement in time, being set just after the Civil War, allows for a distant but

---

[9] Interesting connections have been made between war time and the advancement of gay
literature. Works such as *Coming Out Under Fire* (Bérubé 1990), *The Lavender Scare* (Johnson
2004), *Homosexuality in Cold War America* (Corber 1997), and *The Straight State* (Canaday
2009), among others, help to inform and illustrate my points on this matter, which will become
especially important in the next chapters.

relatable setting. The book was first published as a master's thesis in 1949, then published for

public audiences in 1950, just a half-decade after the end of World War II. The American public

at this time was all too familiar with the dramatic changes brought about by life after a major

conflict[10]. Just as Walt Whitman and his contemporaries were inspired to write about the

American Civil War, twentieth-century gay writers began to write "honestly about their lives and

their sexuality in books, paperbacks, magazines, and pornography" and "an increasing number of

postwar novels and short stories began to deal with the subject of homosexuality" (Bérubé 272).

Phillips's novel is more explicit and sympathetic than many of these, which often "used imagery

that referred to the war" (ibid). In a contemporary review of the novel, Thomas Sugrue writes,

"[Phillips] has brought Louisiana life during the early years of the century into the sort of

believable reality which other Southern writers carefully avoid" (216). The narrative's historical

displacement thus relies on a contemporary trend in gay writing[11] but succeeds where others fail

because it creates an acceptable distance between contemporary readers and the events taking

place in this fictive world. The novel also "implie[s] historical antecedents to the fifties' much-

maligned 'pervert'" (Phillips xvi); or, in other words, it suggests a history for homosexuality in

America, something which contemporary novels dealing only with contemporary issues could

not do.

---

[10] Indeed, the post-World War II period might very well have been the most sympathetic
audience for gay subjects to date. As Allan Bérubé (1990) has noted, "during the war the military
stage had offered gay men a temporary platform on which they could express themselves in
public at a time when few such platforms existed . . . their language was coded, their faces
disguised, and their friendship covert, but they nevertheless chipped away at the barriers
separating them from each other and their heterosexual buddies" (97).

[11] As John Howard describes it in the introduction to *The Bitterweed Path*, "word was out that
homosexuals were everywhere" (viii).

Time is not the only strategic displacement technique, however. The novel's geographic setting, rural Mississippi, makes the provocative subject matter more palatable to northern readers, especially, who, at this point in time, were familiar with the oddities of the southern gothic genre via a legacy of writers beginning with William Faulkner in the 1920s and continuing into the 1950s, when *The Bitterweed Path* appeared, and via writers such as Truman Capote and Carson McCullers, popular authors who explored queer themes and characters in their own works. Although Phillips's work does not work as a southern gothic novel, its regional intimacy to the genre is nevertheless familiar. There is, in addition to the general setting, a theme maintained throughout the narrative that conditions the reader to relate the idea of displacement with homosexual activity. Specifically, it is typically when the main characters, Darrell, Malcolm, and Roger, have left home for one of the larger cities in the region, most often New Orleans or Vicksburg, that their sexual relationships are most clearly defined and expressed.

One significant example of this agreement between displacement and sexual expression is when Darrell leaves home to visit his friend Roger at boarding school. At this point in the narrative, Darrell's parents have both died and he now lives with his grandmother; but the Pitt family, headed by Malcolm, Darrell's primary love interest, has become more of a family to him than his own ever seemed to be. Although Darrell and Roger often think of themselves as, and are described by others as being like, brothers, their relationship is much deeper than familial. It is not realized, however, until both young men are away from home. Roger has told Darrell that he earned perfect grades "so [Darrell] would be proud" (72). The pronouncement is followed by a telling scene:

> Darrell did not move his lips. He sat in silence against the footboard and gazed at Roger and shivered the whole curled length of his body, for Roger was the most beautiful thing he could

imagine in a very real and beautiful world. And he thought, even then, it would be the kind of Christmas he would never again know." (ibid)

This subtle but clear coming-of-age moment for the two boys is almost immediately followed by another experience, this time between Darrell and Malcolm Pitt. It also occurs away from home, when Malcolm takes Darrell with him to Memphis to buy a cotton gin. This trip is what will define the rest of their relationship, spanning more than a decade, and it is appropriately more explicit than the moment shared between Darrell and Roger. During this trip, Malcolm buys Darrell a suit, which Darrell, out of modesty, refuses to accept. Malcolm asks him, "you want to be my boy don't you . . . I thought you loved me a little" (80). It suffices to say that Darrell does accept the suit. The scene in itself could be read platonically: a good man has simply accepted an orphan as his own son; however, the pages that follow are filled with sentimentality and sexual allusion. The chapter closes with Darrell and Malcolm sleeping together, during which Darrell "could feel the great maleness" of the older man and, soon after, felt "Malcolm's lips against his cheek" (83-84). The pathos is heightened by a reference to Darrell's accepting his place in what he feels must be "some old ritual binding them together" (83).

The back-and-forth between Darrell and Roger, and Darrell and Malcolm, continues as the narrative progresses, revealing the slow dissolution of Darrell and Roger's relationship as Darrell and Malcolm's grows stronger. At times, Darrell will go to visit Roger and they will share experiences that reinforce their sexuality. During one of these visits, when Malcolm and Darrell have gone to see Roger at a school tennis match, Darrell sneaks out to be with Roger after Malcolm has fallen asleep. When Roger attempts to introduce Darrell to a female prostitute that evening, Darrell's reaction makes it clear how offended he is personally and also how shocked he is to discover that Roger might be interested in this kind of affair:

Suddenly Darrell thought he did not know Roger at all. He wanted to touch the arm or wrist stretched along the table before him to make sure it was the same body which he had slept warmly against in another and younger day, the body that had whispered to him beside a creek bank in the nights of another and younger time. (120)

The attempt with the prostitute fails. She declines them with a certain understanding about their relationship which they are perhaps unwilling to admit, and the distance between the two young men becomes clearer. After parting, Darrell returns to Malcolm's side, sharing his bed again, and while he lay beside the man, "his body began to grow warm" (125).

While these escapades away from home certainly serve as opportunities for the three male protagonists to explore their sexualities and define their relationships, they also give occasion for Darrell's gradual coming-of-age and coming-out. When Darrell leaves for Littleford Springs to visit Miriam, Roger's sister and the woman whom the reader is meant to suspect Darrell will eventually marry, he finds not Miriam but another woman who does in fact become his wife. Their relationship is of course doomed to misery, and this is portended in their earliest interaction. Miriam, who is at one of the medical centers with her ailing father, tells Darrell, a newcomer about whom she knows nothing, "that's the doctor. If there's anything wrong with you he'll patch it up" (181). Darrell responds, "he couldn't fix what's wrong with me" (ibid). The scene that follows is meant to appear flirtatious, as if what Darrell said should be taken in jest; however, the reader knows by now that when Darrell says he "need[s] a new heart" (ibid), the proclamation is serious, even if he does not yet understand his own meaning. This interaction and the ultimate failed destiny between these two lovers could not have happened had Darrell not left home to find Miriam, and failed.

Darrell will eventually come to understand his own heart. He believes that his failure with Emily is because he was supposed to marry Miriam, but when Malcolm Pitt is tragically killed in a gin accident, "the old feeling" (281) he pretended to carry for her all along suddenly

disappears. It is not until he is with Roger again that he finds "the everlasting magic" (287) and

"wild tenderness" (311) again. He discovers this, of course, only at the end of the narrative when

Roger is leaving home forever, thus permanently cementing the relationship that has been

established between homosexual identity and displacement. Homosexual love can exist, but only

in another time or another place. This possibility is further emphasized in another work, one of

the most successful pieces of the time, published less than a decade after *The Bitterweed Path*.

James Baldwin's *Giovanni's Room*, published in 1956, is one of the few homosexual novels

to become both critically and popularly successful in its own time. What allowed this novel, as

opposed to others published during the early twentieth-century, to be so successful? Certainly,

the fact that Baldwin was already a celebrated author, having previously published, to great

acclaim, *Go Tell it on the Mountain* (1953) and *Notes of a Native Son* (1955), might have helped.

Yet, other homosexual writers, such as Charles Warren Stoddard[12] and Henry Blake Fuller, had

also been successful prior to publishing their openly gay fiction, only to find their popularity

rapidly decline in the aftermath, a fate which James Baldwin did not share. What makes

Baldwin's novel different and perhaps more palatable to the 1950s audience is not simply that

Baldwin has displaced the story, creating a safe distance between the United States and the

narrative from which to explore homosexuality; another distinguishing feature for *Giovanni's*

---

[12] Before publishing his most overtly gay novel, *For the Pleasure of His Company* (1903),
Stoddard's travel writing had been praised by William Dean Howells as "infinitely the best thing
of its kind that I have read" (Tarnoff 214). In addition, his *South-Sea Idyls* and other short works
drew critical comparisons to Bret Harte and Mark Twain. Similarly, Henry Blake Fuller had
established himself as a popular Chicago writer, having published such works as The *Cliff-
Dwellers* (1893) and *With the Procession* (1895), both of which are "accomplished works of
realism that were widely admired in their time by writers such as William Dean Howells,
Theodore Dreiser, and H. H. Boyesen" (Dimuro 141).

Room, in comparison with the other novels of displacement explored in this chapter, is that it draws on many of the then-common literary and cultural tropes about gay men that were often found in gay pulp fiction[13]. In addition, while Baldwin sets his narrative outside of the United States, which allows him the freedom to tell the homosexual story, and while he, unlike Prime-Stevenson and Brown, incorporates the very American expectations of what a homosexual novel *should* be, he does this in order to make the audience complicit in the narrator's (and culture's) guilt about Giovanni's eventual demise. Rather than celebrate the death of the homosexual character or simply accept it as an unavoidable outcome of a tragic condition, as gay pulp audiences may have been expected to do, the reader here becomes, unsuspectingly, a mirror for the narrator's failure to save Giovanni. These two elements, the strategic choice of setting and the ingenious subversion of cultural expectations, helped elevate Baldwin's gay novel to a level of success that earlier pieces from talented writers, such as Phillips and Brown, could not achieve.

In *The Gay Canon* (1998), Robert Drake makes an important point about David, the narrator of *Giovanni's Room*. Drake argues that David is "a coward. Not in the misguided, hypermasculine way in which violent men call peaceniks cowards, but in the honest sense of the word: David shirks what he knows is right" (321). This establishes a significant difference between Baldwin's narrator and the narrators of *Imre*, *Better Angel* and *The Bitterweed Path*, none of whom could be considered cowardly. The dichotomy is especially important because it relates to the cause for David's fleeing[14] the United States for France and, eventually, wanting to

---

[13] These tropes will be explored in great detail in chapter three, though some of the common ones include melodrama, violence, and murder or suicide.

[14] David is not the only displaced character, nor the only coward. In *All Those Strangers: The Art and Lives of James Baldwin* (Oxford 2015), Douglas Field notes that Giovanni, "who has left his

flee France for someplace else, anyplace else. In both cases, David, unlike the other gay

protagonists discussed in this chapter, does not want to leave in order to find himself; instead, he

hopes leaving will help him forget a certain part of himself, the homosexual part that he has

acted on repeatedly and always with regret or shame. Immediately, then, the tone of this novel

becomes closely aligned with the melodramatic environments of the gay pulp genre rather than

the more positive and reaffirming narratives discussed thus far.

The dark mood is established candidly in the first chapter when David introduces himself in

this way:

> I stand at the window of this great house in the south of France as night falls, the night which
> is leading me to the most terrible morning of my life. I have a drink in my hand, there is a
> bottle at my elbow. I watch my reflection in the darkening gleam of the window pane. My
> reflection is tall, perhaps rather like an arrow, my blond hair gleams. My face is like a face
> you have seen many times. My ancestors conquered a continent, pushing across death-laden
> plains, until they came to an ocean which faced away from Europe into a darker past. (3)

In this opening scene, there are multiple references to night and darkness, literal and

metaphorical, as well as indications that the narrator has been drinking excessively, and that he

views himself as one villain in a long line of dangerous ancestors. He is unhappy in France, yet

he cannot return home to the United States because he sees only darkness there as well.

The above scene also establishes what the reader will soon identify as David's incessant

neurosis: flight and failure. He recognizes that he has fled "so far, so hard, across the ocean even,

only to find [him]self brought up short once more before the bulldog in [his] own backyard" (6).

Allusions to flight, darkness, and despair persist throughout the opening chapter as the reader

---

Italian village" and Jacques, "the Belgian-born American businessman" (125) are also part of
Baldwin's "assembly of displaced, sometimes spectral figures" (ibid). The similarity does not
end there, however. Giovanni and Jacques are also homosexuals, like David, and each is a
coward as well. Giovanni fled his home after the still-birth of his son, leaving his wife behind,
and Jacques is described as "a fool and a coward" (23).

discovers that David has had at least two affairs with other men, both of which ended negatively, and that he had proposed marriage to a young woman, as Oswald had in *Imre*. The oppressive, despondent mood and the list of failed relationships lead at last to David's attempt to rationalize just what he was doing in France. He first imagines that he "wanted to find [him]self" (21), a reasonable enough motivation for a young person's desire to travel abroad. Yet, soon after making that claim, David admits that he "knew, at the very bottom of [his] heart, exactly what [he] was doing when [he] took the boat for France" (ibid). In other words, David imagined he was fleeing from his homosexual past in order to make a new start, but he also knew that in Europe he would likely have the opportunity to continue exploring his sexuality. In France, he would be able to do this at a distance from his oppressive home life, away from his dominating and controlling aunt (11) and away from the father who failed him and forced David to tell him only "what he wished to hear" (20). David's father's inability to comprehend his son's sexual difference is explored subtly in the opening chapter; however, in a letter to David, after David has been in Paris for some time, his father writes, "there's nothing over there for you. You're as American as pork and beans, though maybe you don't want to think so anymore" (91). This is one of the clearer explanations for David's need to leave the United States. He may not truly believe that Europe will "cure" him of his desires, but he does know that his homosexuality is perceived as wholly un-American.

Robert Tomlinson (1999) has also stressed the significance of expatriation in *Giovanni's Room*. He makes a critical connection between issues of race and sexuality in Baldwin's work. The two, he writes, "assume a common rhetorical function, evoking the dark side of human nature, and this terror-ridden inability to come to terms with them was not, in Baldwin's view, his problem, but that of White America" (139). Tomlinson's argument is effective in reading

Giovanni's Room through the lens of race (black and white) and culture (European and American); however, although he articulates the "parallel between sex and race" (139) and notes that "the homosexual and expatriate experiences are made to function as paradigms for the African American experience," he stops short of explicitly critiquing *heterosexual* America. Instead, he refers throughout to "White" America and puritanism. This reading, while appropriate if arguing that Baldwin himself, as a black man, creates a white narrator as a mask to express racial inequity in America, does not do justice to the fictive world that exists within the narrative itself. The fact is that a significant impetus for David's expatriation, or necessary displacement, is not his race (he is a white man) but his sexual attraction for men.

The connection between David's homosexuality and the necessity of being out of the United States if he is to pursue it, is reiterated throughout the narrative. For instance, on the many occasions when David thinks of home and his sexuality within the same context, he begins to feel deep shame about his sexual desires. Shortly after they meet, he and Giovanni, along with two older patrons, Guillaume and Jacques, go out for drinks and a late-night meal. While sitting privately with Giovanni, David is confronted by a quick succession of emotions: First, he experiences "a longing to go home" because he feels out of place in Paris and especially out of place being intimate with another man in public; second, he adjusts to consider that "what was happening . . . was not really so strange, so unprecedented" (61); finally, despite his attempt to rationalize and to accept that some men are attracted to other men and act on that attraction, as he knows from personal experience, he rejects this and feels only embarrassment that he could be "so hideously entangled with a boy" (ibid). Emmanuel S. Nelson recognizes this particular struggle for "self-identity" (121) in Baldwin's fiction. He notes that, for Baldwin's protagonists, "reaching a genuine sense of self and forging an identity depend largely on self-knowledge and self-awareness which . . . come only through suffering" (ibid). David certainly satisfies this argument, as he struggles painfully to reconcile his feelings for both Giovanni and Hella and to finally admit his love for Giovanni only when it is too late.

The disturbing fact for David is not that he is American and Giovanni Italian, nor that he comes from a wealthy family whereas Giovanni is poor. It is the sexual nature of the relationship which troubles him, as it has always troubled him. In her essay on expatriation and homosexual panic, Mae G. Henderson writes, "*Giovanni's Room*, Baldwin's novel of expatriation and homosexuality, thus, explores the homosexual dilemma as one of expatriation, or exile—from nation, from culture, from body" (314). When, at the end of the novel, David attempts to flee again, that same homosexual dilemma is forcefully demonstrated:

> I look up the road, where a few people stand, men and women, waiting for the morning bus. They are very vivid beneath the awakening sky, and the horizon beyond them is beginning to flame. The morning weights on my shoulders with the dreadful weight of hope and I take the blue envelope which Jacques has sent me and tear it slowly into many pieces, watching them dance in the wind, watching the wind carry them away. Yet, as I turn and begin walking toward the waiting people, the wind blows some of them back on me. (169)

Preceding this scene, David has reluctantly admitted the truth about himself to his fiancé Hella, and they have parted ways. He has essentially admitted blame for Giovanni's fate and in so doing, attempts to come to terms with his own body and his own sexuality. David spends the morning looking at himself naked in the mirror, telling himself that he must "save it from the knife" and "hold [it] sacred" (168-9). The hope is, then, that some of David's homosexual panic has been resolved by this point. He has decided to return to Paris, not home to the United States. He has exiled himself from his country and from any culture that had been familiar. This is another contrast with a narrator like Kurt, who returns home to continue his life after accepting himself and his sexuality. The pieces of Jacques's letter which are caught by the wind and returned to David signify "the homosexual who cannot reconcile himself with his body and desire . . . one who is a stranger unto himself[15]" (Henderson 322). He has destroyed Giovanni by lying to him and the consequences of that will follow him back to Paris and onward.

James Baldwin sets the majority of the narrative in Europe, necessarily displacing it from the United States in order to, like other gay authors of this period, create a relatively safe fictive space for exploring homosexuality in fiction. Unlike these other examples, however, the reason for the displacement is not to create affirmational experiences for the narrator. David never truly accepts himself, although there might be the slightest hint of that possibility in the concluding moments, and the resolution is certainly not a happy one for Giovanni. Baldwin has utilized gay pulp strategies, such as a mood of despair, homosexual death, and an inability to find happiness or self-acceptance in order to advance his plot, something many of the more literary authors managed to avoid; theirs were in many cases powerful examples for the possibility of early twentieth-century homosexual happiness, including committed relationships, long lives, and successful careers for the novels' gay characters. *Giovanni's Room* is not like the gay pulp novels, however, because despite its tragic overtones, Baldwin creates a certain degree of complicity in the reader, even empathy. Whereas the pulp novels were meant to be enjoyed primarily for their spectacle and often ended in a self-flagellating didactic note, *Giovanni's Room* encourages readers to begin to understand David, including his frustrations and his choices. Most importantly, Baldwin encourages readers to empathize with Giovanni and to feel wounded and

---

[15] The confusion indicated here is represented throughout the narrative by David's many antithetical statements and by the antithetical themes established by Baldwin as primary to the homosexual experience. As Yasmin DeGout notes, "the positive depiction of homoerotic love (its association with innocence and with healing powers) and the subsequent tragedy of David, who denies his homosexuality and therefore cannot save Giovanni, coexist with a negative depiction of homoerotic love and the subsequent implication that society, in producing sexual deviants, has failed to meet traditional standards" (428).

betrayed, as Giovanni feels he has been. The morality tale here is not anti-homosexual, although it might appear so on the surface; instead, it is an exploration of "the failure of love" and the "terrifying . . . effect of its failure" (Hoffman 198). This is illustrated especially well in the argument David and Giovanni have when David returns to the room one last time, in order to end the relationship and collect his things:

> 'You are not leaving me for her,' he said. 'You are leaving me for some other reason. You lie so much, you have come to believe all your own lies. But I, I have senses. You are not leaving me for a woman. If you were really in love with this little girl, you would not have had to be so cruel to me . . . You do not,' cried Giovanni, sitting up, 'love anyone! You never have loved anyone . . . You want to be clean . . . You want to leave Giovanni because he makes you stink. You want to despise Giovanni because he is not afraid of the stink of love.' (140-41)

Giovanni understands about David what David cannot admit about himself, that he equates love with guilt and immorality, with "stink," because the only two people he has loved are men. This realization comes to him only in their last moment together, when David admits, "I wanted to beg him to forgive me. But this would have been too great a confession" (144). The freedom to love which he hoped to find in Europe confronts the fact of his Americanness, and fails, in this moment and also in the spaces constructed by gay men in order to encourage that very possibility.

Throughout the narrative, David is described as being at his most defeated and self-loathing when he is occupying the gay spaces that have supposedly been constructed in order to free him and men like him. Stanton Hoffman notes, "David fears homosexuality, which . . . is his fear of the dangers of love, or selfhood and experience; and he is attracted to a homosexual bar, which identifies him with those things characteristic of the bar, and which identifies those things characteristic of that bar with him" (199). In other words, David hates himself, and this hatred is rooted in the American problem[16] that led him to flee in the first place. The narrator makes this clear when he recalls Giovanni telling him that Guillaume has identified David as "just an American boy, after all, doing things in France which [he] would not dare to do at home" (108). Giovanni also explains that Guillaume thinks David will leave him soon. The older, experienced homosexual Frenchman has located in David the American homosexual, one who may indulge himself for a time but only while abroad and never again once he returns to the United States.

This connection between America and heterosexuality is further illustrated by a scene mid-narrative, when David receives a letter from Hella. When she indicates in that letter that she has decided to accept David's marriage proposal, he feels a sense of relief, even vindication. He orders a "Scotch and soda . . . which had never seemed more American than it did at that moment" and considers that his relationship with Giovanni could now be "something that had happened to [him] once" (94). In that moment, David imagines he can return to Hella and forget Giovanni, the way he tried, unsuccessfully, to forget his first lover, Joey. What David does not permit himself to acknowledge, however, is that he is still haunted by his relationship with Joey, especially by the way he ended it. Giovanni, too, will haunt him. The melodramatic ending invites the reader into the moment of Giovanni's execution, though the narrator can only imagine it. David looks into the mirror and sees Giovanni in his final minutes:

> Giovanni's face swings before me like an unexpected lantern on a dark, dark night. His eyes—his eyes, they glow like a tiger's eyes, they stare straight out, watching the approach of his last enemy, the hair of his flesh stands up . . . My own hands are clammy, my body is dull and white and dry. I see it in the mirror, out of the corner of my eye . . . And I look at my body, which is under sentence of death. (167-8)

---

[16] As Henderson and Tomlinson have discussed and as has been noted earlier in this section of the chapter.

In this instant, David sees himself in Giovanni, and Giovanni in himself. He recognizes that he is responsible for Giovanni's death sentence because he failed to love him until it was too late. This failure in effect sentences him to the same fate. He realizes that Giovanni was right, that he will never be able to love because he has not been able to accept himself, his desires, and his body.

Giovanni's Room was published two decades after works such as Blair Niles's *Strange Brother* (1931) and Charles Henri Ford's and Parker Tyler's *The Young and Evil* (1933), and it perpetuates some of the tropes established by the gay pulp fiction genre that became popular in "the postwar period in America," when the culture "saw a relaxing and a tightening of sexual boundaries" (Field 41). For example, the two deaths in *Giovanni's Room*, Guillaume's and Giovanni's, fulfill the concept of "queer hatred" which was embedded in both the dominate heteronormative culture generally, but also in the homosexual community itself (Bronski, *Pulp Friction*, 12). Baldwin's narrative also sets up a clear distinction between the masculine David, blonde and wholesome, and the "fairies" and "grotesques" with whom he interacts. These are the "twilight" men of gay pulps who are traditionally cast in the genre as loathsome, effeminate, and even dangerous.

Yet, despite employing some of the tropes which saturated gay fiction in the early- and mid-twentieth-century, Baldwin's novel differs from these. It is elevated by the fact that he incorporates an honest analysis of the cultural rationale for the treatment and depiction of gay men. In *Giovanni's Room*, Giovanni is not condemned to death because he is evil; on the contrary, readers are meant to empathize with him. Baldwin manages this by illustrating the effect class has on a gay man's treatment by society and on his treatment by the law. After Giovanni confesses to murdering Guillaume, David relates that "from the press one received the impression that Guillaume had been a good-hearted, a perhaps somewhat erratic philanthropist who had had the bad judgment to befriend the hardened and ungrateful adventurer, Giovanni" (157). This is of course an inaccurate description of Guillaume, who would be more correctly described as a predator and an opportunist. It is his wealth and his important family lineage which create the public narrative, however. Giovanni, a poor immigrant outsider, has no means to combat these impressions. In this way, James Baldwin manages to do what the gay pulps to be explored further in the next chapter did not: he creates a more realistic, intersectional description of the gay world and the gay men who inhabit it. The melodrama created in the final scenes is not gratuitous. Baldwin's pathos makes the reader complicit in David's guilt and creates a sense of outrage regarding the Parisian aristocracy. For Baldwin, the gay man as villain, as psychopathic or diseased, is an inaccurate and overly-simplistic characterization. Baldwin's homosexuals are complex human beings who are as much at risk of being ostracized because of their socioeconomic status and nationality as they are because of their sexuality. Setting the novel in Paris rather than the United States allows Baldwin to develop a homosexual narrative that confronts each of these stigmas through the lens of European immigration and a traditional caste system.

In each of the four principal novels discussed in this first chapter, the author chose to displace, and in some cases, publish, his novel outside of the recognizable United States. In each case, there were specific reasons for and advantages to doing this. By organizing representative texts from this early part of the twentieth-century chronologically, it becomes possible to determine not just how homosexuality in literature was depicted at a certain time, but also how those depictions changed, based on what factors, and through the use of which narrative strategies. In *Imre*, the European setting creates a physical distance which allows for an open treatment of homosexuality by virtue of the locale's exoticism. It also brings the narrative story closer to the European scientific community which was, at the time, much more progressive in its treatment of homosexuality than their American contemporaries. The protagonist in *Better Angel* also becomes familiar with those European sexologists during his coming-of-age, but rather than beginning and ending his story outside the United States, the narrative is a *bildungsroman* that brings the young man to Europe so he can come to terms with himself and then return home a more confident, self-affirming man. In *The Bitterweed Path*, Phillips sets the book in the United States, and publishes it there, but provides himself some protection[17] by composing his narrative as a piece of historical fiction set nearly one-hundred years in the past. *Giovanni's Room*, published at the height of the McCarthy era that gave rise to the "Lavender Scare," again takes the reader outside the United States and employs many tropes found in pulp fiction, but ingeniously subverts them to create pathos between the reader and the narrative subject. The narrative strategy of displacement, then, allowed for a number of open treatments of homosexuality in early gay American fiction, yet the majority of these generally positive depictions of homosexuals in literature have received little critical attention; as such, their influence on the gay American literary tradition has been underappreciated. In contrast, gay pulp fiction, to be explored in the next chapter, was read widely during this same period and has had a number of significant, lasting effects on the genre, some of which have been damaging.

---

[17] This protection would have been absolutely necessary, as other gay writers such as Truman Capote and Gore Vidal, were well-aware; coded narratives, which will be discussed in further detail in chapter four, were prevalent at this time not just for the sake of propriety. John Howard explains in his introduction to *The Bitterweed Path* that, "as reported in the *New York Times* on 1 March 1950, Peurifoy told a Senate Committee that left-wing subversives recently booted out of the State Department because they were security risks were mostly homosexuals. The statement was uttered; the connection was made. Homosexuality represented the worst evil" (ix).

CHAPTER 3

THE POWER OF PULP FICTION: CONSTRUCTING & PERPETUATING STEREOTYPES

"Armand's love was more than this, he believed. It flowed around him, it was an irresistible force, sweeping him to heights or to destruction. He must face it and make an appropriate answer." –Andre Tellier, *Twilight Men*, p. 177

As has been discussed, it is generally believed that gay literature in the United States did not exist in any considerable or cohesive way until the mid-twentieth-century, just before Stonewall, and that it advanced rapidly thereafter. As demonstrated in the first chapter, this argument is unfounded. Another misconception about early twentieth-century gay American fiction is that no one was reading it because no queer presses existed at the time. In *Culture Clash: The Making of a Gay* Sensibility (1984), Michael Bronski correctly notes that "popular novels may have been directed to a gay audience but, by and large, they were not published by gay-identified publishers" (145); in other words, there was no dedicated audience and no clear outlet for reaching any potential audience. In *The Golden Age of Gay Fiction* (Gunn 2009), Ian Young argues as much when he writes that "gay subject matter was taboo in the publishing industry" until "during and after World War II, when gay writing suddenly emerged from the shadows" (3). While it is true that the advent of specifically queer publishers had not yet happened, the gay pulp novels were indeed being read, in fact many earned multiple printings due to successful sales and continued interest. André Tellier's *Twilight Men* was published in 1931, nearly a decade before the start of World War II, and just two years later, Charles Henri Ford and Parker Tyler published their gay novel, *The Young and Evil* (1933). There are a number of other gay novels that found publishers prior to the 1940s, although many of them were much less explicit than the pulps and thus could be easily overlooked, misinterpreted, or relegated to "the shadows."

In this chapter, I explore a selected set of gay pulp fiction novels published between 1931 and 1952, in order to demonstrate how the genre's primary conceits, including melodrama, homosexual panic, gender inversion[1], and violence (often to the point of death by murder or suicide) helped to create and sustain a gay fiction readership and to perpetuate certain cultural assumptions about homosexual men[2]. In addition, I will demonstrate that each of these texts, as well as the genre itself, aided in creating the concept of the "gay space," which meant a location or situation that encouraged, provided for, or presumably "necessitated" homosexual activity; in the case of pulp fiction, this meant one or more of the following: a major metropolis (usually New York City), a prison, or the military or close relationship to it. To pursue this discussion, I will evaluate André Tellier's *Twilight Men*, Charles Henri Ford and Parker Tyler's *The Young and Evil*, Charles Jackson's *The Fall of Valor* (1946), and George Sylvester Viereck's *Men into Beasts* (1952). This will be followed by a conclusion which addresses some of the important similarities and differences between the pulp and literary genres, and a note on the "golden age" of gay fiction. These four representative pulp novels fit squarely into one of the three primary

---

[1] As Eve Kosofsky Sedgwick notes, one problem with the concept of inversion is that it perpetuates the false idea of a binary, established by Foucault, which suggests that masculine/feminine and heterosexual/homosexual, or in other words, gender performance and sexual desire, are somehow codependent (*Epistemology* 157-163). In this chapter, inversion refers specifically to gender performance, in particular the ways in which these authors equate effeminacy (acting or appearing "womanly") with homosexuality.

[2] Indeed, as Paula Rabinowitz notes, "still the residue of pulp haunts us in myriad ways" (*American Pulp,* 2014, 281).

gay spaces suggested above, and they incorporate all of the themes expected from the gay pulp genre.

I have also selected these texts because they have received less critical attention than some other texts of the period, specifically Gore Vidal's *The City and the Pillar* (1948) and Truman Capote's *Other Voices, Other Rooms* (1948). This is not to say that these two texts do not deserve their place in a discussion about mid-twentieth-century gay American novels; however, they have received the critical treatment that the texts I have chosen to evaluate have not. It should be noted, however, that they also fulfill some of the criteria I have outlined above, including the murder of a homosexual character or a melodramatic plot (Gibson, Alexander & Meem, *Finding Out*, 246-247). Of additional interest is the fact that many of these texts engage directly with critical and sociological conversations of the period, including the influence of literary modernism as well as discussions of sex theories generated by the work of Alfred Kinsey, Evelyn Hooker, and others.

André Tellier's *Twilight Men* begins in France but eventually migrates to New York City where the majority of the story, including its climax and resolution, takes places. The location for the setting fulfills one of the criteria for "gay spaces" outlined above: a major metropolitan area. As George Chauncey notes in *Gay New York:*

> By the late 1920s, gay men had become a conspicuous part of New York City's nightlife. They had been visible since the late nineteenth century in some of the city's immigrant and working-class neighborhoods, and since the 1910s in the bohemian enclave of Greenwich Village. But in the 1920s they moved into the center of the city's most prestigious entertainment district, became the subject of plays, films, novels, and newspaper headlines, and attracted thousands of spectators to Harlem's largest ballrooms." (325-327)

It is not surprising, then, that authors of gay fiction would take advantage of the city as an opportunity for creating a gay story that unfolds in a space that had become if not entirely welcoming of homosexuals, at least tolerant of them[3]. *Twilight Men* is in many ways the

quintessential gay pulp novel. The plot is wildly melodramatic[4], the characters confront their

own homosexual panic, the idea of gender inversion is perpetuated, and there is a great deal of

violence, some of which may today be considered gratuitous. These four characteristics of the

gay pulp novel, as effected by Tellier, help to define the city, in this case New York[5], as a kind of

affirmative locale for homosexual men. This reinforces the notion that the city is a "gay space,"

encouraging migration from rural areas or, in this case, other countries. Tellier indicates,

however, that there are nevertheless certain restrictions for a gay existence, even in the city, and

certain prejudices as well. Therefore, while *Twilight Men* successfully creates a specific and

recognizable "place" for gay life, it also perpetuates stereotypes about gay men.

In the introduction to James Barr's *Quatrefoil* (1982), Samuel M. Steward describes *Twilight*

Men as one of "a number of [1930s] wooden productions, portraying the homosexual scene as

giddy or semi-tragic or downright awful" (x). His assessment of both the writing style and the

atmosphere cannot be argued; however, the critique does not consider the ways in which the

melodrama is created, or why Tellier, like so many other gay pulp novelists, relied on such an

atmosphere to tell his story. As Robert J Corber notes in his introduction to Robert Scully's *A*

---

[3] Chicago is another city that had a vibrant gay district before Stonewall. In *Chicago Whispers: A History of LGBT Chicago Before Stonewall*, St. Sukie de la Croix reminds us that "from the mid-1940s until the mid-1960s, Dearborn and Division Streets were 'Queerborn and Perversion,' a gay nightclub area controlled by mobsters" (218). He adds that the *Chicago Sun-Times* and the *Chicago Tribune* printed articles condemning these areas, just as the New York City newspapers condemned their own (ibid). Nevertheless, the gay scenes and nightclubs survived in New York, Chicago, and Los Angeles as well.

[4] Michael Bronski, in *A Queer History of the United States* (2011), calls this "lowbrow" (126).

[5] In their historiography, *Gay L.A.* (Basic Books 2006), Lillian Faderman and Stuart Timmons note that Los Angeles was another major metropolitan area that had an important gay scene, and that some of its gay bars had their "glamour days as early as the 1930s" (1).

Scarlet Pansy (1932), this "spate of novels published in the 1930s . . . explored new constructions of homosexual identity" (5). The melodramatic plot may now be perceived as stereotypical; however, in the early-1900s, when these novels were being published for the first time, they simultaneously fueled readership by adhering to familiar plot devices and readers' expectations about pulp fiction while also engaging the reader with homosexual characters and concerns, perhaps for the first time. Audiences interacting with gay pulp novels then began to become familiar with authors' interpretations of homosexual identity, which introduced or reinforced characteristics about gay men and also promulgated the idea of gay men as a presence, and gay culture as a reality, even if a seedy one. James Levin considers *Twilight Men* to be "one of the bleakest" novels of this period (*The Gay Novel* 42), and this is because of the melodramatic and indeed hopeless way that it treats its "afflicted" characters. The "unsavory" element of homosexuality was often most effectively accomplished through melodramatic portrayals of its characters and situations.

One significant example of how Tellier creates melodrama in *Twilight Men* is in the tension developed between the main character, eighteen-year-old Armand, and his father, Comte Edmond de Rasbon, a tension which is crafted by a perhaps intentional misinterpretation of scientific beliefs about sexuality and heredity[6]. Within the first few paragraphs of the narrative, the reader learns that young Armand has been living with a tutor, Josef Bironge, whom de

---

[6] It should be noted, Nicholas F. Radel offers a brilliant reading of *Twilight Men* as a text of race, wherein homosexuality threatens "white legitimacy" and "the patriarchal family functions" ("(E)racing Edmund White," 771). Although not specifically treated in my research, the perceived threat of homosexuality on white male legacy, as evidenced by the tension between Armand and his father, is a compelling one. Early in the novel, the Comte raises this very concern when he implies that Armand must marry and have a son, not just a child, if he is to fulfill his duty as a son and a man (Tellier 26).

Rasbon hopes will stamp out the unusual elements of his son's character. On the contrary, however, Bironge has notified the Comte that Armand is unchangeable. The significance of this should not be overlooked. We have in this instance a primary character in a gay pulp novel from the early 1930s indicating that this young man, a homosexual, simply is what he is. The moment is subtle, but the idea that homosexuality cannot be changed or cured is nevertheless casually indicated on the first page of the text.

The reaction from Armand's father is swift: "I'd rather know he was dead! . . . Why didn't you put him quietly out of the way? What is death—nothing! But this—a young man of his sort never amounts to anything" (5). The tension built here does not rest simply on the fact that the heterosexual, aristocratic father dislikes his effeminate gay son. Instead, as James Levin aptly argues, one of the overarching issues of the novel is the argument that "homosexuality [was] viewed as an hereditary condition" at this time, "despite the scientific evidence available to the contrary" (41). Thus, when Armand and Comte de Rasbon meet again near the end of the novel, after Armand has left Europe for New York City and spends years away from his father, Armand tells the man, "I am the result of your own folly . . . all sorts of unfortunate things may happen to the child born of a roué and a degenerate" (204). In other words, Armand is a homosexual because his father was a promiscuous man who could not control his own sexual instincts and therefore passed along the trait, in some fashion, to his son. It is somewhat ironic, then, that another of the most important constructions of melodrama in the text is a result of a meeting contrived by de Rasbon in an attempt to cure young Armand of his prudishness (23), which the virile father considers to be a disability (27).

Just as the relationship between Armand and his father creates a melodramatic arc for the text, Armand's relationship with Marianne persists throughout the story and creates points of contention between Armand and his pursuit of happiness. She attempts to stand in the way of each of his romantic relationships. When they first meet, Marianne Dodon is thirty-five-years old, nearly twenty-years older than Armand. Comte de Rasbon arranges the rendezvous in the hopes that Marianne, a sexually experienced woman, can guide Armand into heterosexual adulthood. Although they do sleep together, Armand finds the experience "hateful and disgusting" and begins to understand that "he had acted in a manner outrageous to his true nature" (43). Marianne, meanwhile, begins to wonder if "his sexual needs were perverse in nature" (ibid). They do have sex, but the affair is a failure, one that establishes a primary plot line for the novel: Marianne is the one to fall in love with Armand, not the reverse. Indeed, Marianne follows Armand first to London, when he leaves France, and then to New York City. At every turn, she becomes jealous of the men with whom Armand is involved and continues to attempt to seduce him, to change him, and then, as a last resort, to change herself. When all attempts fail, Marianne lashes out by revealing to Armand that Comte de Rasbon is his father; this knowledge will eventually lead to tragedy. Armand's relationships with these characters are not the only opportunities for melodrama. Perhaps one of the most significantly affected scenes in the text is a result of the homosexual panic experienced by one of Armand's early lovers, Jean Mareau.

The death of Jean Mareau is the impetus Armand needs to move to New York, but as Anthony Slide notes, "the manner of Jean's leaving is more than a little melodramatic" (167). Indeed, beyond being simply melodramatic, it is indicative of homosexual panic and paranoia. The relationship between Armand and Jean is one of opposites, and one that fulfills traditional gender roles. Bironge, Armand's benefactor, hires Jean Mareau to be Armand's tutor when it becomes clear that his current tutor and cousin, Lucien, is dying[7]. Mareau is described as "the

son of parents who had migrated to the West Indies . . . well-read, sophisticated and cultured . . .

He had lived with the Negroes of the colonies, and he had known the aristocracy of France" (59).

In other words, Mareau was older, worldlier, and much more experienced than Armand. In

evaluating their relationship, it is helpful to consider Judith Butler's theories on gender

performance and desire. Butler argues that

> gender can denote a unity of experience, of sex, gender, and desire, only when sex can be
> understood in some sense to necessitate gender—where gender is a psychic and/or cultural
> designation of the self—and desire—where desire is heterosexual and therefore differentiates
> itself through an oppositional relation to that other gender it desires."[8] (*Gender Trouble* 30)

We see this relation perpetuated at the start of their relationship when Armand first flirts with the

idea of sexual intimacy between the two by describing an imagined past-life where Mareau, the

male-performing partner, dressed in expensive suits with "lace ruffles" and where Armand, the

female-performing partner, wore "a silk-frilled petticoat" (63). As Butler suggests, their

relationship requires certain sexual rules be followed in order for it to work, in this case a

gendering of each sex role, despite the fact that both partners are men.

For a time, the relationship continues to grow and progress successfully toward "a mutual

understanding . . . a certain likeness of desire" (68) because Mareau is able to view himself as the

male partner. When he considers Armand, he sees the boy as "frail" and "slim," while Armand

notices Mareau's "well-knit body . . . broad, muscular shoulders [and] manly height" (69). As

---

[7] Another example of the melodramatic, as Armand has quite fallen in love with Lucien despite
being his cousin.

[8] Gender and masculinity will be explored in depth in chapter five, but it is important to consider
it here in regards to the homosexual panic that Mareau faces, considering it is brought on by a
reversal of the comfortable gender roles that Armand and Mareau had been performing.

long as the relationship between the two continues on in this way, with each partner fulfilling his prescribed role, it may last; however, when Armand breaks the rules, when he attempts to assume the dominant role in their relationship, Jean Mareau is faced with his own paranoia about his sexuality, and he panics. The scene that plays out is almost gothic in nature. The prevalence of homosexual paranoia in gothic literature is well-established by Eve Kosofsky Sedgwick. In *Epistemology of the Closet* (1990, 2006), she describes the many "forms of investment that force men into the arbitrarily mapped, self-contradictory, and anathema-riddled quicksands of the middle distance of male homosocial desire" (186). She adds that gothic tales, or gothic scenes in this case, are ripe for homophobia because they create an atmosphere where one man is both feared and desired by another man (187). While this text is not gothic, the pulp genre certainly borrows from its traditions, and this scene in *Twilight Men* fulfills that very rule. Armand had been the desired partner/object, but as he expresses his sexual agency, Jean Mareau's panic causes him to fear Armand.

After Armand comes to Mareau in the library and instigates their first distinctly sexual affair, Mareau admits that he "shall never be happy again" (86). The narrative tone shifts, and instead of describing the two lovers in warm terms, Mareau begins to think of himself as a "leper" and "unclean" (87). Mareau struggles to reconcile his belief that same-sex love and desire "had existed as long as the race, dateless, primeval" (ibid) against a new understanding of "his own nature" (89), which has changed since Armand assumed the supposed masculine role in their relationship by his actions as sexual aggressor. Eventually, after additional encounters, Jean Mareau believes he can no longer live with "his own ugliness" and with memories of "all the fetid, rotten things" he had done (93). In a deeply intimate moment, and just as it seems Jean Mareau may be able to come to terms with his sexuality and to fully accept Armand as a partner,

Armand asks Mareau if he loves him, and the final straw breaks. Mareau admits that he does, then leaps out the bedroom window to his death. His paranoia about homosexuality and the emotional and psychological panic it provokes in him cannot be overcome. Jean Mareau is not the only person in Armand's life to struggle with questions about gender.

Another character who begins to question the rigidity of her gender is Marianne Dodon, and this is brought about by her desire for Armand. She recognizes from very early on that Armand is different; nevertheless, she continues to attempt to seduce him. Marianne follows Armand to London under the guise of caring for him after Lucien dies and Bironge leaves to deal with the funeral and other issues. In considering their fantasy relationship, Marianne notes that "she wanted him to be the aggressor" (72) but realizes in their first encounter that she had to fulfill that role. Part of Marianne's initial strategy had been to place an even greater emphasis on her femininity, to act even more the female part in an attempt at "re-awakening his interest" (ibid). This strategy of course fails. Instead of stirring passion in Armand, she realizes that Armand has begun to think of her "like a mother" (71). The failure brings with it recognition. Armand at last explains that he loves Jean Mareau, and Marianne exclaims: "you're one of those creatures who prefer your own sex" (74) before continuing on to condemn his "effeminacy" and "perversion" (75). Still, despite her initial reaction to Armand's admission, Marianne cannot resist her own desire. Instead, she considers the possibility that she can invert her gender role in order to successfully pursue Armand, just as Armand inverted his sexual role in order to pursue Jean Mareau. It may seem an impossible feat for Marianne, to assume the male role in a proposed relationship between a heterosexual woman and a homosexual man; however, as David M. Halperin notes, "to be recognized and treated as male is inevitably to be socially and subjectively constituted as male. The result of that gender-constitutive process appears in many aspects of masculine subject formation" (*How to Be Gay*, 2012, 333). In other words, despite the biological

impossibilities for her, Marianne can and does nevertheless attempt to constitute herself as male.

This becomes apparent in the following scene:

> She found it strange that Nature was so oddly revealing her to herself, so strangely refuting
> her own arguments in favor of love between opposite sexes only. She wondered whether
> there might not be in her a vein of latent masculinity. The very fact that he affected her so
> deeply was a sign that love did not confine itself to one mode of expression, since she, a
> woman, was loving one who was more woman than man. (77)

This new appreciation for the possibilities of gender roles allows her, rather foolishly, to

continue her pursuit, not just in London but ultimately to New York City and Armand's eventual

end. She reads Havelock Ellis and begins to consider herself something other than "absolute"

(80-81). Ultimately, these sexual and gender inversions fail both Armand and Marianne. In

Armand's case, the sexual role reversal was brought on by Mareau's distancing himself

physically from Armand; the young man wanted to engage in a sexual relationship with the man

he had fallen in love with, but Mareau resisted any relations beyond a certain point. In finally

pursuing Mareau more aggressively, Mareau equated Armand's role in their relationship as the

aggressor, or masculine partner. This caused Mareau to panic and ultimately commit suicide. In

Marianne's case, she attempted to invert her gender role, also in pursuit of a lover. Like

Armand's attempt, however, it fails, not because Armand panics but because he cannot feel

sexual desire for a woman. Marianne misunderstands the nature of Armand's sexuality by

assuming that because Armand is feminine, he will respond favorably to whomever is the more

masculine partner. Marianne survives her mistake, but Jean Mareau does not survive Armand's,

nor is he the only character apparently doomed by Armand's sexuality.

In addition to Lucien, Bironge, and Jean Mareau, all of whom die before Armand leaves

London for New York City, two other characters are destined to an early grave, presumably because there is no happy ending[9] for the homosexual pulp character or those closest to him. Indeed, Anthony Slide goes so far as to write that, "it is probably best that [Armand] should die, because he certainly would not have looked forward to life as an aging homosexual male" (168). David Bergman, in his essay on gay pulp fiction, adds: "For quite some time I imagined that all pre-Stonewall novels followed an unbroken formula: boy meets boy, boy dies" ("Cultural Work" 26). These are just two examples[10] of a trend in gay criticism which equates homosexuality with death and suicide. Despite some evidence to the contrary, as described in other chapters in this book, the belief persists in large part due to pulp novels like *Twilight Men*.

The two most important deaths in the novel are those of Armand and his father, Comte de Rasbon. The fact that the characters are related is significant, but the critical condition is the concept of sexuality as hereditary which Tellier exploits. When Armand confronts his father to claim that he is homosexual because of the Comte's own moral failings, we see that the relationship is almost symbiotic: one cannot live without the other. Indeed, Armand learns, much to his chagrin, that the Comte has been monitoring him from afar, paying his debts and keeping him from too much scrutiny or scandal. This revelation is followed by one of the more melodramatic scenes in the novel, wherein Armand murders his own father. Just before the

---

[9] In *Lost Gay Novels*, Anthony Slide notes that *Twilight Men*, first published in 1931, was republished in 1948 (printed twice) and published again in 1957, quite a success for any novel with an openly gay main character, especially one that is now considered to be "rather silly" and filled with "triviality" (168). Slide argues that there are two reasons for this success. The first reason is that there simply were very few titles available that treated homosexuality so openly, and which were cheap and easy to buy. The second argument, and the most relevant, is implied. This is that the novel sold well because its main character dies (ibid).

[10] See also: Robert McRuer's *The Queer Renaissance* (NYU Press, 1997), Lee Edelman's *No Future* (Duke U Press, 2004), and David Bergman's *Gaiety Transfigured* (U Wisconsin Press, 1991) among others.

dramatic patricide, Comte de Rasbon releases a barrage of criticisms against his son, including

the following which addresses his son's drug addiction and the Comte's promise to have Armand

committed to a mental institution because of it:

> The only way you can be made to stop is by force. He should have beaten the life out of you,
> and you might have become a man instead of something that should be wearing skirts. I don't
> believe all this rot about you people being born that way. You're that way because you want
> to be [. . .] But to want men . . . that's rotten . . . it's beastly [. . .] What filthiness! (205)

This passage near the end of the narrative brings the reader back to the very beginning, where

Bironge suggested to de Rasbon that Armand is simply different, and where the Comte

responded to that suggestion with vitriol. The father and son have been connected all along, so it

should come as no surprise when, after Armand kills his father by bashing his "grizzled head"

(210) with a candlestick, Armand's own body succumbs to the complications and strains brought

about by his drug addiction and his "vile, perverted" (209) lifestyle. While the style may be

wooden and the prose simplistic, *Twilight Men* is nevertheless an important example of the gay

pulp novel before the 1960s. Its commitment to the melodramatic, its depiction of homosexual

panic and paranoia, its exploration of inverted gender and sexualities, and its reliance on the

machinations of death and suicide speak to its place in the tradition of this genre. It is just one of

many in this category to display homosexual men and homosexual spaces openly, if not

pleasantly.

Charles Henri Ford and Parker Tyler are poignant examples of the erasure that gay

American authors have suffered. Despite the fact that the two were prolific writers, editors, and

publishers in their time, and despite the fact that they interacted personally and professionally

with writers and artists such as Gertrude Stein, Andy Warhol, and Djuna Barnes, the two are

nevertheless underappreciated and criticism of their work is severely lacking (Wolmer, "Charles

Henri Ford," 1987). Christopher Looby claims *The Young and Evil* is "one of the truly

remarkable novels of the twentieth century" ("The Gay Novel" 430). In addition, William Carlos

William considered Parker Tyler's long poem, *The Granite Butterfly* (1945), to be "the best long

poem written by an American since *The Waste Land*" (Watson, Introduction, 24).

Ford and Tyler's modernist gay pulp novel, *The Young and Evil* was published in 1933,

just two years after *Twilight Men*. As with the latter, *The Young and Evil* is set in New York

City, including specific areas of the city which at this time are becoming clearly identifiable as

gay spaces. George Chauncey identifies some of these spaces, including bath houses, cafeterias,

and gay bars (*Gay New York* 1994); however, Ford and Tyler also address specific

neighborhoods and public areas. For example, when Karel and Frederick are arrested for

disorderly conduct after being attacked by a group of sailors, one of the officers tells the gay

men, "if you'd stayed on Broadway this wouldna happened" (184). Clearly, there are areas of the

city where it is acceptable for gay men to "appear" homosexual, and others where it is not.

While it is unknown whether or not Tellier based his narrative on his own life, Ford and

Tyler certainly did; indeed, each character can be traced to the person he or she is based on in

Ford or Tyler's experience. Steven Watson, drawing significantly upon information from the

Parker Tyler Archives at the University of Texas, Austin, notes in his introduction that the novel

tells "the parallel story of the real lives lived" (3) and that Ford and Tyler together "embarked

upon the escapades immortalized in *The Young and Evil*" (11). This is not unusual in the pulp

novels. George Sylvester Viereck, for example, based *Men into Beasts* on his own experiences in

prison. This distinction aside, other similarities include the fact that *The Young and Evil* is told in

a melodramatic albeit experimental fashion, and it, too, deals with issues of homosexual

paranoia, as well as sexual inversion, particularly in terms of gender expression. In addition,

Ford and Tyler, like Tellier, emphasize the seemingly inextricable relationship between homosexuality and violence.

Ford and Tyler's melodrama is crafted quite distinctly from the type expected from pulp narratives. There are two elements that best demonstrate how the authors play with melodrama. The first is in the style itself, which is a type of modernist surrealism characterized "by a sense of determinism and fatality" (See 1092). The very nature of the novel's form results in an oppressive, near-nihilistic pathos. In addition to the form and style, the narrative's resolution recalls a gothic terror resulting in a dénouement that is both shockingly violent and maddeningly inconclusive.

A representative example of the surrealist style which creates the melodrama that persists throughout the narrative occurs in the very first paragraphs of the first chapter, revealingly titled, "Well Said the Wolf":

> Well said the wolf to Little Red Riding Hood no sooner was Karel seated in the Round Table than the impossible happened. There before him stood a fairy prince and one of those mythological creatures known as Lesbians. Won't you join our table? They said in sweet chorus. When he went over with them he saw the most delightful little tea-pot and a lot of smiling happy faces. (11)

Although the melodramatic features of the gay pulp novel are traditionally interwoven with a darker mood, the passage here is representative of the sensationalist approach that Ford and Tyler take to storytelling, as well as their commitment to plot and style over characterization. Indeed, in this bizarre introduction, we learn just one character's name, Karel, while the rest of the characters and elements are equated with mythological or fairy tale types, including the wolf and Red Riding Hood (alluding to the fairy tale as well as the "trade" market for supposedly straight men who would sleep with male prostitutes[11]), the Round Table (of Arthurian legend),

---

[11] i.e. "The erotic system of wolves and punks" (Chauncey, *Gay New York,* 88).

the fairy prince (fairy being a common term for an effeminate homosexual), a chorus (dramatic

device), and a tea-pot (likely alluding to both *Alice's Adventures in Wonderland* and tearooms[12]).

This melodramatic stream-of-consciousness narration is maintained throughout the text, and it is

meant to signify celebration of "the sexual freedom of New York's bohemian milieu" and to

"dissolve the rapidly solidifying opposition between heterosexuality and homosexuality"

(Corber, Introduction, 9).

Despite the fact that *The Young and Evil* appears more celebratory in tone[13], which is at

odds with much of the gay pulp genre, it does demonstrate one of the key characteristics of these

works: homosexual paranoia and panic. This paranoia expresses itself in three ways: first, in the

casual swapping of sexual partners by the main characters, which is suggested to be a kind of

bohemian free-love but is in reality a result of the failure to believe in "the sincerity of the people

[they] saw living together supposedly in love" (72). In their world, sexuality and love and

sexuality and commitment cannot coexist. Indeed, as Joseph Cady argues, their disguised panic

"implicitly endorses a 'feminine' and depressive picture of male homosexuality" which makes it

impossible for them to "fall in love with each other" ("American Literature," *Gay and Lesbian*

Literary Heritage, 33).

In the second case, sexual paranoia is expressed in the way the gay characters adjust their

gender performance when they appear in public spaces that are beyond their safe boundaries, as

---

[12] Chauncey helpfully explains that tearooms in Greenwich Village "served as the meeting grounds for its bohemians" (*Gay New York* 237), including homosexual men and women. It is important to note that *The Young and Evil* is set in the Greenwich Village neighborhood of New York City, which makes this allusion all the more apt.

[13] Byrne R.S. Fone argues the same in *The Columbia Anthology of Gay Literature*. According to Fone, "while many other books of the thirties . . . ruled that homosexuals should lead melancholy and tragic lives, *The Young and Evil* triumphantly derides that convention" (654).

on Broadway or 72nd Street, where they can be their natural selves. When they appear elsewhere, however, they sometimes "imitate the straight" and match their gaits to "the inconspicuous left-right balance-turn-on-either-foot of the gangsters" (128). For all their talk of freedom, the men still fear being "found out," they still fear the raids, and they still fear the heteronormative system, illustrated in this case by the New York City mafia and the police department, both of which will take advantage of them and then punish them for the trouble.

Finally, homosexual panic presents itself when Gabriel, slighted by his former lover who has left him for a mutual friend, visits Theodosia, the only significant female friend in this Greenwich group, and attempts to have sex with her. The scene is one of the more melodramatic in its description. In his attempt to free himself from loving another man, Gabriel's body reacts violently:

> She kept her eyes closed as she felt Gabriel beside her. Her nightgown was being raised and she breathed faster and faster. She felt Gabriel's hands on her ankles and her legs slowly bending at the knees. Oh, oh she gasped, her eyes still closed. Then she opened her eyes some and saw Gabriel on the bed kneeling in front of her with his hands holding her legs apart, his mouth descending.
>
> Gabriel felt her faint. He was standing in the middle of a merry-go-round and saw a nude woman walk up behind him. She kicked his head off. He saw his head whirl brilliantly from his shoulders. His head was a bottle whirling in the sun. He could see the blood gushing from his headless trunk. It gushed like vomit.
>
> He had vomited. (84)

Thus, this scene combines two of the major pulp features, melodrama and panic, to create one of the more bizarre moments in the narrative. The juxtaposing of Gabriel's horrific fantasy, imagining himself on a merry-go-round being decapitated by a naked woman just as he is about to perform cunnilingus on said woman for the first time, reminds the reader that much of the positive treatment of homosexuality in this text is façade. As James Levin notes, "a casual reading might convincingly lead one to believe that we have here an early gay liberation statement, but this would be too simplistic a view" (49). While it is clear that these men are "out" to an extraordinary extent, given the time period, and that they at least appear to accept themselves—with perhaps the exception of Gabriel, as noted in the passage above—and have helped to create a make-shift community of like-minded individuals, they yet suffer from many of the same insecurities as are expressed in other gay pulp narratives that are more overtly negative in their portrayals of gay characters. They may run happily, but they are still running.

For this reason, Levin argues that the novel is "overvalued" (63). I cannot wholly agree with this claim, though he is correct to question readings which suggest that Ford and Parker's narrative is a cheerful treatment of homosexuality. Roger Austen is one critic whom Levin may be criticizing in this regard, as his evaluation of the text is glowing. Austen claims, for example, that "there is nowhere in the novel the sense of being overwhelmingly oppressed in a homophobic society, because everyone in madcap Greenwich Village has about as much sex as he can handle" (*Playing the Game* 61). This argument is reductive; it constricts the freedom to live openly as a homosexual to the ability to have sex with other men in private. The pulp novels are especially notable for incorporating public gay spaces into their narratives, which means they are explicitly concerned with sexual freedoms beyond the bedroom. Austen's argument also ignores certain fears that do arise throughout Ford and Tyler's narrative, such as fears of raids, rape, eviction (due to discovery), and arrest.

The Young and Evil, like many of these pulp novels, also explores gender and sexual inversion. Within the first few paragraphs, for example, a mysterious "little girl with hair over one ear" asks Karel: "why don't you dress in girls' clothes?" To this interrogation, the mythic Lesbian adds, "yes your face is so exquisite we thought you were a Lesbian in drag when we first saw you," and the chorus notes, "for two long hours they insisted that he would do better for himself as a girl" (11). The suggestion is made from the start, incorrectly, that homosexuality and gender expression are corresponding traits; however, this is a theme that continues throughout the narrative, as the main characters display their obsession with physical appearance, including jewelry, dress, and make-up.

An early scene that demonstrates this fixation on physical appearances and stereotypically feminine gender expression occurs when Karel returns home from prostituting himself. He has a new bracelet on his wrist, which Julian immediately asks to see. When Karel hands it over, he notes that his "jewel boxes will be bursting if last night should be repeated often" (38). To this he adds a description of his night, beginning with the fact that, upon reaching the club, he "went directly to the bathroom and retouched [his face]." The scene is meant to reveal the casual relationship that these men have with sex, and the fact that they are willing to sell their bodies for money or other "lucre" (ibid); however, the more important consideration is that the men are being described not just as prostitutes, but as prostitutes who perform the female gender in order to seduce their trade. Rictor Norton (1997) offers a helpful explanation for this phenomenon:

> The possibility that fairies were easier and cheaper than female prostitutes is not an adequate explanation for what really seems to be a preference . . . wolf/punk relationships were very often found in circumstances which are now dismissed as "situational" . . . but in fact they often persisted even when women were available . . . Fairies were sometimes even "married" to wolves or jockers [sic], masculine men who positively preferred male sexual partners and who were regarded as being different from normal yet not quite queers. (264)

Not only does this analysis describe one of the reasons[14] why the main characters may have preferred to "invert" their gender expression, to wear make-up and jewelry as a sign that they were available to men, for a price, but it also refers specifically to the type of man who would be referred to as a "wolf," which is one of the fantasy creatures introduced at the very beginning of the novel. In addition to being a signal for trade, however, dressing in drag was also a cultural phenomenon in New York City at this time. The penalties for cross-dressing could be severe, so the characters decide to dress in costume rather than risk being arrested: "Frederick was not made up more than usual except his eyebrows were plucked thinner but Julian had on his face the darkest powder he could borrow, blue eyeshadow and several applications of black mascara; on his lips was orange-red rouge and a brown pencil had been on his eyebrows showing them longer" (151). Thus, unlike the gender and sexual inversions described in *Twilight Men*, which were devices performed in an attempt to win a lover, and unlike situational inversion as depicted in *Fall of Valor*, to be discussed later in this chapter, Ford and Tyler's inversions are first, economically necessary, and second, expressive of the bohemian freedom that this fictive Greenwich Village of the 1930s is meant to signify.

Lastly, although no one dies in *The Young and Evil*, the suggestion of violence nevertheless permeates the text in three ways: first, in the mafia threat, both economic and physical, that looms over the characters' daily lives; second, in the physical threats posed by

---

[14] This is not to say that the "inversion" in and of itself is antithetical to any particular homosexual experience. Gender and sexuality must not be conflated; however, it is important to acknowledge the context of the text and the cultural realities it depicts. It is well-established (Chauncey, Faderman, de la Croix, etc.) that the "true" homosexual in the 1930s was assumed to be effeminate, and that the trade industry functioned in large part based on binary rules: wolves were the masculine, assertive partners who usually considered themselves to be heterosexual, whereas the feminine, passive males, known as fairies and pansies, were the homosexual partners.

appearing homosexual in public; and third, in the gothic threat that conflates sexual desire with

violence (or threat of death), which is a significant feature of the gay pulp novel as demonstrated

in *Twilight Men*. We see the first example, the ever-present mafia force, described most clearly

near the end of the narrative, when Julian learns that Gabriel and Louis have hired a mafia thug

to rob Julian of his possessions:

> Do you know two guys named Gabriel and Louis? he asked
> Julian said yes he knew them.
> Have youse seen them lately?
> Not recently Julian said.
> Youse don't know where I could find them?
> No.
> Well if youse see them again, tell them to look out for me because they're going to get it!
> Julian wanted to know why.
> What I'm going to do ot them will be plenty, see. They told lies on me to the big boss!
> They did? said Julian knowing nothing about the big boss.
> Yeah. I'd seen the bastards around and the other day they asked me how much I'd take to
> clean out this place. (206)

Without steady income, and living in an apartment controlled by the mob, Julian would have had

no recourse had their plan succeeded. This scene is significant in that it creates an awareness of

how solitary, and thus compromised, a homosexual life could be. As Michael Bronski notes,

Greenwich Village and other gay neighborhoods "were often in the less prosperous sections of

cities" (*Queer History* 171). He adds that, "having made the decision to be more open about their

sexuality, [gay men and women] understood they might have a difficult time finding

employment" (ibid). Thus, gay men like Julian were at risk of losing everything, including their

home and job, if they were "outed" to the wrong people or, more significantly in this case, forced

by physical threat to leave a neighborhood where they had been accepted.

The threat of physical violence is indeed explored in this text, though ultimately it is not Julian who faces it. Instead, Karel and Frederick are attacked by a group of sailors simply because they appeared homosexual in a part of the city where it was not acceptable to be such:

> They got up on Riverside Drive again. Soon there was a lot of sailors and civilians who must have started to follow them. Karel and Frederick could hear them, at first a crowd of them but neither dared look back. Let's hurry Karel said. Let's cross. He heard them coming and calling out things. He would not stop nor would Frederick. [. . .] When Karel did turn around they were leaping at Frederick and him. He saw Frederick get swiped. One swung, one sailor, at Karel who had to run then across to two automobiles parked where some people were. He heard pad pad after him but was Frederick being killed. (182)

Fortunately for Frederick and Karel, the automobiles that Frederick dashed to for help happened to be occupied by plainclothes police officers. In many cases, the gay pulp genre established police offers as antagonistic to homosexual men, primarily because they often were; however, there were degrees of tolerance[15]. As Vern L. Bullough notes, although police and law enforcement officials were sometimes tolerant, "there was, however, never any guarantee that this would always be the case; often out of the blue the police would one day suddenly intervene and charge individuals with crimes against nature or, more likely, with lesser crimes such as indecent behavior, creating a public nuisance, or any number of greater or lesser crimes" (69). Ford and Tyler, residents of the village themselves, accurately describe a possible scenario between gay men and the police in this scene. Although the characters, Frederick and Karel, were doing nothing wrong, they were nevertheless charged with disorderly conduct; of

---

[15] George Chauncey describes arrangements made in Greenwich Village between police and the gay and lesbian establishments as largely cooperative, although he adds that between 1924-1926 there was a series of "crackdowns" on gay establishments, which both heightened anxiety and animosity, but which also helped to further solidify the specific gay spaces in New York City where gay men and women could be left relatively un-harassed by law enforcement (*Gay New York* 238-241).

significance, however, is the fact that the sailors were also charged. This demonstrates the fact that the police officers were not necessarily targeting gay men, but neither were they eager to protect them more than was absolutely necessary.

As in *Twilight Men*, Ford and Tyler end their narrative with a scene of gothic melodrama. The majority of the unusual affect is constructed, as discussed earlier in this section, by the combination of surrealist-modernist form and style. The book's concluding scene, however, is a direct appeal to the gothic melodrama so often found in these pulp novels, and it conveniently follows numerous ponderings on death, such as when Julian personifies fate and time. He thinks of fate as a fencing partner bringing fortune or misfortune, and of time as a deceptive monster (196-197). These musings introduce a scene where Louis and Gabriel, about whom Julian had just been thinking, are bantering about death. Louis tells Gabriel that, "death will touch you" and adds that, "he's a friend . . . I asked him to keep away from me but gave him your address" (197). Later, after the mobster has visited Julian, Karel hears Julian mumble about "terror and sickness" (207). These are twin concepts, to Karel, whose third is "sex . . . whose shadow, too, is death" (ibid).

The way the men treat these concepts of fate, time, sex, and death, is in keeping with the gothic tradition associating desire and violence. Julian's former lover has taken a new one, and together those two have collaborated with the mafia, a violent organization, to take everything away from Julian. This same treatment of love and violence is affected with heightened drama in the final scene, when Louis, having left Gabriel, returns to Karel and entreats him to leave Julian so that they can be together. This is another threat of separation committed against Julian. Their tête-à-tête is almost hypnotic, Louis stripping Karel of his clothes and forcing him to bed all the while Karel tries, in vain, to resist:

Louis stepped up closely to him and clutched one of his lapels. Who do you think you are? Karel's lips pouted and quivered. He did not resist having his topcoat taken off, then his jacket, then his vest and, lastly, falling over on the bed, his trousers. Louis leaned over and Karel saw him kissing him before he felt the bite. Then Karel screamed. (215)

The final moment is Vampiric, recalling the drama, erotic energy, and threat of violence established in the tradition of Bram Stoker and Sheridan Le Fanu.[16]

Sam See claims that *The Young and Evil* "disrupts critical narratives that relegate queerness to a 'niche' realm of scholarly and literary interest" (1075). In considering the importance of this text and of the gay pulp genre generally, this is indeed a significant argument to make. Much of the appeal of the pulp novels at the time of their publication was that they incorporated both recognizable details, such as relatable New York City locations and events, with melodramatic storytelling. As demonstrated, *Twilight Men* and *The Young and Evil* manage to describe gay men and gay lifestyles, sometimes unflatteringly, as just another element of metropolitan life. The concept of the city in literature, and in reality, as a space for perpetuating and disseminating information about queer culture, cannot be overlooked. There are, however, other common spaces for treating homosexuality in the pulp genre, such as in military and mentorship relationships.

Charles Jackson's *Fall of Valor* was originally published in a pulp press in 1946, then reprinted by Signet in 1949. As Michael Bronski notes, that novel was so successful that its cover image has become "a common refrigerator magnet and illustration of books on 'queer pulp'" (Jackson, "Introduction," v). The fact that the book received numerous reviews in 1946 and 1947 demonstrates that people were beginning to treat homosexual literature as culturally

---

[16] Sam See also notes the significance of this Vampiric kiss, though he argues it is "the bite's mythic resonance" which matters, particularly as it might relate to "Little Red Riding Hood's" wolf, introduced at the start of the book ("Making Modernism" 1083).

relevant and homosexuality as a subject that was open to discussion. The majority of these reviews are either ambivalent or positive regarding the book itself, yet they are filled with homophobic or stereotypically naïve considerations about homosexuality in general. Harrison Smith, in *The Saturday Review* (1946), writes that homosexuality, "is an uncomfortable and an ugly theme" and that the main character suffers "the slow growth of an evil seed" (12). Diana Trilling's review is less damning than Smith's, but in it she claims the book is a "study of disease" (450) and a "fiction of pathology" ("Fiction in Review" 451). The Kinsey Report, which shattered stereotypes about sexuality and which broke open the dialogues surrounding such, would be published just two years after *Fall of Valor* and these reviews.

In addition, while some critics, such as Felice Picano, have praised *Fall of Valor* as being "the first significant work of American literature to confront the subject of homosexuality" (qtd. in Crowley, "Charles Jackson's," 259), we must be careful not to confuse the first critically attended works with the "first significant work." The fact is that the time period, and particularly the effects of World War II[17], made the possibility for writing about, reading about, and discussing homosexual issues possible, but as has been established already, the first gay works did not suddenly appear in the mid-1940s.

Fall of Valor takes as its main subject the latent homosexuality of a middle-aged English professor, John Grandin, who begins to understand his desire for men after meeting a young marine. The professor has a history of interest in soldiers but it takes a direct encounter in close

---

[17] The military—and the prison, as will be demonstrated in the next section of this chapter—are often labeled as places of "situational homosexuality." This term is typically applied to spaces and circumstances where absence of the opposite sex has resulted in sexual relationships with members of the same-sex, not due to "real" desire or romantic attachment, but out of necessity. George Chauncey rightly challenges the concept as "culturally blind" (*Gay New York* 91), but in literature, and the gay pulps in particular, these situational stereotypes linger.

quarters with this particular man to bring his desires to consciousness. Margot Canaday notes

that in the time period immediately following World War II, military and governmental officials

were already discussing the possibility that "military life itself created conditions that

encouraged homosexuality[18]" (*Straight State* 161). While this demonstrates a clear lack of

understanding regarding homosexuality, it does reveal that conversations about homosexuality

were taking place both at the popular cultural levels, in pulp novels, for example, and at the

highest levels of government, and that the parallels between sexual desire and military men were

already being drawn.

It is clear that Jackson's text perpetuates situations of war and wartime as a "gay space,"

one which at least instigates homosexual yearnings, if not allowing for successful sexual or

romantic acts themselves. The narrative, grounded as it is in its fascination with military youth

and sexuality, also delivers key features of the pulp novel: melodrama created through use of

atmosphere and mood; homosexual panic which, in this case, often masquerades as confidence

and scientific awareness; gender and sexual inversion as relative to heterosexual marriages and

"effeminate" homosexuals; and a close relationship between sexuality and death or violence, as

demonstrated in Grandin's obsession with death and in the melodramatic, violent final meeting

between Grandin and his object of desire, the marine Cliff Hauman.

---

[18] John W. Crowley adds, "World War II significantly lowered the cultural threshold of homoeroticism. Not only did homosexuals from across the country . . . find one another in the armed services, but they also found validation in their 'deviant' sexuality. Moreover, under the guise of admiring manly valor . . . it became easier and more socially acceptable for Americans to gaze upon the young warriors and to celebrate the spectacle of their sheer physicality" ("Charles Jackson's," 268). Thus, wartime and sexuality are inextricably linked, and this becomes reflected in the culture and in the literature of the time. See also: David K. Johnson's *The Lavender Scare* (U Chicago Press, 2004), Robert J. Corber's *Homosexuality in Cold War America* (Duke UP, 1997), and Allan Bérubé's *Coming Out Under Fire* (UNC Press, 1990).

The melodramatic atmosphere that Jackson creates in *Fall of Valor* becomes apparent within the first few pages of the novel. John Grandin is an accomplished academic. He is a college professor with a book deal from Scribner's and an apparently happy life with his wife and two sons. Yet, for some inexplicable reason, he is depressed and self-critical to the point of neurosis. In introducing Grandin to the reader, the narrator explains that "his happiness, his success, his marriage itself, seemed founded on sand" and that Grandin "was sometimes tensely aware of some unnamable force which momentarily menaced the whole structure of his planned life" (5). The melodramatic tension being crafted here recalls that of *Twilight Men* and *The Young and Evil*. There are notes of the gothic in it, as the narrator hints at dark and secret evils that cannot be contained much longer. These descriptions are meant to keep the reader on edge, wondering what could possibly be wrong with such a seemingly-accomplished, well-adjusted middle-aged suburban man. Even Grandin himself feels that "something was about to happen to him, something untoward, perverse" (6) and that "relief would only come when the secret was out (if secret it was), the nature of the crime named and accepted" (7). A number of early reviews suggest that Grandin was taken by surprise when he realized his sexual attraction for men. Ben Ray Redman (1947), for example, argues that Grandin "discovers in his middle forties that he is a homosexual" ("A Cross Section" 245) and that Grandin is meant to be "an innocent victim of fate" (ibid). These early scenes, however, as well as future revelations such as Grandin's hiding pictures of men in his study and staring at youths playing sports, make it clear that he was at least subconsciously aware of his sexual desires. Early reviewers either missed these clues or conveniently ignored them.

Just a few pages further into the narrative, as the plans for John and his wife Ethel's trip to Nantucket are revealed, the narrator makes clear that the couple's primary impetus for scheduling their trip at this particular part of the summer is because "a full moon was due" (14). Thus, the melodramatic mood is enhanced by the symbol of the moon, a symbol that persists throughout the text and continues to generate a suspicious and eerie atmosphere. In his 1946 review of the book, Walter McElroy makes an interesting point about the nature of melodrama in queer pulp novels appearing just after the war: "Now as we face an insecure and uneasy peace, these themes of guilt and doom appear likely to occur more often in writing that aims at serious understanding of reality" (20). This is a significant connection to make between the opportunity provided by the "gay space" of the military and the melodramatic themes persistent throughout the novel. Although the story does not take place in combat, the "gay space" of wartime is created by virtue of the professor's obsession with military men. His object of affection is a wounded but recovering marine who is bound to return to war in the near future. As such, war time and the strange attraction it holds for the main character permeate the text and coordinate with the sensational unraveling of John Grandin's heterosexual life, right up to the final, violent altercation between himself and the marine which will lead to Grandin's ruin. In addition to the melodramatic atmosphere, *Fall of Valor* maintains another trademark of the gay pulp genre, which is the panic and paranoia of its primary queer characters.

As Georges-Michel Sarotte rightly notes, "John Grandin comes to the realization that the ideal, virile homosexual relationship is not viable in American reality" (20) and that "the homosexual American dream can only be a mirage" (21) in the mid-twentieth-century. Mark Connelly adds that Grandin recognized his homosexuality as a neurosis (86-87). His desire for young men, and for Hauman in particular, might be irrepressible, but he can choose not to act on those feelings and thus remain a moral person. This desire for what is ultimately impossible in coordination with his refusal to act on his homosexual desires underlies the feelings of paranoia about homosexual relationships developed throughout the novel. Both Grandin and Cliff Hauman entertain ideas of homosexual attraction, but it is only the idea which can be allowed, and even then, only subconsciously or in discreet flirtation. When in the presence of an overtly gay male, Hauman's and Grandin's first reactions are to be caustically disparaging toward the young man or to be repulsed by him. This is despite the fact that Grandin himself is beginning to understand his own sexuality as male-desiring and that Hauman in essence admits to having enjoyed near-homosexual experiences with his marine comrade in the past. One of the more noteworthy examples of how Grandin's homosexuality is treated as a type of disease or neurosis[19] occurs in the third section of the novel, when his wife Ethel begins to treat him as if he is sick. This occurs following their bizarre experience in the moonlit, foggy walk home from the dance, when Grandin finally consciously recognizes his desire for Hauman:

> This morning she had begun and torn up a letter to the University dean, the gist of which was to ask him if it might be possible for her husband to be relieved of his teaching duties for the summer. She considered following this with a letter to her parents-in-law to tell them that their son was in need of a long rest, away from the boys and herself, and could he spend the summer with them in his home town? (233-234)

Her reaction is significant because it in many ways recalls depictions of women in literature,[20] suffering postpartum depression or other "afflictions," whom men could understand only as psychologically disturbed or neurotic. In this case, the situation is inverted and it is the sensible

---

[19] In *Homosexuality and Civilization* (2003), Louis Crompton reminds us that this perception of homosexuality as a medical problem dates back to Aristotle. Crompton argues that Aristotle's views on homosexuals "smack of the clinician who seeks a scientific explanation for human behavior" (65), adding that Aristotle considered homosexuality to be, in some cases, a "morbid propensity" and in others a result of "natural disposition" (ibid). While Charles Jackson's arguments rely more heavily on Freudian and pre-Kinseyan interpretations, it is important to note that the context of homosexuality as an illness or mental weakness is millenia old.

[20] See, for example, Sandra Gilbert's and Susan Gubar's seminal, *The Madwoman in the Attic* (Yale 1979).

wife who is struggling to understand and care for her afflicted husband. Jackson's reversing of the stereotypical gender roles played by husband and wife, while significant, is not the only case of inversion in the narrative.

John W. Crowley remarks that *The Fall of Valor* "questions [stereotypically masculine] sentiments by showing their naiveté in a post-Freudian universe of ignoble unconscious desires. The quaint romantic notions of 'immaculate manliness' or 'fortitude' or 'the soul' or 'character' itself are illusions over which Jackson refuses to throw 'the robe of concealment'" (262). Consideration of such illusions is demonstrated quite expertly in the scene where Grandin questions his ability to be a role model to college men. "Professors in personal conference with the young," thinks Grandin, "were supposed to serve as examples of behavior, to represent an exemplary manhood" (238). In other words, if Grandin acts on his desires for Hauman, he will be unable to avoid thinking of himself as unmanly[21], as effeminate, and thus "a hypocrite through and through" (239). The perception of homosexuality was that it affected every aspect of one's life, including a man's ability to perform completely non-sexual duties, such as a professor's ability to be a faculty advisor to his students. The perception stems, of course, from broader gender constructs of the 1940s which continued to prescribe the professional and academic spheres to men, and the domestic spheres to women[22]. As such, if Grandin allows himself to perform the "role" of the woman in his own private affairs with Cliff Hauman, he

---

[21] Grandin fears Ethel will naturally ascribe to this same philosophy, adding that, if she were to discover his desires, she would realize that "the man she loved was no man at all" (241).

[22] For an excellent and thorough history on the concepts of private and public spheres, see Ulla Wischermann's "Feminist Theories on the Separation of the Private and the Public" (*Women in German Yearbook*, U Nebraska Press, 2004).

disqualifies himself from a professional life. Charles Jackson also creates opportunity to consider

Hauman's gender performance as a disguise.

As Diana Trilling notes, "we are given many convincing evidences of Cliff's own quite

unconscious homosexuality. This is a good insight of Mr. Jackson's—his perception of the

sexual ambivalence of the ultra-masculine, football-player type of man" (451). What Trilling

labels sexual ambivalence, however, I would argue is actually an unwillingness to act on his

sexual desires. Hauman is indeed the hypermasculine character Trilling describes, but this

masculinity is a cover he applies in order to flirt with and seduce Grandin without having to

formally act on or publically acknowledge those desires himself. Hauman's subconscious desires

are intimated when he describes his best sexual conquests as being those which occurred as a

result of his ménage-a-trois with another man:

> I'd give anything to have you know my buddy Walt, and him to know you. You'd like
> him a lot, Johnnie. He's a swell guy to pal around with [. . .] I don't think either one of us
> ever laid a dame on leave that we didn't do it together. He loved it and so did I, but it was
> never any good, I don't care how hot she was, unless Walt was there too. We used to
> keep it up all night—not just once or twice, you understand, but seven or eight times.
> (304-305).

This confession takes place near the end of the novel, just before John Grandin reveals his

feelings for Cliff, and it follows a series of flirtations where Hauman hints and probes just

enough to cause Grandin to consider the possibility that Hauman might have same-sex desires as

well. But when Grandin does make his feelings explicit, Hauman reacts violently. This reaction

is caused by the fact that Grandin has broken the rules. In order for their friendship to work, and

for any possibility of a sexual experience between the two, Hauman's masculinity cannot be

challenged. In speaking the words, Grandin threatens to invert Hauman's gender performance, to

unmask his same-sex desires, ones which can only be acted upon when at least the appearance of heterosexuality (i.e. he and another man he is attracted to make love to the same woman) must be upheld. In the end, it is not that Hauman fears homosexuality or homosexual experiences, per se, but that he fears being treated like a woman, forced to respond to sentimental appeals rather than physical urges. Blake Bailey calls attention to the fact that Cliff Hauman "is afflicted by the same tortured latency as Grandin" (221). Bailey adds that Hauman sometimes expresses his repressed homosexuality through "egotistic perversity" and sometimes through seemingly accidental flirtation (ibid). Significantly, however, is the fact that, when he does treat homosexuality directly, it is in response to the one overtly gay character, Arne Eklund, whom Hauman calls a "pretty boy" and "fag," and whom he teasingly claims as his own (Jackson 202). Because neither Grandin nor Hauman is able to get beyond associating his homosexual desires with a fear of effeminacy, the violent ending is perhaps unavoidable.

Although there is just a single act of violence in the novel, it is anticipated throughout. Both the pre-violent anticipation and the explicitly violent final dénouement are instrumental in maintaining the melodramatic mood of this pulp novel; however, they also reinforce the notion that violence and homosexuality are codependent in American literature. Interestingly, one of the first clues the reader has in regards to the potential for violence in this novel comes from Ethel's observations about Cliff. She finds him animal-like:

> Cliff seemed almost a creature to beware of. His feet turned in when he walked, like an aborigine's, and the ponderous half-closed fists at the ends of his long arms swung monkey-like at his sides. How a girl could have fallen in love with such a man, whose physical attraction lay only in being massive, was beyond her. (157)

Of course, Ethel does not yet realize that her husband is attracted to Cliff partly because of that massive stature, which demonstrates both youth and masculinity. Had she known, she may have found occasion to warn Grandin about her observations.

Another hint of violence occurs in a beach scene forty pages later, when Hauman and Grandin touch intimately for the first time. Cliff Hauman, preparing to take a swim, lathers himself in sunscreen and then proceeds to do the same for one of the groups' new acquaintances, Bill Howard, an older gentleman who is also vacationing with his wife and with whom Hauman joked about "the fag," Arne Eklund. After finishing with Howard, Cliff moves on to do the same friendly service for John Grandin. There are two interpretations for Hauman's actions: first, that he is simply a well-mannered young man who honors his elders; or, second, that this is another flirtatious set-up, an excuse to be able to touch Grandin intimately without revealing the nature of his desire. It is difficult to understand Hauman's motives in this moment until later in the text, but Grandin's reaction is certainly revealing:

> The job finished, Hauman moved over to Grandin. 'I'll do it for you too, Johnnie'
> 'No, thanks. I can manage myself.'
> But Cliff ignored this. 'I can do it much easier than you can, Johnnie.' He bent down and placed his hands on Grandin's back.
> Grandin pulled violently away. 'I said I didn't want it!' He was surprised at the sharpness in his voice. (195)

The reaction is a "painful embarrassment" (ibid) to the entire group, but it serves to demonstrate that Grandin's desires are becoming explicit, and that others, Hauman in particular, will begin to notice. It also hints at the nature of Cliff Hauman and John Grandin's final meeting, where it is Grandin who reaches out to the younger man. That action, Grandin admitting his feelings to Hauman and Hauman, in turn, beating Grandin on the head with "brass-handled tongs" (307), runs the gamut of expectations set up by the gay pulp genre. It fulfills the requirement of a melodramatic ending, it reminds us of Hauman's paranoia and insecurities surrounding his own sexuality, and it reinforces the stereotype that where there is a gay love story, there must also be a violent, unhappy ending.

As described above, Charles Jackson's *Fall of Valor* fits squarely into the tradition in a number of ways, such as in its use of melodrama, its dependence on characters who exhibit paranoia over their homosexual desires, its exploration of gender inversion in gay men, and in its close association between violence and homosexuality. On the other hand, the novel differs from many gay pulps in that it sets its story outside of the city. Nevertheless, it manages to adhere to a "gay space" by exploiting homosocial situations created during wartime. This contributes to the long-standing perception that some instances of homosexuality are "situational." Another pulp novel that explores situational homosexuality while observing traditions of the pulp genre is George Sylvester Viereck's *Men into Beasts*.

A review of the literature concerning George Sylvester Viereck reveals two important considerations: first, Viereck's problematic political positions, specifically his reputation as a Nazi sympathizer[23] [24], which ultimately caused him to be imprisoned[25]; and second, notable interest regarding the homoerotic overtones of his more popular novel, *The House of the Vampire* (1907). Catherine Geddis describes this novel as one of a series of twentieth-century

---

[23] George Sylvester Viereck interviewed Adolf Hitler in 1923. The interview was republished in *Liberty Magazine* in July of that year, and *The Guardian* lists it as one of their "Great Interviews of the 20th Century" ("No Room for the Alien," *The Guardian*, 2007).

[24] It should also be noted that Viereck was a respected figure in literature and the arts as well. His publisher mentions that Viereck received accolades in *The New York Times* and the *Saturday Evening Post* (Viereck 10). Niel M. Johnson adds, Viereck "was a many- sided person who gained fame as a neo-romantic poet and peripatetic journalist" (1). Meanwhile, Susan Stryker describes him as a "minor poet who ran in avant-garde circles" (104).

[25] Justus D. Doenecke provides a concise description of Viereck's criminal history: "In October 1941 Viereck was arrested for failing to comply fully with the Foreign Agents Registration Act of 1938. Convicted in March 1942 and sentenced to prison, Viereck experienced a temporary reprieve when, a year later, the U.S. Supreme Court reversed the conviction on the grounds that the jury had been improperly charged. But in July 1943 he was again convicted, and this time he remained in jail until 1947" ("Viereck, George," *American National Biography*, 2000).

texts which provided "sympathetic portraits of gay, lesbian, and bisexual vampires" (325). Less available, however, is scholarship pertaining to his autobiographical piece detailing his time spent in prison, a work in which he describes a number of same-sex encounters, from the orgiastic to the romantic.

Men into Beasts is ostensibly a personal case study about the American prison system as described by the author who experienced it; however, the primary audience upon the book's original publication as a softcover pulp, intended or not, was likely those who were more interested in the homosexual aspects of the text. Viereck's publisher makes this point explicit in the introduction to the hardcover edition, where he asks, "is it far-fetched to assume that a few of the million persons who bought this book in its paper-covered edition . . . bought it with the sly notion that it might be useful to them to find out what life in prison is like?" (7). In other words, the publisher reinforces a notion about prison life which was widely accepted at that time, if not a point of public conversation. This is the idea, reinforced by the work of Havelock Ellis and John Addington Symonds, among others, that prisons, segregated as they are by sex, are an ideal location for situational homosexuality. Viereck's memoir, published in 1952, appeared at an interesting moment in time. Alfred Kinsey's work was beginning to reshape perceptions of gender and sexuality, and others, such as Evelyn Hooker, began their own "study of homosexuals not incarcerated in mental hospitals or prisons" (Gibson, Alexander, and Meem, 2014). Thus, Viereck, informed as he was by sexology and the work of Kinsey, Ellis, Magnus Hirschfield, and Sigmund Freud (Viereck 13), utilizes his personal experience in prison to create a narrative where prison fulfills the expectation of a situational "gay space," but wherein a fuller and far less homophobic treatment of homosexuality is explored.

Despite its being largely autobiographical, Viereck's text manages to satisfy the four primary criteria of the gay pulp genre as established in this chapter. First, Viereck creates melodrama by providing his first-person perspective in relation to the tensions, dangers, and "incredible things" (13) that happen inside prison walls. In addition, the idea of homosexual panic and paranoia is evidenced in some of the sexual relationships Viereck depicts, particularly those which are not consensual, and also in the way that "true" homosexuals, those who would act on same-sex desires whether or not they were in jail, are described and treated by the other men. The concept of inversion in gender or sexual roles appears as well, especially in the stereotypical way that masculine and feminine roles are perpetuated, although Viereck-as-narrator is careful to incorporate arguments which undermine these stereotypes in favor of more progressive theories of homosexuality. This subversion distinguishes his text from others in this chapter and from the pulp genre generally. Finally, given the setting, the relationship between violence and sexuality could not be more explicit, but Viereck also connects this concept to important moments pertaining to his own personal predicament.

Viereck's reliance on melodramatic formulae to create pathos and advance the plot becomes clear at the start of the text, when he introduces himself and his story by writing, "the incredible things I describe are true. They really happened" (13). The reader should know, of course, that the book is based on Viereck's own experiences, so the reinforcement of truth and the use of such emotive language function as a conscious effort to generate tension. The melodrama does not necessarily detract from the significance of the narrator's experience; in fact, the combination of melodramatic technique and autobiographical perspective make the events described arguably more powerful. David Halperin suggests such a possibility when he writes, "to live one's love life as melodrama, to do so knowingly and deliberately, is not of course to refuse to take it seriously" (294). As an observer, Viereck is not doing the "living" in this text, but he is describing the lives and relationships, some romantic and some not, of his fellow inmates. In this way, he is making serious observations of gay love "more widely available" (ibid) to an audience with preconceived notions about homosexuality and about the pulp genre which had traditionally styled it in certain uncompromising ways.

The melodrama is best effected in descriptions of sexual encounters among the inmates and of the way prisoners comport themselves when left unattended. An excellent example of this occurs early in the text, just after "lights out" on the narrator's first day in jail:

> I started to undress when strange noises began. It was like the awakening of a menagerie. Animal sounds, lascivious howls, caterwauls, screams shook the jailhouse [. . .] I caught a word here and there. They were the words seen on the walls of latrines. Some of them I had never heard before, but a sort of bestial vitality made their meaning unmistakable [. . .] It was a foul hurricane of obscenities. It was a physical and emotional explosion. All the suppressions of long days and nights in an Eveless hell were washed to the surface like scum from the deep. (47)

In this passage, Viereck creates a sensational scene where sounds in the darkness, jungle-like, correspond with the "Eveless hell" or woman-less setting, to hint at the actions in which these prisoners are now engaged. Some of them are masturbating, while others, as becomes clearer later in the text, are engaging in sexual relations with fellow prisoners. It is not any overt description of the acts themselves, however, so much as the draw of the melodramatic moment, which builds suspense and intrigue and that carries the reader tantalizingly forward.

In contrast, some of the melodrama created by sexual scenes is indeed more explicit and in keeping with the tone of the gay pulp genre. For example, later in the text, the narrator explicitly recounts a "wild orgiastic scene" (170) that occurred among "a parade of satyrs and fawns[26]" (171). The scene is littered with phrases such as "huge buttocks," "like a worshipper in a temple," "joyously inviting," and "a sort of Hallowe'en when the witches ride out on their broomsticks" (170-173). The narrator devotes three pages to the orgy itself and another two pages reflecting on it, making it one of the lengthiest and most extravagant single episodes in the entire narrative. This is not to say that all of the melodrama is sexual. Indeed, one of the most productive uses of melodrama is also one of the quaintest. Earlier in the text, the narrator describes a riot that took place at his prison in Atlanta shortly after he had left. He assures the reader that "fantastic events took place" (144), even going so far as to detail "a marriage between two inmates" (ibid). This scene is an important and illustrative example of how Viereck at times upsets the conventions of the gay pulp genre. While the marriage is in essence a camp-like farce, just one example of the rioting prisoners having good fun, it nevertheless underscores other moments in the book that illuminate the truly genuine relationships between prisoners in—given the circumstances—loving relationships. While the moment itself is melodramatic, "a heyday," the implication that same-sex male relationships could be successful is not lost. The success of said relationships depends on the willingness of both partners to engage, however, and as has been demonstrated in each of the three pulp novels so far, homosexual paranoia is nearly ubiquitous in the genre. *Men into Beasts* has its share as well.

---

[26] The description of "satyrs and fawns" refers to the sexual role, based on gender, that each of the men performs. Satyrs are the masculine or active partner, whereas fawns are the passive or receptive partner. In *Gaeity Transfigured*, David Bergman describes a study of same-sex sexuality in prisons that was conducted by Bruce Jackson in the 1970s. He notes that, "male prisoners divide themselves sexually into three groups: queens, those who are homosexual outside of prison; studs, those who while in prison play the inserter role with other men; punks, those who while in prison play the receptor" (28). Although the terms may change depending on the time and location, fiction, theory, and social science suggest consistent reliance on traditional gender dynamics in sex acts, even in the "situational" sexual circumstances of the prison.

If we have come to expect nothing else from the gay tradition in American literature, it is that the homosexual character will at some point in the novel express doubts, from the mild to the extreme, about his sexuality and his sexual desires. These doubts often become character flaws that create neuroses, addictions, or suicidal and even murderous tendencies. It is no surprise, then, to find similar cases in Viereck's novel, especially given that the text is set in a prison. The prison system itself, after all, had its own institutional anxieties about homosexual activity. As George Chauncey notes:

> Most authorities did not think that men isolated from women would randomly engage in homosexual behavior, but they did assume that such men would be susceptible to the fairies [. . .] Indeed, their fear was not just that fairies would induce other men to engage in homosexual practices but that rivalries between men for a fairy's attentions would escalate into violent confrontations. (92)

There are three important points to extract from this explanation. First, that situational homosexuality itself is not a danger. Second, that homosexual men *are* dangerous in that they have the ability to seduce heterosexual men who are isolated from women. Third, that the homosexual's seductive powers, in the right setting, are so far-reaching as to cause concern for the general safety and security of the entire prison, lest physical conflicts arise over a desired sex-object ("fairy"). George Viereck does describe each of these scenarios in his memoir, but he also creates opportunity for assuaging some of the homosexual panic or paranoia by rejecting certain stereotypes.

Viereck's portrayal of prison as a place for accepted homosexual activity certainly corresponds to Chauncey's first condition[27]. The fact that these men have same-sex sexual

---

[27] Viereck is not the only author to write about situational homosexuality in prison. Another is Chester Himes, whose novel, *Cast the First Stone* (1952) appeared in the same year as Viereck's. Gregory Woods notes that not only is Himes's novel autobiographical, like Viereck's, but it, too, suggests "a commonplace plea for tolerance" (291). A study of prison memoirs written by homosexual and bisexual authors in this regard is, I think, warranted.

relations does not particularly bother the guards; in fact, some of them even participate. For example, one of the guards, Mr. Colt, is described as a "somewhat corpulent individual with tremendous buttocks, a high voice, and a mincing walk" (45). The description is coded in such a way as to hint at his sexuality, but if this is not explicit enough, the guard is soon propositioned by an inmate who asks Colt to let him out for exercise and, in exchange, the prisoner will "make it worth [his] while" (46). Colt will be present at the infamous orgy scene later in the narrative as well, and we learn that he has preferences for "rough trade," or young black men (170).

The second condition, that homosexual men might take advantage of otherwise "straight" prisoners, is also fulfilled in the text. One of the most descriptive and disturbing accounts of homosexual paranoia occurs early in the narrative, not long after the narrator has arrived at the prison. He learns that a new inmate was "had by two guys" at his former jail, and the inmate now fears that he may have "a blood baby" (56). Put another way, the prisoner, having been raped by two men—it is unclear whether the rapes occurred simultaneously, though the phrasing suggests such—begins to think he is cursed with some kind of demonic pregnancy. In fact, the prisoner was so convinced that he had become pregnant, that he "expected to be taken to the maternity ward" (ibid) in the near future.

The final institutional fear regarding homosexuality in prison, the possibility that two men might become physically violent when competing for a "fairy," is also present. This is most apparent in the love-triangle created by the characters, Davey, Goldilocks, and the Alley Cat. Both Davey and the Alley Cat are attracted to Goldilocks, who is described as "a handsome lad whose slender sturdy body would have inspired a statue of Apollo. His legs were straight and gracefully curved [. . .] The light tan he had acquired under the southern sun set off the golden hair of his head; his chest was hairless" (82-83). In other words, he was young, boyish, and effeminate. The two roughs, both Don Juans in the extra-penal world, cannot help but compete over this "fairer" of the male sex. Chauncey's point, that much of the anxiety arises from the fact that the "true" homosexual would intentionally provoke this competition, is also affirmed in Viereck's experience. Goldilocks, upon admission, is stripped in front of the other prisoners and forced to bend over and be "probed . . . with a gloved finger" (83). As it happened, "Goldilocks himself, his face wreathed in smiles, took the inspection as a lark . . . he seemed to take a delight in the public exposure of his charms" (ibid). He instigates the competition, fulfilling one of the institutional fears about homosexual men.

Having met these conditions, as established by the prison authorities, Viereck's memoir seems at first to cater to the stereotypes readers might expect from a gay pulp novel. This is not always the case, however. Following the Goldilocks storyline, for example, Viereck describes for his readers a change in the romantic situation. After some time, it becomes clear that Goldilocks and Davey's relationship, strictly sexual, has dissolved. In its place arises a romantic relationship between Goldilocks and the Alley Cat. Indeed, Viereck describes their romance as "reaching an emotional climax . . . genuine, passionate, sincere" (115). So, despite perpetuating some expectations of situational homosexuality in prison, Viereck also adds a new dimension, the element of genuine affection and romantic love between two men. At the same time, even this achievement is made to fit neatly into prescribed gender roles.

It is laudable that Viereck includes in his prison memoir romantic relationships as well as physical ones. This is significant and unexpected. In so doing, however, Viereck perpetuates the notion that there are clear masculine and feminine roles in same-sex relationships, and that the supposedly gendered-male, the one who seems most like a man, will be the dominant sexual partner, while the gendered-female partner, the one who seems in appearance or actions most feminine, will be the passive partner. This makes it necessary for at least some of the male

prisoners to be "inverted" regarding gender, because, according to Viereck's descriptions, the

same-sex sexual and romantic relationships must still be predicated upon a gender binary. We

can see this clearly in the relationship between Goldilocks and the Alley Cat.

When the narrator encounters the two young men together in the shower, he describes

both their present condition and the condition, or roles, of their relationship by establishing each

man's place in the supposed binary, both in terms of physical appearance and masculinity or

femininity:

> [W]hen I came near the showers I beheld a scene that might have been taken from an
> ancient Greek frieze. Goldilocks and the Alley Cat were standing intertwined in an
> embrace that blotted out the world for them [. . .] The dark hair of the Alley Cat
> contrasted startlingly with the fair ringlet of Goldilocks. Whatever the moralist might say,
> it was a symphony in gold and black, youth calling to youth. [. . .] They clung together
> like two statues welded together by some mischievous god [. . .] The Alley cat was
> obviously the stronger, the more masculine of the two. And he had met a perfect
> complement in the gracefully epicene Goldilocks. (115)

This description is significant in a number of ways. First, it conforms to the narrator's

progressive view of homosexual relationships in that it treats the two lovers as a natural, even

beautiful, pair, one which could have been ordained by the gods. The "moralists" are rejected,

for who can deny a "symphony" such as this? He adds that they were so lost in each other that

the world was "blotted out," which gives credence to the notion that their attachment is more

than just sexual. This view that homosexual relationships are naturally occurring is certainly

informed by Viereck's knowledge of sexological and psychological perspectives on gender and

sexuality. On the other hand, the scene also reinforces the notion that gay relationships require a

masculine/feminine dichotomy, and that the coupling could not exist if not for the fact that one

of these men is "stronger," or manly, and the other "epicene," or womanly/androgynous. It is important to note that, while Viereck may not have specifically intended it, the scene reminds us that this argument supposing a link between gender expression and sexual desire has been perpetuated for millennia. As Rictor Norton indicates, "the important fifth-century medical treatise *De morbis chornicis* [describes] 'soft' or unmasculine men, as men who depart from the cultural norm of manliness in so far as they actively desire to be subjected by other men to a 'feminine' (that is, receptive) role in sexual intercourse" (29). The allusions to Greek beauty is certainly a homosexual code, as will be discussed in Chapter Four, but in this case, it also serves as a reminder that homosexual expression has been enmeshed in gender constructs since its earliest recorded iterations.

Despite this minor failing, Viereck does what much of the pulp novels do not, which is to describe a same-sex male couple as both normal and beautiful. Indeed, shortly after this description, when the two young men's relationship is challenged by "an unsavory old jailbird" (116), the narrator makes his approval all the plainer. When the jailbird, upon being rejected, asks the men, ironically, if they are married, Goldilocks responds, "No, we're not married, we're only lovers" (ibid). To this, the narrator is compelled to add, "And so they were, in a strange fashion" (ibid). Thus, Viereck's approach to expressing gender and sexuality in his memoir is both similar to and different from other texts in the pulp genre. His treatment of violence and death in relation to homosexuality is also unique.

Considering the fact that *Men into Beasts* is a memoir about prison, it is to be expected that violence will play some part in the narrative; however, the violence is described not only as a condition of life in prison, but specifically in regards to, first, the narrator's personal situation, and second, as intimately connected with sex. In the first place, we know that the narrator is in prison for crimes against the United States. He describes this moment in time as "when war psychosis was at its height" (14). Indeed, the fact that the memoir was published in 1952 is somewhat astonishing[28], given the fact that Senator McCarthy's persecution of homosexuals and subsequent purging of them from government, military, and civil service were well underway by 1950. Indeed, David K. Johnson notes that in 1947 there was a "media and legislative campaign to pass a harsh sexual psychopath statute" and that the "U.S. government quietly launched its own campaign to combat homosexuality" (59). In Washington D.C., police even instituted a "pervert elimination campaign" to rid the public parks of homosexuals (ibid).

The fact that Viereck was under suspicion for treason *and* a well-known poet with bisexual tendencies made him a rather conspicuous target. In his memoir, Viereck casts the prison censor, Stanley Lubiak, as the metaphorical embodiment of the oppressive government agencies that had begun their assault on homosexuality[29]. He describes the censor as "a swarthy man with a brutal face and mannerisms" with an "enormous bulk . . . like a mountain" (44). As the prison censor—and a governmental official—Lubiak has total control of all messages that transfer in and out of the prison. He takes an immediate disliking for Viereck because he is a traitor and "an intellectual" (ibid). Lubiak's menacing presence and psychological attacks on the narrator persist throughout his time in prison, symbolically echoing the same attacks being perpetrated against homosexual men and women outside the prison system during the McCarthy-era "Lavender Scare."

---

[28] Viereck's publisher, who had been imprisoned for printing so-called obscene material, writes in his introduction to *Men into Beasts*: Today, "every citizen is a potential criminal, threatened by . . . the atavistic laws of forty-eight states governing sex" (7).

[29] The suggestions went beyond simple surveillance and threats of dismissal from employment or service. In the military, there were "secret proposals to incarcerate homosexuals more systematically in formal detention camps" (Bérubé 214).

In addition to the narrator being oppressed because of his sexuality[30], violence and sex function together throughout the narrator's period in jail. A link is often drawn between violent reactions and sexual desire, for example. This is demonstrated quite clearly when the narrator, having learned that an inmate, Carl, is in prison for executing black men, wonders if Carl is "jealous of the alleged sexual superiority of the negro" (104). The question arises as a consequence of Carl having invented a penis pump. The narrator thinks he may have invented the device because "nature endowed him indifferently" (ibid). In other words, Carl's penis envy motivates him to commit murder. Later in the text, when describing some new arrivals to the prison, the narrator makes the observation that "sex seems to be at the root of most crime" (112). He subsequently adds that certain kinds of sex acts "can get you a life term at hard labor" (174). In including these brief but specific comments on the relationship between sex and violence, or sex and punishment, Viereck demonstrates both his own disapproval for treating sexuality as a crime and his awareness of the contemporary perspectives on gender and sexuality being posited by Kinsey and others sexologists and psychologists. Whereas some of the earlier pulps maintained the idea that homosexuality was a neurosis or disease, Viereck's approach is to view it as natural, if unusual. Indeed, his narrator writes, "you cannot drive out Nature with a pitchfork. If you do, it always comes back" (110).

Despite the relative lack of scholarly attention for Viereck's memoir, the success of *Men into Beasts* as a gay pulp narrative and as critical artifact of the gay American literary tradition should not be ignored. As Phyllis Keller remarks, "its inherent sensationalist appeal brought

---

[30] And it is his sexuality more than his political views that we should be concerned with. Homosexuals during this period were notoriously attacked as "threats" against the government, as immoral or weak-willed people who were susceptible to corruption or blackmail and thus likely targets of foreign influence (Canaday 152) (Bérubé 268).

sales to the half-million mark" (104-105). Viereck's reputation was certainly tarnished by his sympathy for Germany during both World Wars, but prior to the political fall-out, he was a respected poet and journalist. His pulp memoir, at times sensational, adds a necessary and perhaps more honest perspective about prison as a particular kind of "gay space." In addition, it fulfills the criteria of the gay pulp genre in that it is conveyed melodramatically, it explores concepts of homosexual panic and paranoia, it depicts clichéd notions of gender and sexual binaries, and it equates violence with sexuality. In many respects, however, Viereck's work is most notable for its progressive treatment of homosexual issues, even as some of the traditionally accepted tropes are being realized.

Christopher Nealon describes homosexual pulp fiction as "survival literature" (144-149). This is an appropriate description, both for the context of the period in which it was being first printed and read, and also currently in retrospective analyses of the function of this genre and these texts. Some critics, such as Susan Stryker and Drewey Wayne Gunn, have focused their attention on what they describe as the Golden Age of gay fiction[31], i.e. the 1950s and 1960s. Others, such as Robert McRuer, describe the 1980s and 1990s as "the queer renaissance." Each of these arguments has merit. These periods surely reflect significant changes in the number and types of gay texts being published and read, aided greatly by the sexual revolution and by landmark wins in obscenity trials, such as William S. Burroughs's historic 1966 victory for *Naked Lunch* (1959), which changed the publishing landscape in the United States. Nevertheless, many of the pulp novels of the 1950s and later, such as those written by K.B. Raul and Jay Little, continued to rely on themes and stereotypes established in the gay pulps published during the

---

[31] The vast majority of anthologies devoted to gay pulp fiction begin with texts published at/after 1950. See Susan Stryker's *Queer Pulp* (2001), Drewey Wayne Gunn's *The Golden Age of Gay Fiction* (2009) and *1960s Gay Pulp Fiction* (2013), and Michael Bronski's *Pulp Friction* (2003).

first half of the twentieth-century. It is unacceptable to overlook these earlier novels simply because they were less widely read. In addition, tracing the progression of the pulp genre through the first half of the twentieth-century illustrates important changes, such as the way pulp writers incorporated contemporary medical, criminal, and sociological perceptions of homosexuality into their texts. We can see, for example, how the "neurotic" and suicidal homosexual evolves from the 1930s-type found in Tellier's *Twilight Men,* to the repressed but rational academic of the 1940s, as portrayed in Jackson's *Fall of Valor*, and finally, to the progressive and accepting depiction found in Viereck's *Men into Beasts*. In this way, the gay pulp novels, though more sensational and perhaps more influential, given their wider reach and numerous re-printings, reflect some of the very changes that were happening in the literary texts at this time. Overall, the literary texts were more likely to embrace favorable views of homosexuality, and even offer happy endings for their gay characters, which may have limited their possibility for gaining successful readership. Meanwhile, the pulp novels helped to create and perpetuate the lingering, negative stereotypes of gay men in fiction, particularly because their willingness to censure or punish the gay character resulted in a readership more amenable to books with homosexual content. Another commonality between the two genres, and indeed a key feature of the gay American literary tradition, is participation in a type of coded communication, an intertextuality that allowed gay writers to present themselves openly to readers who spoke the language, and to communicate with other gay writers, both historical and contemporary. Chapter Four will evaluate this interesting feature of gay writing in the early twentieth-century

CHAPTER 4

INTERTEXTUALITY: THE SELF, THE OTHER, AND CODED COMMUNITY

"It irks me to find more praise bestowed on the praised-enough, —even on groups of
secondary importance, sometimes just because they are remote (in England, perhaps), and so can
be treated with an easy objectivity. To dig in your own day and your own community is harder,
but I should feel it more rewarding." –*Bertram Cope's Year*, p. 107

As has been demonstrated, texts within the gay tradition in American literature share

necessary plot features, such as displacing the fictive world in time or place. They also tend to

rely on characteristics that are perpetuated by the dominant genre from this period, the gay pulp.

In addition, homosexual narratives of the early twentieth-century share a certain intertextuality

that creates a dialogue between gay writers, historical and contemporary, as well as gay culture

and readership. In this chapter, I consider four novels written by homosexual men and published

prior to 1940. In it, I continue the argument that there is substantial gay literature before the

"golden" era of the 1950s and 1960s, but I focus on the concept of intertextuality in order to

illustrate how gay male fiction began to develop a unique tradition within the context of the

greater twentieth-century American literary tradition. Specifically, gay texts of this period share

three significant characteristics: First, they deal with a protagonist who at some point

acknowledges his own homosexuality. This might mean that the character is already aware of his

sexuality at the start of the narrative and either reflects on it or deals with it over the course of the

text, or the character comes to discover his sexuality as the narrative progresses. Second, the

main character or characters articulate their understanding that they are "different from" or "other than" the characters who surround them. In some cases, this understanding is expressed through the narrator's observations, but in other instances the character himself makes this knowledge clear. Lastly, the authors communicate their primary messages through coded language, rhetorical techniques, and veiled themes that a sympathetic audience would understand. The texts being explored include Charles Warren Stoddard's *For the Pleasure of His Company* (1903), Edward Prime-Stevenson's *Imre: A Memorandum* (1906), Henry Blake Fuller's *Bertram Cope's Year* (1919), and Forman Brown's *Better Angel* (1933). Each of these novels satisfies, in various ways, the three conditions mentioned above.

Charles Warren Stoddard is best known for his contributions to magazines and newspapers[1] and for his friendships with prominent literary figures such as Mark Twain, Robert Louis Stevenson, and Bret Harte. In the *American Authors, 1600-1900* biographical entry for Stoddard, first published in 1938, the editor explains that Stoddard was admired "more for his charm and kindliness than for his slight writing talent" (Kunitz par. 3). It seems true that he was well-liked, given his numerous correspondences with friends and acquaintances, as well as the emotional responses to his death[2]; however, the assessment that his writing talent was only "slight" is less accurate[3]. It is more appropriate to say his talent was inconsistent. Interestingly, though perhaps not surprisingly, the entry makes no mention of the fact that Stoddard was a

---

[1] He often contributed under the pseudonym "Pip Pepperpod" (McGinty 154).

[2] The writer Joaquin Miller immortalized Stoddard in a short poem titled, "Say Charlie!" (McGinty 167) and Robert Louis Stevenson, upon visiting Stoddrad's home but finding that he was away, "pinned a lament to the door" (160).

[3] Ben Tarnoff calls Stoddard "the boy wonder of the Bohemians" (4) and a reviewer for *The Dial* noted that "when we say that the author is Mr. Charles Warren Stoddard, nothing need be added for those to whom this name has already made its magic appeal" (155).

homosexual man[4], despite the fact that this was common knowledge among his friends and

literary acquaintances[5] and that he explored homosexual themes in his major works, including

South Sea Idylls (1873) and *For the Pleasure of His Company: An Affair of the Misty City*. It is

the latter, which is largely autobiographical, that is to be explored in this chapter. As Christopher

Looby notes, "sexual identities . . . need to be articulated in order to be received and adopted and

performed, and this requires a literary public sphere" (843). Despite some arguments to the

contrary, *For the Pleasure of His Company* exhibits all three of the major features of

intertextuality as outlined in the introduction to this chapter, and this marks it as one of the

earliest examples in American literature to help create that literary public sphere for gay writers.

The main character, Paul Clitheroe, never admits explicitly to being homosexual, but he does

have a certain self-awareness that makes it clear he understands his own desire for men and has

no qualms about pursuing same-sex relationships. In addition, he indeed compares himself to

others and understands that he is different in many ways, and those closest to him often reinforce

this perception. Finally, the narrative frequently communicates ideas about gender and sexuality

through coded language and descriptions of its characters.

      The first intertextual theme that helps us to establish a tradition of gay male literature in

America is that of self-identification. The writers explored in this chapter are known to have

---

[4] In his biography of Stoddard, Roger Austen notes that "after they have been in their graves for a decade or two, it is a grand old American custom for homosexual writers to undergo curious transformations. Literary historians and critics and biographers set to work heterosexualizing or at least neutering these writers for posterity" (*Genteel Pagan* xliii).

[5] Stoddard "aired his passions in public—and [his friends] loved him for it" (Tarnoff 38). While they did not necessarily understand his sexuality, they were aware of it and accepted it, perhaps due to Stoddard's "all-conquering warmth that made people lower their defenses" (ibid). James Gifford notes that "Ambrose Bierce, William Dean Howells, and Bret Harte detected Stoddard's 'difference'" and that Mark Twain, who enjoyed Stoddard's company so much that he hired him as personal secretary, called him, "a nice girl" (93).

been homosexual, but what is of greater importance is how the gay male protagonists in these narratives learn to self-identify. *For the Pleasure of His Company* is, perhaps, the least successful attempt at a homosexual novel of those to be explored in this chapter. I agree with Roger Austen who writes that the failure is due in large part to the novel's "obliquity" (qtd. in Stoddard 7). It is also accurate to argue that "Stoddard had little choice but to write as he did" (ibid), which is to say, to write about homosexuality through use of innuendo, obscurity, and veiled allusions. Still, the main character, Paul Clitheroe, does ultimately realize his true sexual identity and is witness to a variety of transgressive sexual and gender situations along the way.

Paul Clitheroe is a young man who is not "manly, or even masculine" (20) and who sleeps "like a faun." The narrator indicates that "his was a nature which had never been warped by the various social and moral and religious influences brought to bear upon it" (ibid). This early scene immediately implicates social, moral, and religious teachings as antagonistic elements that would strive to divert Clitheroe from his nature and toward a "normal" life; this of course necessarily implies that Paul Clitheroe is somehow abnormal. Taking this into account, and considering it in relation to the character's description as an "aesthetic Bohemian" and a "sensuous young poet" (34), it is understood that the oddness is in his lack of masculinity, or, in this case, his sexuality.

It is in Clitheroe's relationships with Foxlair and with Grattan Field, and in Clitheroe's active and willing acceptance of both, that the *otherness* becomes more apparent. We know, for example, that Clitheroe and Foxlair sometimes spend their nights together (41) and even share lodgings. At one point, the two are "for a week . . . inseparable" (33). This is especially significant when, after Foxlair announces to Clitheroe that he "loves [Clitheroe] better than any fellow" (40) and then unceremoniously disappears from his life, Clitheroe refuses to admonish him or think poorly of him. Roger Austen argues that this scene plays out like a marriage proposal. He notes that "Paul is tempted [to leave with Foxlair] but answers that he has no money" (*Playing the Game* 14). Austen might be implying that, had Clitheroe means, he would have left with Foxlair after all; however, this ignores the character's general inability or unwillingness to commit, a trait that becomes apparent throughout the rest of the narrative. Paul Clitheroe wants to love, surely, and he loves often, but it is not insufficient economic status that keeps him from commitment. To Clitheroe, love is meant to be spread freely and widely. Marriage would restrict this. Much of the reason he eventually disappears with the primitive island men at the end of the novel, is because he desires the freedom to love openly and broadly, a love of "comrades" which reflects Stoddard's own philosophy, as evidenced by his correspondence with his hero Walt Whitman (Fone 585-586). Nevertheless, Clitheroe is indeed, at this point in the narrative, devoted to an unrequited and unworthy lover.

The difficulty in reading this early novel as a gay one arises when considering that the sexual preferences of the protagonist are primarily revealed only through suggestion. Stoddard's work is heavily coded, as will be discussed later. Still, there are moments of overt romantic sentiment between Clitheroe and other men. For example, after Clitheroe and Grattan Field have a passionate argument and it seems that their friendship might sever forever, the narrator writes:

> Something in Grattan's manner; something in the warm, manly pressure of the arms that encircled Paul, something in the deep distress of his friend, won Clitheroe in a moment: All at once he began to love that wildly impulsive, strangely contradictory, utterly ungoverned and ungovernable nature . . . henceforth they found such pleasure in one another's society that they were seldom more than two days separated. (143)

While all of these moments, from the descriptions of Paul Clitheroe as feminine, to his uninterrupted and private time spent with other men, to the warm embraces of a man he is described as loving, can perhaps be read as nothing other than "manly love" and affection, the conclusion of the novel at long last proves Clitheroe's true nature.

In the concluding pages, Clitheroe decides to abandon his life in San Francisco for one that is more atavistic, more natural. While on a cruise, he espies "out of the darkness . . . the slender hull of a canoe, the wild, many ribbed sail, and the dusky forms of three naked islanders" (188). Clitheroe's final decision is to leave society, a place where he cannot be himself, behind. So, "with a sudden impulse" and "with never a glance backward," he strikes out like Huck Finn going west. He joins these naked men, his "old friends . . . from an island he had loved and mourned" (ibid) and realizes that being away from them, being unencumbered by social, moral, and religious control, is what he had been mourning; it is with passion and joy that he recognizes in the naked chiefs his true self and the nature he has been suppressing all along. The island freedom is a metaphor for something in him that had been missing, a freedom he could not explore fully. Leaving, then, signals an active decision to embrace his identity.

Although self-identification is difficult for Paul Clitheroe, there is certainly an awareness of his own "otherness." As Aldrich and Wotherspoon indicate, "Paul's same-sex desires place him outside the norms of American culture; he must therefore seek out an alternative to the repressive patterns of nineteenth-century American thought and action" (423). In this way, the second condition, an awareness of self-as-other, is demonstrated, and it is demonstrated at a number of points throughout the novel. One such example is when Paul Clitheroe is described as having "narrowly escaped" being a young woman[6] (88). At another point, Clitheroe is acting in a play—a coded activity that will reappear in *Bertram Cope* and *Better Angel*—and must engage in

---

[6] "If Paul had been a young woman — some of his friends thought he had narrowly escaped it and did not hesitate to say so — he would instinctively have become [Miss Juno's] confidante."

a love scene with a young woman. He finds this to be a "perilous predicament" and a "great trial," and is haunted by nightmares of the scene, bad dreams that cause him to awaken "in a cold sweat" (55). Clitheroe understands that these feelings might be strange to some, but in his own estimation of himself, he is normal. This is best articulated in his conversation with Miss Juno. When she admits to Paul that some have described him as odd, he responds, "I know . . . it's been said in my hearing, but I don't care in the least; it is natural for the perfectly natural person *not* to care in the least" (97). There are just a few moments in the narrative when Paul expresses his awareness that others gossip about him, but in each instance, he reiterates his belief that he is "natural," different, perhaps, but no better or worse than anyone else. It is in recognizing this difference without qualifying it that he distinguishes himself as a sexual minority, and it is his acceptance of himself as *natural* that challenges some readings of this text as one which fails to be "gay enough."

It might seem reasonable to conclude, based on early reviews of the book which omit any reference to homosexuality, such as Florence Jackson's 1903 review in the *Overland Monthly* and William Payne's review in the same year, published in *The Dial*, that the homosexuality is too coded; however, as Roger Austen notes, "this novel is almost as gay as Edward Stevenson's *Imre* . . . the key difference is that while Stevenson discusses homosexuality per se, Stoddard persists in the use of such euphemisms as 'chum' and 'pal'" (*Playing the Game* 15). Indeed, *For the Pleasure of His Company*, published before *Imre*, is much more coded in its language and more elusive in its form. It reads in some ways more like *The Young and Evil*, but this is not a failing; in fact, it is a testament to Stoddard's creative heights.

It is not just in the language where one can locate Paul's awareness, however, but also in the structure of the novel itself. In his dissertation, Mark Isola writes that Stoddard "initiated a distinctly modern gay male American literary tradition, which reaches its fullest aesthetic expression in his 1903 novel *For the Pleasure of His Company: An Affair of the Misty City*" (ii). Isola is referring to textuality and form, a thread which Christopher Looby investigates in his own study, "The Literariness of Sexuality" (2013). According to Looby, "originally, Stoddard drafted this tale as a sequential story that would follow Paul Clitheroe along a single chronological passage of time. But late in its composition, he shuffled the chapters . . . re-sorting them into three gatherings and reordering them so as to produce three overlapping narratives" (852). Looby explains that this reshuffling results in a narrative that describes "the action of all three books" as it happens simultaneously, and thus argues that "Paul is circulating between separate social worlds that do not overlap; in each of these worlds he appears, so to speak, as a different person" (ibid). This is crucial to understanding Paul's awareness of himself as someone who exists outside the mainstream of heteronormative sexuality. Paul is most comfortably and expressively himself when he is with Miss Juno, whom Roger Austen describes as "a lesbian" (*Playing* 14), although that term is never used in the text. This is significant because it creates a sphere, one of three in the text, wherein Paul, being with Miss Juno, can openly communicate his ideas about sexuality, marriage, and love. These conversations make it clear that both Paul and Miss Juno, or "Jack," as she likes to be called by her "comrades," are indeed "different."

In one exchange, Paul and "Jack" discuss boys who wish to be girls and girls who wish to be boys. It becomes obvious that they are in fact talking to each other about themselves. "Jack" adds, "I know an old gentleman who used to bewail the degeneracy of the age and exclaim, 'Boys will be girls!'" (98). Christopher Looby draws an important distinction between Stoddard's treatment of homosexuality in *For the Pleasure of His Company*, one that is essentially pre-identity, and Prime-Stevenson's treatment in *Imre*, which "fully assimilates the scientific and medical vocabularies that were coming to frame the understanding of same-sex intimacy around the turn of the century" (849). In passages like the one described above, however, we see that Stoddard is not rejecting the concept of a homosexual identity; instead, he is framing it within gender constructs and perpetuating it through codes[7]. This is reinforced at the close of the scene, when "Miss Juno had rested her hand on Paul's shoulder and said in a delightfully confidential way: 'Let it be a secret that we are chums, dear boy – the world is such an idiot.'" To which Paul responds, "All right, Jack . . . little secrets are cozy" (99). This illusion of secrecy is supported by the convoluted structure of the narrative itself and by the coded language throughout; but ultimately, Paul and Juno having made their admissions to each other and the reading audience having borne witness to it, the secret is out[8].

Clearly, Paul Clitheroe knows that he is different and, in the end, he is able to admit this to himself. In a 1989 review of the book, Thomas Yingling laments that "there is no sense at all of what it would take to make [Paul Clitheroe] happy: there is no psychological depth at all to his figure" (92). While it might be argued that Clitheroe's happiness is elusive and that the structure of the novel, experimental as it is, does not make it easy to decipher Paul's developing awareness and personal desires, the fact is that his awareness of himself as an outsider leads to the last decision he makes within the narrative itself, and it is that choice which will ultimately bring him

---

[7] In "Sexuality's Aesthetic Dimensions," (2012), Christopher Looby describes this as an "explicit disavowal of compulsory heterosexual romance" and a "critique of sexual and gender norms" (164). Although *For the Pleasure of His Company* may be heavily coded, its refusal to offer an obviously heteronormative storyline is in itself an act of destabilizing heteronormativity and, as such, encourages a queer reading. I argue that Stoddard has written a gay novel in its own right, but queer readings of it are certainly compelling.

[8] In many ways, this is what Mark Mitchell and David Leavitt meant when they write that homosexual texts have always been there, "if only you had known where to look" (xvii).

happiness. This is the decision to leave the western world and to return to the south sea islands, accompanied by three naked men, "old friends," whom he greets passionately. In many ways, this departure recalls the necessary displacement explored in the representative texts of Chapter Two. Paul Clitheroe leaves not in order to find himself, however, but because he has *already* identified himself and understands where, and how, he will find satisfaction.

Finally, what most qualifies this novel to be considered in a discussion of early twentieth-century gay literature is the fulfilment of the third condition, a willingness to communicate. While Stoddard avoids doing this overtly, he undoubtedly uses codes to get his point across[9], as when Clitheroe admits to Miss Juno that most girls have no flavor, "neither have they form nor features, nor tint nor texture, nor anything that appeals to a fellow of taste and sentiment" (92) and concludes with the declaration that "they are not [his girls], and not one of them ever will be" if he can help it. This is one of the more obvious codes, but others include descriptive words that are applied to Clitheroe throughout the novel, such as "pretty," "dainty," and "very feminine" (130), all of which signify to the reader if not homosexuality, at least femininity[10]. The narrator further establishes Clitheroe's homosexuality by communicating his relationships with other men in coded fashion, especially self-awareness brought on by his relationship with Foxlair, but also his romantic relationship with Grattan Field. In the first instance, not long after Foxlair declares his love for Clitheroe and then disappears, Paul sees him at a club wearing his clothes and carrying his cane, an accessory to which Clitheroe is particularly attached:

> Presently his eye fell upon a figure he seemed to recognize. It was familiar, and yet it was not familiar. The form was that of one person, and the chief outer garment was that of

---

[9] Thomas Yingling rightly notes that Clitheroe's "homosexuality is depicted in a highly coded (and thus possibly invisible) language" but that the codes are "familiar" (91).

[10] Which, as has been noted, has often been conflated with homosexuality.

another. Paul grew more perplexed the longer he strove to explain the mystery. It was as if his astral body, clothed even as in flesh, had adjourned to an adjacent table, and there seated itself with its back to him. (42)

Paul soon comes to his senses and realizes that the figure is Foxlair in Clitheroe's clothes. The obvious connection to be drawn from this is that Foxlair is a thief. The scene is meant to emphasize more than this, however. It is not just Foxlair whom Paul sees, but himself, and in so doing, he cannot help but see himself the way others see Foxlair, the way he saw Foxlair after the man admitted his love for Paul. The moment is described in such terms as "mysterious" and "sensational," not because Paul is shocked to see Foxlair again, nor because he is disturbed to discover that Foxlair has stolen from him. Instead, these descriptions emphasize the self-realization that Paul Clitheroe is experiencing, the mysteries he is revealing about himself. He *is* Foxlair, and Foxlair is a man who loves men.

In the second case, where romance is involved, we find certain coded terms being applied to describe the nature of those relationships. For example, when the narrator depicts Paul Clitheroe writing a letter to Grattan Field, following a disagreement, it is described thus:

Now if ever they should have been the closest friends; now if ever they two might have joined hands and been in complete sympathy . . . he arose again and penned a long and affectionate letter to this quondam chum. He made a careless and playful allusion to a childish spat that had for a time estranged them, and then related at some length the experience of the last few weeks, and tried to give expression to the emotions, all so new, which now possessed him. Having freed his mind and heart, he returned to his pillow and slept. (56)

Roger Austen has noted the importance of such coded terms as "chum," but in this scene, there are other terms and phrases to be acknowledged, such as being "in complete sympathy" and emphasizing the closeness of their relationship with words like "affection" and "heart." The term "sympathy" is applied at significant moments throughout the text, as when Little Mama explains to Paul the "coterie, all sympathetic," she creates (167). Known as the "Order of Young

Knighthood," this sympathetic group is one where all members, except for herself and her husband, are homosexual men. Indeed, when a heterosexual man, courting one of Little Mama's female friends, is considered by the group, Little Mama exclaims, "I don't see much of knighthood in him" (155). This is, of course, because he conforms to traditional sex roles. The narrator, in describing Clitheroe's experience this way, is echoing the very "new emotions" that Paul himself is trying to express to Grattan Field. As Clitheroe begins to understand what he is feeling for Field, the narrator reveals, just as tentatively, Clitheroe's mysteries to the reader.

In addition to the use of coded language throughout the text is the use of certain coded themes which refer to larger cultural ideas about homosexuality. The first is the theme of "manly friendship" or camaraderie, heavily influenced by Stoddard's admiration for Walt Whitman. Indeed, in part three of the novel, the term "comrade" is used at least three times: First, Little Mama uses it to describe Calvin Folsom, whom we later discover is her husband (133); then, Paul uses it to describe Miss Juno, or "Jack" (138); and finally, Little Mama uses it again to describe the young men whom she recruits to join the "Order of Young Knighthood" (146). The link, here, is that each instance of comrade is used to describe a certain kind of love and attachment, and it is used only for those in "sympathy," which is to say, those who exist beyond the boundaries of gender and sexual conformity. Another coded theme is that of Westerner-Easterner sexual relationships, particularly relating to Orientalism and the idea that the white western man is sexually aroused by foreign men of the far east[11]. Other homosexual narratives,

---

[11] Robert Aldrich rightly notes that Stoddard's *South Sea Idyls*, like others in the "western explorer" genre, "says a great deal about attractions between men of two cultures, about the desire of the American (or European) to escape the confines of his own society . . . travel to the Pacific is discovery of one's inner self" (*Colonialism and Homosexuality* 132). This fascination with the islanders and Stoddard's own discovery of self is carried over into *For the Pleasure of His Company*.

such as *Twilight Men,* have relied on this same exoticism as code for a return to the narrator's "natural" state. When Paul Clitheroe flees San Francisco on a cruise ship, and then flees the cruise ship for the islands, he does so because he misses the "brotherhood" of the tribe and being "a native among natives" (186). Clitheroe recollects that "their thoughts were his thoughts, their tongue, his tongue" (ibid). This recalls the scene where Clitheroe sees himself in Foxlair. He does not just think as the islanders do, nor speak the same language; he is an islander. When they arrive "out of the darkness" (188), nude and excited, Paul recognizes them as "old friends" and "pals" whom he greets passionately and then disappears with. In the end, Clitheroe finds clarity and embraces his identity. He leaves San Francisco, "with never a glance backward" (188) to return to the islands, the naked men, and the freedom to be himself.

Although some have described *For the Pleasure of His Company* as a failure, a novel without "a convincing excuse for telling the tale at all" (Jackson 265), it is in fact an important artifact in the gay American literary tradition. Paul Clitheroe is understood to be a homosexual character, one who has no doubt about his sexuality nor any expressed remorse about his same-sex relationships with Foxlair, Grattan Field, or the islanders to whom he returns. While these relationships must be read through coded language and themes, and through an intentionally convoluted narrative structure, they are nevertheless present and affirming. Ultimately, if we are to understand homosexual literature in the United States, it is important to recognize how homosexual writers chose to express their ideas either within the constraints of their cultures or in spite of them. Writers like Charles Warren Stoddard often created characters, sometimes autobiographical, whose sexuality is located in the character's own self-awareness, in his recognition of himself as *other*, and in the coded language and themes the author creates or perpetuates, which are shared across the genre and became recognizable to an audience "in the know." While homosexual sentiment in Stoddard's narrative is relatively vague throughout, other early novels are surprisingly forthright in their depictions of positive homosexual male characters. Edward Prime-Stevenson, for example, creates, in *Imre: A Memorandum*, two masculine military men—upright and honorable in every way—who just happen to be attracted to other men.

Edward Prime-Stevenson, like Stoddard, Henry Blake Fuller, and other gay writers who have been essentially forgotten, was in his time a respected "man of letters" with a reputation as an accomplished writer and critic (Bullough 35). He published *Imre* privately in 1906. Stevenson's biographer, James J. Gifford, explains that only 500 copies of the book were printed in its first run (qtd. in Gunn and Harker 30). *Imre* has often been celebrated as the first gay American novel, although this claim has been tested by scholarship of the last decade which argues that Bayard Taylor's *Joseph and His Friend: A Story of Philadelphia* (1870) or Charles Warren Stoddard's *For the Pleasure of His Company*, deserve that honor[12]. Still, as recently as 2006, some gay historians were claiming that *Imre* was "probably the first American homosexual novel" (Edsall 141). How can this be? The greatest difficulty in classifying these early gay texts as "homosexual" is that they are, of necessity, heavily coded. In the case of Stoddard's novel, an analysis of the codes and themes certainly support the argument that it is a gay novel, as does the fact that it was written by a homosexual man who incorporated a great deal of autobiography into the work. On the other hand, *Joseph and His Friend* is much more problematic. It, like so many other possibly gay novels, not only relies heavily on codes, but also denies a homosexual ending

---

[12] There is no evidence that Bayard Taylor himself was homosexual. He was married twice (1849, 1857) and likely based the novel on the relationship between Fitz-Greene Halleck and Joseph Rodman Drake. See *American Byron: Homosexuality & The Fall of Fitz-Greene Halleck* (University of Wisconsin, 2000).

for its protagonist[13]. This is not the same as the pulp novels, which in many cases presented their gay characters quite openly, only to punish them with death or tragedy in the end. *Joseph and His Friend* instead "turns" the homosexual character straight before the end of the narrative. His friend marries a woman and, it is assumed, lives happily-ever-after with her, and the narrator seems destined to do the same. Thus, Taylor's novel should be rejected as an openly gay novel for many reasons and most significantly because it does not provide narrative space for gay identity the way that *For the Pleasure of His Company* does. *Imre* progresses even further than these two earlier examples. Prime-Stevenson still relies on codes and themes to enhance the homosexual elements of his novel; however, he also develops two characters who are unequivocally homosexual men, men who fall in love with each other and who, apparently, enjoy a happy ending. As such, it may not be the first gay American novel, but it is certainly the boldest.

James J. Gifford, in his introduction to the novel, notes that *Imre* might be "the first overtly gay American novel." He qualifies this, however, by adding: "there are no scenes of physical intimacy, no rollicking Tom-Jones style bedroom romps, no kisses save of the most formal and chaste kind. No subterranean visits to gay brothels or bathhouses" (13). Gifford suggests that readers will be surprised to find an early gay American novel that does not read in the style of the pulp novels. I agree that readers coming to *Imre* and early-American gay fiction

---

[13] Indeed, at the end of the novel, when Philip sees his friend Joseph happily engaged to a woman, he at first laments losing the "precious intimacy of a man's love" (360). Then, however, he exclaims, "if there is not now living a noble woman to bless me with her love . . . I will wait: but I shall find her!" (361). Taylor comes close to concluding the novel with clear homosexual sentiment, but in the end, he cannot do it. The implication is that, no matter how closely intimate two men grow, they must ultimately reject same-sex relationships. For this reason, it is difficult to cast *Joseph and His Friend* as the first gay novel, since homosexuality is finally denied.

for the first time may indeed be surprised by this, but it is important to note that this is not a

failing of these early novels. Instead, it is a symptom of the popularity of the gay pulp genre and

those cultural stereotypes they perpetuated. *Imre* may not be sexually gratuitous, but it is

surprisingly open in its treatment of homosexuality, despite the fact that Prime-Stevenson still

relies on a number of codes in his attempt to reach an intended audience, i.e. gay men.

In arguing for the naturalness of homosexuality, which he does quite confidently, Prime-

Stevenson nevertheless relies on the intertextuality of homosexual language and themes

established by writers before him. This includes his characters' willingness to identify

themselves as homosexual, a self-awareness that helps create the concept of gay identity and

which is lacking in some of the earlier examples such as Bayard Taylor's. In addition, the

characters recognize that they are different from heterosexual men, and they describe their

experiences of being "othered." Finally, Prime-Stevenson utilizes coded language and themes to

appeal to historical threads of homosexuality in making his case that same-sex desire is normal,

and to speak to an audience who would understand those codes. These codes are significant

because they create a language for the narrator and main characters, allowing them to

communicate within the fictive world. Perhaps even more importantly, however, is the

"community" that this kind of intertextuality creates. Mark Mitchell and David Leavitt refer to

this phenomenon in their aptly titled anthology *Pages Passed from Hand to Hand* (1998), and

Gifford notes that "such networking among homosexual readers was widespread" (Prime-

Stevenson 18).

It is surprising to consider that this text was published just three years after *For the

Pleasure of His Company*, given how differently the subject of homosexuality is treated. Prime-

Stevenson is able to accomplish this unguarded treatment because the book, though written by an

American, was published anonymously and outside of the United States. These two circumstances perhaps allowed the author to be bolder than the time would otherwise have allowed. Even more significantly, however, is the author's treatment of self-identification in the book. It differs from Stoddard's in two important ways: First, it is more direct, such as when, very early in the novel, the narrator unequivocally states that he is "a young man who loved other men" (33); second, it depicts the two homosexual men as masculine— "normal" men—rather than effeminate or "abnormal." While it is dangerous to draw comparisons between masculinity and "normalcy" in men in general, the clear purpose, here, is to make the case that homosexuality, and homosexual men, are not what common stereotypes, those stoked by stories of Oscar Wilde and other flamboyant dandy-type figures, would have people believe[14].

Imre also offers characters who fully accept themselves not only as homosexual, but as homosexual *naturally*. This is true at multiple points throughout the narrative, such as when the characters refer to the works of Havelock Ellis and other sexologists and psychologists who had begun to make the case that homosexuality was a natural occurrence. For example, late in the novel, when Imre is sharing his story with the narrator, he describes how he finally gave up on the idea of being cured:

> I had no disease! No…I was simply what I was born! – a complete human being, firm, perfect physical and mental health; outwardly in full key with all the man's world: but, in spite of that, a being who from birth was of a vague, special sex; a member of the sex within the most obvious sexes; or apart from them. I was created as a man perfectly male, save in the one thing which keeps such a 'man' back from possibility of ever becoming

---

[14] James Wilper accurately notes that at this time "medicine consigns same-sex desire to the realms of decadence, effeminacy, and pathology" (54). Thus, Prime-Stevenson's characters are "beginning to form a distinct identity" (Bronski, *Culture Clash,* 77) despite science and psychology's stance that homosexuality was a kind of medical defect. This is a bold treatment that predates Kinsey's conclusions by decades, and which in some ways foreshadows the 1970s decision by the American Psychological Association to declassify homosexuality as a pathological problem.

integrally male – his terrible, instinctive demand for a psychic and a physical union with a man. (121)

This particular passage is significant for a number of reasons. There is, for example, an acknowledgement of the common belief that homosexuality is a disease followed by an immediate refutation of such philosophy. Then, Imre addresses the general misconception that homosexuality is a choice, instead stating that he was "born that way." Next, he notes his maleness—his masculinity—and how very much like any other man he is. Finally, he debunks the myth that homosexuality is simply about deviant sexual desires when he expresses not just a physical desire for men, but also a psychic—a spiritual—desire for male love and companionship. In a strikingly bold and comprehensive moment, Imre, through Prime-Stevenson, comments on virtually every prejudice and stereotype pertaining to homosexual men and counters with the realities of a self-identified gay male character succeeding in a staunchly masculine world: the military.

Prime-Stevenson satisfies the second feature of intertextual themes in gay literature in that his characters are aware that their identity is beyond the boundary of "normal" society's expectations: they are "different." A common way this is expressed in gay fiction is through the theme of isolation and loneliness[15]. Not only is this isolation rejected by Prime-Stevenson, but his characters, drawn together in confidence by their mutual condition of being sexually othered, proceed to converse openly and extensively about themselves and about their sexual histories. As

---

[15] Aldrich and Wotherspoon claim that *Imre* "was the first novel by an American to deal with homosexuality positively and openly, and not as some unspeakable secret leading to an inevitable suicide" (303). As has been noted, this is not entirely accurate, but the rejection of secrecy is indeed important, particularly as it corresponds, in this case, with a rejection of loneliness as well. Because Oswald and Imre are able to reveal their secret to the other, they are able to build a relationship together.

John Lauritsen notes, "following an intense discussion of friendship, Oswald begins a confession, which goes on for almost fifty pages" (qtd. in Bullough 36). The narrator of *Imre*, though no longer doubting his sexual identity by this point in the narrative, nor doubting his friendship with Imre, recalls his moments of "darkness" and "sadness" (29) and remembers being "horrified" and "filled with suicidal guilt and shame" when first realizing his desires for other men. Later, when the narrator and Imre tell each other their personal stories, the narrator juxtaposes the "most brilliant minds and gifts, of intensest [sic] energies . . . scores of pure spirits, deep philosophers, bravest soldiers, highest poets and artists" against "the Race-Homosexual" which "apparently ever would be . . . ignoble, trivial, loathe-some, feeble-souled and feeble-bodied creatures! . . . the very weaklings and rubbish of humanity!" (112). This juxtaposition in many ways predicts Foucault's thoughts on the function of sexual discourse. In the first volume of *The History of Sexuality*, he writes that "discourse transmits and produces power; it reinforces it, but also undermines and exposes it, renders it fragile and makes it possible to thwart it" (101). He goes on to argue that discourses dealing with homosexuality[16] balance "extreme severity" with a widespread tolerance. *Imre*, in dealing openly with homosexuality, certainly provides an opportunity for reclaiming power over one's identity, locating and encouraging tolerance where possible, but it also anticipates attacks on moral and medical grounds and relays moments of despair and rejection that both Imre and Oswald experienced before meeting each other.

A clear example of this rejection, which demonstrates the isolation foisted upon homosexual men and the "extreme severity" of reactions from some heterosexuals, is described in Oswald's long narration describing how he revealed his sexuality to a male friend for whom

---

[16] Foucault uses the term "sodomy" (101).

he had developed romantic interest. His friend, having "pledged his word" (98) that he would not tell Oswald's secret to anyone else, listens as Oswald describes his love. His reaction, then, is biting:

> I have heard that such creatures as you describe yourself are to be found among mankind. I do not know, nor do I care to know, whether they are a sex by themselves, justified, because helpless, play of Nature; or even a kind of logically essential link, a between-step, as you seem to have persuaded yourself. Let all that be as it may be. I am not a man of science nor keen to such new notions! From this moment, you and I are strangers! I took you for my friend because I believed you to be a … man. (99)

The friend goes on to describe his loathing and hatred for Oswald, but this first reaction is important because it reinforces a number of notions and incorporates a number of codes that Prime-Stevenson relies on in developing his narrative. In the first place, the friend is willing to admit that there might be some natural explanation for homosexuality, but he has no desire to know about it. This satisfies Foucault's point that homosexual discourse is often treated simultaneously with extremes of severe punishment and a certain degree of acceptance. In addition, it reinforces the idea that science may be able to change the discourse, to offer answers and thus, eventually, convince the public that homosexuality is naturally occurring. Finally, it perpetuates the theme of loneliness and rejection that helps to construct the "outsider" experience of gay men in American fiction. Georges-Michel Sarotte warns that, in *Imre*, Prime-Stevenson applies "protective devices," which include the "inner sufferings" and "long suffering" of both primary characters; however, he appropriately adds that Prime-Stevenson's reliance on the device of suffering is temporary (14). This is important because the "boldness" of the novel rests in large part on the fact that Imre and Oswald overcome their suffering and solitude upon finding each other, communicating their otherness, and developing a happy relationship together. Imre and Oswald both acknowledge that they are different, but they are notable in that they survive the expected censure this brings, accept their otherness as natural, and ultimately seek out another with whom they can share the experience and build a romantic future.

It may seem that because both of the homosexual characters have such a strong awareness of their gay identities and because they both accept, even celebrate, their difference, there would be little need for coded language in the novel; however, Prime-Stevenson does indeed employ such codes, including themes which speak to the generations of homosexual figures to come before him. He mentions, for example, the prevalence of homosexuals world-wide and their various professions, in an attempt to legitimize their contributions as upstanding citizens. The narrator also points out that certain men are "speaking the language" (41-42) of homosexuality while simultaneously forced to wear the metaphorical "mask[17]," a trope which becomes ubiquitous in gay fiction. Two of the most important and pervasive codes throughout *Imre* are the use of lists as a rhetorical strategy and the use of music as it relates to sexuality.

The use of lists is a noted feature of gay literature. It helps to create historical and contemporary, even forward-looking, "databases" of homosexual people, places, and contributions. As such, it has been an important stylistic practice in gay American fiction, used especially by writers who aimed to create a space for their voices within the larger canon. Mitchell and Leavitt describe this "list-making impulse" as a feature of Prime-Stevenson's fiction, but also as a common trait of those who hoped to find an audience that would understand them and pass on their works to sympathetic readers (xiv-xv). Gregory Woods expands on this to add, "the writing of such lists pre-dates the Victorian age" (3) and lists Christopher Marlowe's *Edward II* and Edmund Spenser's *The Faerie Queen* as textual examples. In addition, Byrne S.

---

[17] Another significant code, which was explored in Chapter Two and will be again later in this chapter.

Fone writes that "it was in the latter eighteenth century that writers began compiling lists . . . to bring legitimacy to what the world called perversion" (*Hidden Heritage* 163). An illustrative example of such a use in *Imre* occurs in the second section, where the narrator provides a long history of confirmed or supposed homosexuals:

> Themistocles, an Agesilaus, an Aristides and a Kleomenes; to Socrates and Plato, and Saint Augustine, to Servetus and Beza; to Alexander, Julius Caesar, August, and Hadrian; to Prince Eugene of Savoy, to Sweden's Charles the Twelfth, to Frederic the Great, to indomitable Tilly, to the fiery Skobeleff, the austere Gordon, the ill-starred Macdonald; to the brightest lyrists and dramatists of old Hellas and Italia; to Shakespeare, (to Marlowe also, we can well believe,) Platen, Grillparzer, Holderlin, Byron, Whitman; to Isaac Newton, a Justus Liebig; to Michelangelo and Sodoma; to the masterly Jerome Duquesnoy, the classic-souled Winckelmann; to Mirabeau, Beethoven, Bavaria's unhappy King Ludwig; to an endless procession of exceptional men, from epoch to epoch! (87-88)

A number of these examples might be problematic, as Gifford explains in his footnote to the section. Nevertheless, the list as a feature of gay American literature is an important one. Whether or not Prime-Stevenson was accurate about each of the individuals he includes, what he does accomplish is to raise the consideration that a number of prominent and potentially homosexual historical figures, of all backgrounds, talents, and nationalities, and from age to age, existed and contributed to their cultures and to the record of world history generally. As such, this list of "exceptional men," possibly gay, might provide both a sense of pride and reassurance for gay men reading the novel and an avenue for dialogue about contemporary society's stereotypical beliefs about homosexual men being perverse, damaged, or diseased.

Included on the list are also a number of artists and musicians whom the narrator describes as "the brightest lyrists and dramatists." This relationship between music and homosexuality is another coded theme prevalent in gay fiction[18]. Prime-Stevenson himself was

an accomplished musician and music critic, but the importance of music as a feature of the text is

not simply in its autobiographical concern. As Joe Law notes, "music and homosexuality are

inextricably linked" (195). For Oswald, music and identity-formation are codependent[19]. Having

read the prominent studies of homosexuality as written by medical practitioners, psychologists,

and sexologists, Prime-Stevenson would surely have been aware of the argument that music and

the arts are somehow intimately related to homosexuality. As such, he incorporates this in his

descriptions of Imre, as a code to his readers:

> He took uncertain because untaught interest in painting. Sculpture and architecture
> appealed more to him, though also in an untaught way. But he was a most excellent
> practical musician, playing the pianoforte superbly well . . . his musical enthusiasm, his
> musical insight and memory, they were all of a piece, the rich and perilous endowment of
> the born son of Orpheus. His singing voice was a full baritone, smooth and sweet, like his
> irresistible speaking voice. He would play or sing for hours . . . he would go without his
> dinner (he often did) to pay for his concert ticket or standing-place in the Royal Opera.
> (55-56)

There are two important codes being delivered through language and theme in this particular

example. First, the perpetuated theme as described above, of musical or artistic interest and its

relationship to homosexuality. While the narrator repeatedly emphasizes Imre's—and

Oswald's—total masculinity, here we discover that Imre is more than attracted to music, a

traditionally "feminine" interest; indeed, music absorbs much of his time and his meager income.

---

[18] It has also been a feature of sexological study, as in Havelock Ellis's and John Addington
Symonds's *Sexual Inversion* (1897). Ellis writes that in "musicians and artists . . . sexual
inversion prevails beyond the average" (124).

[19] Law's claim extends beyond *Imre*, however. He argues that music and homosexuality are
linked in gay writing broadly at the turn of the nineteenth century and that this feature can be
located in works such as George Grossmith's *The Society Clown* (1888), Oscar Wilde's *The
Picture of Dorian Gray* (1890), and Edward Carpenter's *The Intermediate Sex* (1908).

In addition to this clue into his character, which naturally occurs in an early section before Imre and Oswald have revealed their sexual interests, is the equally important coded language that is used to describe how Oswald views Imre. Describing his singing voice as "smooth and sweet," comparing him to the "son of Orpheus[20]" and noting his "irresistible speaking voice" all serve to demonstrate that Oswald is taking more than a passing interest in the young man. Thus, through coded language, through strategic use of lists, and through use of sexological studies such as the relationship between music and homosexuality, Prime-Stevenson creates a discourse that welcomes readers who will understand these features and that challenges the perception of readers who may not.

Ultimately, despite being one of the more, if not the most, blatant depictions of homosexuality in early gay American fiction, Prime-Stevenson relies on the same strategies applied throughout the tradition, such as including protagonists who come to terms with their sexuality over the course of the narrative, developing characters who accept that they are different and somehow demonstrate that difference, and creating a narrative that relies on coded language and devices to reach its intended audience and add to the intertextual conversation being slowly generated and circulated. Using these codes, as well as cultural and historical references, in addition to addressing the individual concerns of self-identity and awareness, functions to form a recognizably gay tradition within American literature. *Imre* is perhaps the first gay American novel to do this candidly, and while Prime-Stevenson is comfortable enough to write a descriptive love scene complete with "kissing," "throbbing members," and "electric

---

[20] As John F. Makowski notes, Orpheus was not only a mythological god of music but he has also been read as bisexual or homosexual dating back to "the third-century Phanocles" who described Orpheus's same-sex relationship with Calais (27). Thus, this reference alludes to musical ability and to same-sex desire, and it further develops the strategical "listing" device employed throughout the text as a stylistic code.

seed" (130-132), authors like Henry Blake Fuller are not quite as provocative. Nevertheless, *Bertram Cope's Year* is another successful novel that, in addressing identity and difference, sometimes through codes, adds to the rich and varied tradition of gay American literature.

Henry Blake Fuller was a well-known Chicago author who "wrote scores of book reviews, editorials, magazine essays . . . three opera librettos and their musical scores . . . dozens of short stories, translations from contemporary Italian literature, plays, and poems" (Dimuro 148-149). He was so talented that Theodore Dreiser called him "the father of American realism" (Anesko 116). Despite his reputation as a leading Chicago writer and foundational figure in American Realism, Fuller has been relegated to the margins of American literary studies. The majority of scholarship on Fuller is limited to his earlier works, especially *The Cliff-Dwellers* (1893), while his later work, including *Bertram Cope's Year*, is often ignored. It is likely that the commercial failure for *Bertram Cope's Year* was instrumental in his loss of stature in literary circles, and in the subsequent absence of his name and influence in the context of American literary studies. Keith Gumery explains that Fuller was forced to finance publication for the book himself because no publisher wanted to take the risk of printing a novel about homosexuality. Fuller did manage to work with a small publisher, but "invoices show that . . . a year after it appeared, Fuller still owed his publisher $336.14" and that "Fuller's gamble that his book would be read, valued, and become a commercial and aesthetic success had not paid off" (48).

Still, there were at least seven reviews for the book published within a decade of its appearance in 1919, four of which are generally positive and three of which mention, in some fashion, the book's treatment of homosexuality. Of those that broach the subject, only one reviewer treats *Bertram Cope's Year* negatively. Burton Rascoe, to his credit, disparages "the literary squeamishness" of some critics and publishers while noting the book's "delicate theme," before concluding that he "tried valiantly on five occasions" to get through the novel, but fell

asleep each time (qtd. in Fuller 275-276). That being said, Rascoe adds, significantly, that Fuller,

despite this apparent misfire, "is unquestionably an important figure in contemporary American

fiction" (276). In contrast to Rascoe's opinion that the book was boring, some reviews published

in minor journals between 1919 and 1923 noted many of its redeeming qualities. In a 1919

review from the *Boston Evening Transcript*, for example, the reviewer writes: "There can be no

question but what [sic] Mr. Fuller knows how to write. *Bertram Cope's Year* proves this" (qtd. in

Fuller 277). To this, H.L. Mencken adds that the novel is "a very fair piece of writing . . . a bit

sly and pizzicato; even a bit distinguished" (141); in addition, Keith Preston finds that "Mr.

Fuller marks out a small plot of ground and cultivates it intensively" (qtd. in Fuller 282).

The most important review comes from Carl Van Vechten's piece "Henry Blake Fuller,"

which appeared in *Excavations: A Book of Advocacies* (A.A. Knopf 1926), perhaps one of the

first titles to begin arguing in favor of treating American literary study as a distinct field within

the study of English literature. It can also be argued that Van Vechten paves the way for queer

studies, as the book explores openly not just the work and homosexuality of Henry Blake Fuller,

but of other American writers such as Herman Melville[21]. In his piece on Fuller, Van Vechten

argues that homosexuality in *Bertram Cope's Year* "is so skillful, so delicate, so studiedly

---

[21] Joseph Dimuro notes that "another way to understand Van Vechten's purpose in writing about Fuller and Melville is to see those essays as early contributions to the institutional development of American literature as a specialized field of academic study" (146). As he notes earlier in the piece, special attention was paid to "the literary contributions of 'gay' authors" (ibid), probably because Van Vechten himself was homosexual. Dimuro notes in the introduction to Van Vechten's essay on H.B. Fuller that Van Vechten's "papers, unsealed 25 years after his death, were found to include scrapbooks of photographs and clippings related to the subject of homosexuality" ("From Carl Van Vechten" 283). This has been explored more fully in *The Homoerotic Photography of Carl Van Vechten* (Temple University Press, 2006) by James Smalls.

restrained, that there should be no great cause for wonder . . . that this . . . should drop from the presses still-born, to meet with absolute silence on the part of reviewers, and to find itself quickly on sale at the 'remainder' tables of the large department stores" (qtd. in Fuller 283). Van Vechten's analysis is important because it identifies both the fact that homosexuality is an obvious, but coded, reality in the narrative and that one of the reasons why the text was near-universally ignored by contemporary readers and reviewers was because of its treatment of homosexuality. While some critics disregarded or somehow overlooked the text's homosexuality, and others acknowledged it in passing, the majority simply refused to read the book, and almost all of them refused to write about it. It would be a mistake, however, as Van Vechten suggests, to misread the situation. *Bertram Cope's Year* deserves scholarly attention because of its literary merits, certainly, but, most importantly for the purposes of this investigation, because it is a foundational gay American text written by a gay man, one who had an impeccable reputation for most of his long career.

In *Bertram Cope's Year*, there are in fact three gay characters. Two of these are young men in a relationship and the other, an aged professor, acts as both a pining lover and a type of mentor figure for Bertram, the novel's protagonist. Fuller's approach to sexuality is more reminiscent of Charles Warren Stoddard's than it is of Edward Prime-Stevenson's, in that it relies much more heavily on codes than it does on overt description. However, the homosexual elements in *Bertram Cope's Year* are not nearly as ambiguous as those in *For the Pleasure of His Company*. An evaluation of the text for the three intertextual features of gay American literature, an awareness of self, an identification of self-as-other, and a readiness to communicate about sexuality and homosexual identity, openly or through coded language and themes, places

Bertram Cope's Year clearly in the tradition of American literature that is developing the means and methods for a gay narrative discourse.

One of the most important features of gay intertextuality is a character's willingness or ability to understand himself as a man who desires other men, which is to say, one who is homosexual. Bertram Cope, a rather guarded and mysterious figure to those who surround him, and intentionally so, nevertheless reveals himself through the text's narrative voice and observations. The narrator describes him, in the first chapter, as a young man with "a high degree of self-possession," but when another character, Medora Phillips, asks Cope why she cannot place him, he tells her that it is because he has not been there, at the college, "to be known" (44). In other words, Bertram Cope is perfectly aware of himself[22], but he is quite cautious in revealing anything about himself to anyone else, stranger or friend. There is just one exception to this rule which is evidenced, for example, in an epistolary scene where Bertram Cope describes, in a letter to his lover Arthur Lemoyne, whom he misses "all the time" (41), his views on dancing:

> Why dancing should be done exclusively by couples arranged strictly on the basis of contrasted sexes…! I think of the good old days of the Renaissance in Italy, when women, if they wanted to dance, just got up and danced – alone, or, if they didn't want to dance alone, danced together. I like to see soldiers or sailors dance in pairs, as a straightforward outlet for superfluous physical energy. (76)

The combined nature of the start of the letter, where one man describes his feelings of loneliness due to his separation from another man, followed by this description of soldiers and sailors dancing together, is a rather bold admission of homosexual sentiment. The epistolary delivery is

---

[22] Anthony Slide, who cautions readers against interpreting the homosexuality of *Bertram Cope's Year* as "more than the author originally intended" (94) nevertheless agrees with this when he writes, "is Bertram Cope gay? Yes, but very much at ease with himself" (95).

important in this case because it allows for Bertram Cope to be perfectly forward in his opinions without the risk of anyone, save his lover and the reader, becoming aware.

In addition, the nature of the relationship between Bertram and Arthur is repeatedly signaled throughout the novel in a number of ways. For instance, the old invalid, Foster, believes the two men "made their partiality too public" when they "brought the manners of the bed-chamber into the drawing-room" (168). Foster clearly recognizes that these two men are lovers. In addition, Hortense, perhaps the only woman savvy enough to realize the true extent of Cope and Lemoyne's relationship, comments that theirs is a "preposterous friendship" that "cannot go on for long" (194). Some scholars have found their relationship to be unsatisfying. Georges-Michel Sarotte, for example, writes that "the homosexual couple in American literature is not a happy couple. In *Bertram Cope's Year*, Bertram felt contempt for Arthur" (27). The initial generalization is understandable in the larger context of gay American literature, particularly if one is critiquing primarily the "popular" gay novels, such as pulps or other melodramatic examples like *Giovanni's Room*; however, the latter point is a misreading of Bertram and Arthur's relationship. For the vast majority of the novel, they are quite happy in their domestic relationship. It is only when Arthur threatens to expose the nature of their relationship to the public, by virtue of his overzealous stage performance as a woman which he continues off-stage, that their relationship becomes strained. Still, when Arthur is forced to leave, Bertram soon follows him. It is problematic to suggest that any same-sex relationship in gay fiction that does not last to or beyond the end of the narrative is necessarily an unhappy one. Thus, while Fuller, in *Bertram Cope's Year,* is subtler in depicting homosexuality and homosexual relationships than Prime-Stevenson, he does not obfuscate them as Stoddard felt the need to do; indeed, there are even moments where physical expression is directly narrated, such as when "Cope, standing alongside, would lay a hand on [Lemoyne's] shoulder" (163).

A final important depiction of Bertram's self-awareness comes during a swimming episode in chapter nine. Bertram and Basil Randolph have been invited to Medora Phillips's house in the Indiana dunes and they decide, or Randolph orchestrates, that they will make the trip together. As such, the two are left to make the trek across the beach together and, not long before reaching their destination, Bertram decides that he wants to swim. During their recreation, for which they both strip naked, they discuss women, marriage, and children. Randolph is, of course, trying to understand Cope better. He wants to determine whether Cope is interested in women at all, or just men; the latter would encourage Randolph to continue his own version of courtship, which in many ways appears like mentorship. When Randolph explains that the "usual crowd" (90) is comprised of the three young ladies who live with Medora, plus a few ever-changing gentlemen who are responsible for the masculine tasks, such as "looking after the stove and the pump" (91), Bertram explains that "there's a knack about [looking after women] . . . a technique" that he does not have, and "nor [does he] seem greatly prompted to learn it" (ibid). This is a significant moment. Bertram seizes the opportunity for discussing "manly" tasks in order to reveal something about himself, which is rather out of character for him, a young man committed to his privacy. Even more important, however, is that he continues the conversation by adding that there is no reason to suggest "that every adult male will make a good citizen, desiring the general welfare and bestirring himself to contribute his own share to it" (ibid). To this he makes special note that he feels unlikely to do so. In other words, Cope recognizes that good citizenship means marriage and that "contributing" to the general welfare means having and raising children.

For Cope, both ideas are repellant because he has no interest in marriage and certainly sees no future for himself as a father.

Keith Gumery makes an important observation about this scene when he explains that "for all the sexual charge and desire that Randolph feels for Cope, the naked swim together on their way to the house on the dunes is remarkably chaste . . . despite the fact that the two men are sitting naked side by side on a deserted beach there is less sexual implication than in some of the hand-shakes and looks elsewhere in the book" (51). This assessment is accurate, but it overlooks one important consideration of the scene, which is that it is here in this intimate moment where Bertram Cope makes himself most clear to Basil Randolph. The scene may not be sexually or physically charged, as one might expect from such a situation, but their physical nakedness certainly reflects the metaphorical bearing-of-self in which Cope engages. He says, as plainly as possible given the time and circumstances, that he is a man who desires men, and he will not participate in society's expectations to wed and have children.

In addition to his self-identification, Bertram is also acutely aware of his otherness and takes active measures to protect himself from exposure despite minor lapses such as those mentioned above. For example, in a letter to his lover, he writes, "I have been pretty careful, and they still treat me with respect" (72). He is referring specifically to his students, and particularly the male ones, but the larger danger is certainly underscored in these words. If his sexuality becomes known to the general academic community, he risks losing his place as an instructor and possibly his ability to complete his graduate studies there. This very risk becomes all the clearer late in the narrative, after Arthur Lemoyne, Bertram's lover, performs too realistically in drag. Christopher Looby rightly claims that, after this social misstep, "Bertram comes to feel that Arthur is a psychic burden and a social liability" ("The Gay Novel" 423). Looby also claims in his piece that "Arthur is more devoted to Bertram than the reverse" (ibid), but this is problematic for two reasons: first, over the course of their correspondences, Arthur reveals that he has been vacationing with another man, a situation which makes Bertram jealous and causes him to actively encourage Arthur to end his affairs in Wisconsin and relocate to Illinois, where they can be together and begin searching for possible employment opportunities for Arthur; second, when the community turns on Arthur, he leaves right away, and it is Bertram who follows after him.

Thus, the fear of exposure that is articulated at the opening of the novel comes to fruition near the end of it, despite Cope's attempts to be discreet throughout. Arthur Lemoyne is forced out of his position at the college, and then Cope himself, after graduating, flees without warning or goodbye. His would-be benefactors, Basil Randolph and Medora Phillips, as well as the critical Joseph Foster, cannot understand this decision because they have never been quite sure of Bertram Cope in the first place. His self-awareness informs his personal choices, most of which result in others' misunderstanding him. Cope is fully aware that he is a homosexual man who has different desires and expectations from those engaging in the rather comedic courtships taking place around him.

Cope does not take caution with just his own personal identity, being aware that he is different from the majority surrounding him. His relationship with Arthur Lemoyne, too, is carefully guarded. Late in the narrative, Bertram Cope's health begins to fail. Mrs. Phillips, who has more than a friendly interest in him, pays him a visit to see how he is doing. Bertram, perhaps in an attempt to entertain her and Amy, who has come with, brings them a number of photographs from his former college to peruse. This scene is similar to the beach scene with Basil Randolph in that Cope reveals, or attempts to reveal, something about himself without necessarily speaking it plainly. As Mrs. Phillips is reviewing Cope's personal photographs, she notices the same man, Arthur, appearing over and over again, and she asks, "Who is this?" (127).

Cope, rather than responding honestly, as would perhaps be impossible at the time, gives an

answer that is described as "prompt, but vague." Cope knows that his relationship with Arthur

will be questioned, even demonized, so he calls him his "chum" (ibid) and says just enough to

raise the question, without putting himself or his relationship too directly into harm's way: "He is

coming down here early in January. To look after me . . . we shall look after each other . . . we

are going to live together" (128). He expresses the nature of their relationships without having to

explain it overtly, just as he used the ruse of "manly service" at the dune house to describe how

he is not suited for, nor desiring of, a heterosexual relationship.

    In addition to Bertram Cope understanding himself as "other" and his relationship with

Arthur as "different," there is a third important character and relationship that demonstrates this

feature of the narrative's intertextual awareness. That is the character Basil Randolph and his

relationship to, or attempted relationship with, Bertram Cope. The first clue that Randolph has

more than a passing interest in Cope is that he admits to being "interested in" (60) Cope, so

much so that he goes to the admissions office to consult his personal records. While this could be

read simply as an elder faculty member's curiosity about a new instructor, Randolph's secretive

approach raises questions. While investigating, he notes that there is "no reason why his new

interest should be widely communicated to others" (ibid). There is a self-consciousness, a fear of

discovery, causing Randolph to be deliberately guarded in his investigations. He is also

persistent. When the records agent tells Randolph that Cope has not yet submitted his

information, Randolph decides to return again in a few days, when he can see Bertram Cope's

own handwriting. The fact that Randolph both searches out more information on Cope and then

returns again simply because he wants to see the young man's handwriting, is telling. A clearer notion forms, however, after Randolph assesses the handwriting, which he finds "open and easy," and adds that "he felt disposed to find his earlier self in this young man" (63). Clearly, something about Cope is drawing Randolph to him, some similarity they share which must be investigated carefully and privately. As Roger Austen remarks, the attraction is so immediate and intense that Randolph, a lifelong bachelor, quickly moves "into a lovingly described larger apartment so that he can better entertain Bertram overnight" (29). Much of this attempt at discovery is then communicated in codes throughout the rest of the narrative.

Thus, Fuller, like Stoddard and Prime-Stevenson, engages in the necessary practice of writing in code. One of the more obvious and persistent is that the narrator repeatedly refers to historical gay figures and concerns, dating back to the classical period. For example, the narrator describes one scene at Medora Phillips's house as one of "Lesbos - - with Sappho" (57). Lesbos, of course, is a Greek island historically associated with lesbianism, largely due to the work of the poet Sappho, who directed many of her poems to other women (Aldrich and Wotherspoon 391-393). Writers aware of this history would not miss the allusion[23]. In a later scene, Cope and Lemoyne take a walk to celebrate the fact that Cope has been "saved" from his inadvertent engagement to Amy Lefingwell. The narrator describes their happiness in this way: "Urania, through the whole width of her starry firmament, looked down kindly upon a happier household" (174-175). The narrator employs two codes in this chapter-ending statement. The latter is found in the intentional use of the word "household." This implies that Bertram and Arthur are not simply roommates, but that they are creating a home together. It is a single word, easy enough to

---

[23] In his review, Charles Van Vechten makes special note of the way that a homosexual reader would find more to appreciate in *Bertram Cope's Year*: "The story . . . would prove unreadable to one who had no key to its meaning. Once its intention is grasped, however, it becomes one of the most brilliant and glowingly successful of this author's brief series of works" ("From Carl Van Vechten" 283)

overlook, yet it connotes the romantic nature of their relationship. The former code is another

reference to Greek mythology, which is significant due to its contributing to the narrative's

pattern of classical references; however, as Joseph Dimuro indicates in his footnote, there is

added significance in the use of this specific mythological reference:

> "Uranian" is a nineteenth-century term for a person of a third sex, originally someone
> with a female psyche contained within a man's body who is sexually attracted to men. It
> is believed to be an English adaptation of the German word "Urning," which was first
> used by Karl Heinrich Ulrichs in 1864 and 1865 in a series of booklets about male same-
> sex love. The term "Uranian" was adopted by English-language advocates of homosexual
> emancipation in Victorian England, where writers used it to describe a comraderly [sic]
> love that would bring about true democracy. (174-175 n.1)

Unlike Prime-Stevenson who, in writing his novel much like a case study, relied heavily on

scientific terminology to support the naturalness of homosexuality, Henry Blake Fuller relies on

artistic, historical, and literary allusions to make the same point. The code would be an opaque

one, as Van Vechten suggests, for those unfamiliar with it; but those who followed the work of

sexologists and psychologists, as well as the literature of earlier gay writers, would understand

Fuller's meaning.

There is also an underlining Greek sentiment throughout the novel, as demonstrated by

two primary themes: the relationship between age and youth, and the relationship between

teacher and student[24]. These themes and the classical aura they generate are expressed through

Randolph's infatuation with the younger graduate student, Bertram Cope. "Greek love" in its

iteration as mentorship between scholar and student is often invoked in gay men's literature

because of the historically evidenced acceptance of such relationships in ancient Greece. As

---

[24] See also: *Hidden from History* (Duberman et al, NAL Books, 1989), *The Gay Canon* (Drake, Anchor, 1998), *Greek Homosexuality* (Dover, Harvard, 1989), *A History of Gay Literature* (Woods, Yale, 1998), *Greek Love Reconsidered* (Hubbard, W. Hamilton, 2000), and *Homosexuality in Greece and Rome* (Hubbard, U California Press, 2003).

Louis Crompton notes, there are a number of relationships in ancient Greek religion, mythology, art, etc. in which "male attachments are presented in an honorific light" (2-3). Crompton adds that "probably the most notable defense of male love" comes from the mouth of Phaedrus, in Plato's *Symposium* (3). A notable example of this mentor/mentee construct between Randolph and Cope is found in the former's decision to move to a larger apartment in order to begin securing a permanent place in his residence for Bertram Cope. Under the pretense of guiding Bertram Cope through his early years as an instructor, he begins to picture their lives together in a domestic fashion. Randolph considers that, "before long, [he] shall have to buy a few sticks of furniture . . . and a trifle of crockery. And a percolator" (139). Then, upon learning that Bertram already has plans to move in with another man, Randolph "[asks] himself if his trouble in setting up a new ménage was likely to go for nothing" (140). If, as the surface narrative suggests, their relationship is meant to be purely that of mentor and mentee, then Bertram's decision to live elsewhere should not affect Randolph in the least; however, the narrator reveals that Randolph has much more intimate designs on the young man[25].

There are other hints of Cope's homosexuality, coded in phrases such as "artistic temperament" (157). Many of these codes are expressed through the points of view of Basil Randolph and Joseph Foster, who are concerned with a particular "type" of homosexuality. Randolph, in particular, finds Cope's homosexual type to be attractive and appropriate, whereas Arthur Lemoyne's type is wholly disagreeable. Arthur Lemoyne also reacts negatively to Basil Randolph, "the little gray man" (185), whom he sees as both a potential rival and a sort of

---

[25] This domestic offer, in addition to offers of patronage, as well as Randolph's multiple inquiries into Cope's thoughts on marriage, are indicative of what James Levin calls "veiled offers of a sexual relationship" (22).

ridiculous figure, too old to be vying for Bertram's attention. Following Arthur's performance as

the woman "Annabella," the narrator indicates that Randolph "felt that Lemoyne had shown

himself in a tolerably clear light" (209). Randolph further suggests that "the right sort of fellow,"

meaning either a heterosexual one or, more likely, a socially-conscious homosexual man, would

have broken character on purpose in order to demonstrate that he was not "epicene" (208).

Lemoyne plays his part too well, which indicates to Randolph that he is too womanly[26] and thus

the wrong kind of gay man. In this way, judgments about acceptable types of homosexual men

are levied. To Arthur Lemoyne, Basil is ridiculous because he has "aged out." To Basil

Randolph, Arthur is ridiculous because he is effeminate. Bertram Cope seems to agree with this

latter perspective, considering his first moments of frustration with Arthur occur when the lover

is so taken with his role that the accessories of it become pervasive in their home life. As the

narrator describes:

> Their room came to be strown [sic] with all the disconcerting items of a theatrical
> wardrobe. Cope soon reached the point where he was not quite sure that he liked it all,
> and he began to develop a distaste for Lemoyne's preoccupation with it. He came home
> one afternoon to find on the corner of his desk a long pair of silk stockings and a too
> dainty pair of ladies' shoes. "Oh, Art!" he protested. (208)

It is no surprise that Bertram, in whom the elder gay man sees much of himself, reacts as

distastefully to Arthur's effeminacy as the others do. Joseph Foster and Basil Randolph are

attempting to cultivate Bertram in their own image. Indeed, Foster is open to considering

Bertram Cope as potentially acceptable, but after multiple interactions with him, and especially

---

[26] The fallacy that equates homosexuality with effeminacy, and vice versa, has been explored
thoroughly in a number of works, including in chapters three and five of this one, but another
notable inquiry is Lee Edelman's *Homographesis* (Routledge 1994). In his book, Edelman
explores the genesis of homosexual identity and notes, significantly, that the earliest connotation
of homosexuality, denoted by the actions of men who participated in sodomy with other men,
dealt specifically with the idea of effeminacy (11).

following the upsetting developments with Arthur's performance as a woman, Foster quickly and

definitely dismisses him by asking, "what hope for him . . . so long as he goes on liking and

admiring that fellow?" (218). In other words, Fuller's narrative both affirms and rejects the

historical signification of the effeminate gay man by creating characters who either fulfill or

disrupt this assumption. The text ultimately reaches a verdict: Arthur Lemoyne, the effeminate

homosexual, is ejected from the community, Bertram leaves it willingly and successfully, and

Basil and Joseph remain members of it. Clearly, the outcast, the wrong type, is Lemoyne.

Bertram Cope's Year, "the most venturesome American gay male publication of the

teens" (Cady 31), is a successful novel for a number of reasons, not the least of which is that it

functions as a masterful piece of American Realism as well as an example of the highly effective

regional Chicago writing of the period,[27] which included such works as Theodore Dreiser's

Sister Carrie (1900). It is particularly important in helping to define the gay American literary

tradition in that it distinctly but effectively employs the three signature features of the early gay

American text. It describes a protagonist who is aware that he is homosexual and, in this case,

comfortable with that fact. Furthermore, the protagonist understands himself to be different in

that regard, and the caution he takes to maintain his place in society by managing his image is a

focal point of the narrative. Finally, the text communicates homosexual issues by means of coded

language and themes throughout, such as its reliance on classical references, its use of the

thematic mentor-mentee relationship as a kind of same-sex relationship, and its coded discussion

---

[27] Joseph Dimuro notes that "Fuller came of age at a time that witnessed many changes in the city's aspirations toward a more refined civilization," which included "the 1893 World's Columbian Exposition," the development of the University of Chicago, "the formation of Theodore Thomas's Chicago Symphony, the founding of the Art Institute . . . and the establishment of many local literary and artistic clubs" (11).

of the right "type" of homosexual. In this way, *Bertram Cope's Year* continues the work of writers such as Charles Warren Stoddard and Edward I. Prime-Stevenson, who accomplished the same objectives by different means. A fourth text that develops on these formative examples is Forman Brown's *Better Angel*.

As noted in chapter two, Forman Brown's *Better Angel* was first published in 1933. It was later reprinted with a pulp press and given the dramatic title, *Torment*. Brown's novel is the most complete and complex of the four discussed in this chapter, and it is perhaps "one of the earliest programmatically 'affirmative' treatments of homosexuality" in early twentieth-century American literature (Looby, "Sexuality's Aesthetic," 172). While it is true that, contrary to popular belief, a number of early gay American texts treated homosexuality with empathy and even acceptance, Forman Brown's semi-autobiographical[28] text is an American novel, first, whose protagonist's sexuality just happens to be a part of the character's identity. The narrative not only allows for self-identification, awareness of self-as-other, and intertextual communication through coded language, but it is, in addition, a classic American *bildungsroman* whose central theme is the character's *journey toward* self-realization. In the three novels already discussed, the characters are aware of their sexual orientations and desires at the start of the narratives, and they do not necessarily need to come to terms with their identities (except in the case of *Imre* where it occurs through mutual storytelling of the "coming out" experience, but that experience had already taken place prior to the start of the narrative). *Better Angel*, on the other

---

[28] According to a short biographical entry in *The Puppetry Journal*, Forman Brown "started his creative life by doing puppet shows" with his gay cousin, Harry Burnett. He then met his lover and lifelong partner Richard Brandon at Yale in 1927. They remained together for 57 years (Abrams 26). Brown's novel is influenced by his life with his cousin Harry and his partner Richard (Brown, "Epilogue," par. 7).

hand, recounts the full gamut of the human experience, from childhood to adulthood, but, in this case, it is the life of a homosexual being narrated. This is a treatment largely unavailable for homosexual characters in American literature before 1950, and it would perhaps not be fully realized again until Sanford Friedman's *Totempole*[29] in 1965.

Despite the fact that *Better Angel* is one of the most successful early gay American texts, one described by Peter Carey as "the first homosexual novel with a truly happy ending" (482), it has received little critical attention. It is probable that early readers and reviewers were reluctant to discuss it because the subject of homosexuality is treated so openly and positively in the novel. As Michael Bronski appropriately notes, "in a cultural climate that fostered fear of public homosexuality, the privacy of reading even popular material on the subject" was significant (*A Queer History* 126). Unlike readers of the more ambiguous or sensational gay novels of the period, then, readers of *Better Angel* confined their reactions to that private sphere. Nevertheless, the book was clearly popular, given that it was reprinted in the 1950s and again in the 1980s. The 1951 pulp edition, however, would have left much to be desired by that particular reading audience, as the book fails to deliver on the genre's traditional promises. Specifically, *Better Angel*, despite being titled *Torment* on its republication, offers little melodrama, no violence, and a happy ending that promises an enduring romantic relationship for its protagonist. Thus, it is far removed from what pulp readers would have expected from such a novel, and it would have been difficult for readers and reviewers to know how to deal with it. Ultimately, in addition to being a remarkable piece of fiction, *Better Angel* is an important example of early twentieth-century gay literature that engages in the critical task of intertextual communication, helping to create and

---

[29] To be discussed in Chapter Five.

disseminate a history of homosexuality within the fictive world that would transmit to its

readership the presence of and possibilities for gay men in the United States.

One benefit, and joy, of reading a gay *Bildungsroman* is that, in the right hands, the self-

identification process, the "coming out" process, becomes a significant part of the protagonist's

coming of age; this is absolutely the case in *Better Angel*. When the main character, Kurt Gray, is

a child, he is described by the narrator in coded language that would make the fact of his

homosexuality clear to an aware audience. He is called a "sissy" (8) by his peers, and the

narrator indicates that he is "like a girl" (9). Early in the text, a description of Kurt at play hints

to the reader what Kurt himself will eventually discover, that he is gay:

> His imagination was keen. He had read all the books he could find to read, particularly if
> they had in them an element of the miraculous . . . His great delight, when he had a few
> of the younger children about him, was to enact a play—something he had read or
> something of his own invention. The plays were always romantic, as fairy tales are
> romantic, for Kurt loved to pretend being a prince, or, still better, a princess. (19)

Despite problematic elements which stereotype gender roles (that all gay boys are "bookish,"

fanciful, and feminine, and that all feminine boys enjoy romance, fairy tales, and princesses) the

passage is still significant in helping to communicate with the reader two things: first, that Kurt

is a gay boy and, second, that, yes, contemporary audiences, and this writer, perhaps understand

homosexual men to be a certain way, to perform certain gender acts that are out of the ordinary[30].

These descriptions do not only help the reader understand Kurt but, more importantly, they also

signify Kurt's budding awareness of himself.

Over the course of the narrative, as the protagonist grows up, his sexual identity becomes

clearer to him. One of the earliest examples of Kurt's self-awareness comes at the start of the

---

[30] An evaluation of the "types" of homosexual male, including the spectrum of masculinity and
femininity, featured in early gay American literature is the focus of Chapter Five.

second section, which details Kurt's college years. Kurt has met another young man named

Derry, and "the two got along unusually well" (72). Not long into their friendship, they discover

the same longing in each other, and that desire is eventually physically consummated:

> They had been quiet at first. Then something in the white silence of the May moon had melted down the reticence their eighteen years of living had built up. Talk, slowly undertaken, had drifted little by little to forbidden things, to exchanges of confidences— and, at last, to the thing Kurt had fought so stoutly for the last four years, complicated now because shared with another. After it had happened, the joy of it turned to fear. (74)

After his first sexual experience with another man, Kurt struggles with his "guilt" over

committing such a "heinous" sin (ibid). He has trouble reconciling the hypocrisy of his feelings,

a simultaneous awareness of guilt and persistent longing for Derry (75). His coming of age and

coming out experiences begin here, but the doubts that he feels are not long lived. As James

Levin notes, Brown's characters are "relatively free from neurosis and gender confusion" (48).

Brown creates an experience that he feels reflects the realities of the young gay man's

experience: some childhood confusion, a struggle with young impulses, and guilt over his first

"indiscretion," but then, acceptance.

Another important moment in Kurt's self-acceptance happens just before he leaves for

Europe, and is inspired by Derry's sister, Chloe, who falls in love with Kurt. When Kurt realizes

what she truly wants from him, he finally begins to consciously assess his own desires and to

admit to himself the nature of his sexuality, which he had surrendered to in his experiences with

Derry and another character, David. Now, in comparing those experiences with the potential for

a similar one with a woman, he can see himself clearly:

> He had seen the same look in David's eyes, but that he now understood and could cope with. He looked about him in the streets and was ashamed. He seemed sometimes to be surrounded by boys younger than himself, who were years older in experience. He almost hated his parents at such times for not letting him dance, for not making him want girls. Or was he, really, incapable of loving a girl? Was he really different, really one of the

beings he read about so zealously? He was, of course. It had all been decided and the ground fought over a thousand times. (138)

This moment of epiphany is rather brilliantly designed, as it incorporates numerous avenues of doubt, which are to be expected in a realistic portrayal of the coming out experience, while still allowing Kurt to reach his moment of admission and acceptance. First, he compares Chloe's desire for him with David's and notes that he can appreciate David's, but not hers. This leads to a comparison of himself with the young men around him, all of whom, he is sure, have experience with women. He wonders, for a moment, whether that makes him a failure in some sense, and if so, who should he blame? His parents and their religion are the tentatively accused. Anthony Slide notes that "there is something poignant and wholesome here, even in the pages dealing with Kurt's introduction to masturbation and the physical dangers he fears from it" (125). Indeed, while some critics have rightly claimed that perhaps this very wholesomeness is why the book received such little critical attention or acceptance as realistic (Levin 47), it is also what makes the narrative remarkable for its time. Ultimately, though, he acknowledges that neither Chloe, nor the other young men, nor his parents, nor even he himself is to blame, as there is no blame warranted. He simply does not desire women.

Although Kurt Gray is able to self-identify as a man who desires other men, and although he does eventually admit this to others, he remains consciously aware of the fact that he is a kind of "other" in the world. While this is true for each of the protagonists in the three novels discussed earlier, what is of particular interest in *Better Angel* is that it is not just the heterosexual world that makes Kurt feel like an outsider or aberration. For example, when he is in Europe, Kurt meets another young man, a bisexual actor named Tony, who cannot fathom that Kurt has never loved or had sexual intercourse with a girl. To Tony, all men are bisexual, a sentiment that would be taken up by Gore Vidal[31], among others, in another decade. When Kurt

explains that he only desires men, Tony responds by saying that a boy wanting a girl is "animal

and normal. If he doesn't, he's abnormal" (171). As the discussion continues, and Kurt tries to

understand what Tony's motives are, Tony responds, "I'm trying to find out what's wrong with

you" (172). This new character, the bisexual, thus adds further complexity, including renewed

guilt and self-doubt, to the protagonist's already troubled psyche. Additionally, the inclusion of a

bisexual character further demonstrates how Forman Brown willingly disrupted traditional

conceptions of sexuality in his fiction. Just as he creates a narrative that allows its gay characters

to find a happy ending and to reject notions of psychosis or illness, so too does he reject "the

reduction of bisexuality to the opacity of 'uncertainty and doubt'" (Angelides 48). It is clear that

Kurt Gray, and therefore Forman Brown, had read a great deal of sexological theory, yet he, and

the author, reject certain of the limiting factors in order to create a more realistic portrayal of

multiple sexualities, as experienced by Brown himself. Ultimately, the experience, far from

permanently disrupting Kurt's perception of himself, strengthens his self-awareness and his

understanding of the spectrum of sexuality.

In addition to the somewhat clinical understanding of the nature of sexuality that Kurt

begins to develop through his extensive reading and by virtue of his experiences with

heterosexual women, gay men, and bisexual men, he also discovers that he is different from his

peers, other gay and bisexual men, in that their first priority seems to be the sexual act. For Kurt,

on the other hand, the priority is love and spiritual connection. He believes, for example, that his

---

[31] As Steven Angelides reminds us in his landmark work *The History of Bisexuality* (Chicago 2001), "Gore Vidal . . . refused the ontological categories of sexuality, suggesting in 'The Bisexual Politics' . . . that 'there is no such thing as a homosexual . . . all beings are bisexual'" (236 n.82).

relationship with David is a "marriage" (269), a belief that, if not uncommon at the time, was rarely expressed. Kurt articulates his romantic priorities by repeatedly referring to his "ideal." This is first communicated in a conversation he has with David, on the night before his departure for Europe:

> It's all to be a new adventure, David—for you, for Derry, for me, for Chloe, too. What better time to start a new adventure? Only please remember, and make Derry remember, that I'm alone. You two will have each other—I will have only the ideal. It's high enough and fine enough to carry me through, if you both will help me. Will you?" (149)

The adventures Kurt refers to are ostensibly his trip to Europe and the others' new lives in New York City; what he is actually referring to, however, is his split from the physical relationships, the "love triangle," that he, Derry, and David have been involved in, as well as his corporal separation from Chloe, whom he knows must be physically removed from him if she is to get over her feelings for him, and, finally, his pursuit of the ideal. To him, the ideal is a solitary pursuit, one which must necessarily be separate from physical relationships because it is an emotional and spiritual connection he seeks.

While he is away, Kurt receives a letter from Chloe in which she acknowledges his pursuit and, while chastising the physical obsessions that Derry and David have cultivated, reminds Kurt not to "let an inferior ideal possess" him (160). Eventually, as he experiences more of the world and accepts everything and everyone as natural, his concept of the ideal takes shape. By the end of the narrative, Kurt, having returned to the United States and accepted a position at a local college, is able to articulate something quite profound and unique:

> He read, finding new delights in the sonnets of Shakespeare, in Shelley and in the patterned brilliance of Proust. The Baron de Charlus and Ozzy, Robert de Saint-Loup and Tony—and yet in all that flayed and slightly nauseous society of "*les hommes-femmes*" no figure, he knew, comparable to David or himself, or Derry, blundering through an unavoidable and uncharted fate. Somewhere, somewhere there must be an honest picture

of it all—Plato and Michelangelo and Shakespeare as well as de Charlus and Jupien and the wry and sorry streets of Sodom. (146)

Forman Brown allows his protagonist to rely on the intertextual device of the list in order to compare himself, and his lovers, to historical homosexual figures. This strategy is not new[32], but what is unique is that Kurt comes to the conclusion that an "honest picture" of all of it has yet to be formed, and that there seems not to be, as many would have it, any one universal "homosexual man." Instead, there are and always have been many kinds of homosexual men, all of them individuals and every one of them genuine. In this way, Kurt is able to accept that he is different, not just from the heterosexual majority, but unique even in the long history of same-sex desiring males. He is also different from his closest friends, David, Derry, and Tony, with whom he has had sexual relations. It is this discovery that offers the opportunity for his and David's happy ending because it allows them to come together as complementary individuals, creating a possibility for an affirming and lasting domestic relationship that had not been made available in gay American fiction before this. This is Kurt's ideal realized.

Codes are important communicative tools throughout this novel. Roger Austen claims that "after Kurt Gray discovers he is 'different,' Meeker's innocuous *Bildungsroman* turns into a problem novel in a way that must have been unsettling for heterosexual readers of the thirties" (84). I have already pointed out that Forman Brown's treatment of homosexuality in this book, as something natural and potentially positive, likely explains why it received virtually no critical attention. Austen's point further reinforces why coded language and themes are important to this text, despite the fact that it is comparatively less abstruse than other gay texts published in the preceding decades. I further submit that the treatment was likely unsettling for homosexual men

---

[32] George Chauncey notes that such practices "had become part of the folklore of the gay world by the 1910s—used by men to legitimate and even exalt their identities as homosexuals (285).

as well, though perhaps not with the same negative connotations. Gay readers of the 1930s may have privately rejoiced at this clearly-written and affirming view of homosexuality, but it was nevertheless an innovative and transformational treatment. The use of familiar codes and themes surely helped the reader to situate this book in the context of others treating the same topic.

One motif that would be familiar to gay readers is that of "the mask[33]." It occurs in a number of early American gay texts, including *Imre* and *Giovanni's Room*, and always in the context of hiding one's identity, usually from the public but, on occasion, from one's self as well. In *Better Angel*, an example of this occurs, logically, near the start of the text, in the first section, which details Kurt's adolescence: "All his life he had been pretending to things he was not, in order to simplify the task of living . . . The whole situation into which he found himself drifting bothered him, but to accept the masquerade made things easier" (58-59). Here, Brown's narrator adds to "the mask" the important idea of pretense. The narrator noted earlier that Kurt, as a child, enjoyed acting. In addition to this, we learn that he uses that skill not simply for recreation but also to navigate through life while maintaining his secret sexual identity. Kurt will continue to "simplify the task of living," but ironically, the way he achieves this is by shedding the mask and beginning an open and accepting life with his lover David.

Other codes and familiar themes arise throughout, such as references to historical figures like Shelley—who was also mentioned in *Imre* and who was, if not homosexual, certainly bisexual—and Abraham Lincoln (18), both of whom have sexually ambiguous pasts and who

---

[33] See for example: "Mask Maker, Mask Maker: The Black Gay Subject in 1970s Popular Culture" (Picheon and Stanford, *Sexuality & Culture*, 2001), "'A Different Story to Tell': The Historical Novel in Contemporary Irish Lesbian and Gay Writing" (Walshe, *Facing the Other*, 2008), "James Baldwin: Expatriation, Homosexual Panic, and Man's Estate" (Henderson, *Callaloo*, 2000), "We Wear the Mask: African American Contemporary Gay Male Identities" (Brown, *Journal of African American Studies*, 2005), and "Lesbian and Gay Male Language Use: A Critical Review of the Literature" (Jacobs, *American Speech*, 1996).

have been the focus of gay iconography, as in Walt Whitman's poems. The theme of loneliness, too, is prominent, especially in Kurt's youth. What is interesting, however, is that this theme of loneliness is introduced at the very moment when Kurt is finally able, or willing, to self-identify, to accept his homosexuality. Just after Kurt admits that "he was in love with Derry" (87), he reflects on what this means for him:

> He knew that he felt [his love for Derry] to be beautiful and worthy of praise, but he knew too that he must endure always the martyrdom of silence. No boasting of his love—his first love—no word of it dared he breathe. Always, always, it seemed to him, life demanded secrecy and silence. (87)

For Kurt, this reflection proves not to be entirely true, as he is eventually able to tell a few select others about his sexual identity. In fact, not very long after Kurt admits to himself this reality, he confides in another, David, "his secret": he loves Derry (100). This scene recalls the confessional moments of *Imre* in that there are again two young gay men who find each other, recognize each other in "fellowship" (88), and, despite their fears, decide to tell each other their truths.

In addition, Kurt is quick to debunk the myth that he, as a gay man, would naturally be attracted to young boys, as was commonly believed[34]. In a conversation about their relationship, Kurt tells David that he is "not interested in seducing adolescents" (242) but, instead, only interested in David. This offers to readers the rather unexplored notion of fidelity and maturity in same-sex relationships. Furthermore, when Kurt is talking to Chloe about his, and her brother's,

---

[34] Although the concept of "Greek love" is often used in gay texts to demonstrate that homosexual men have existed for at least as long as western civilization, the counterargument has been that in many cases the Greek ideal was *paiderastia*. Louis Crompton explains that "in Greek love affairs, an older man, or *erastes*, became the mentor of a young boy, or *eromenos* . . . men met, exercised in the nude, discoursed on politics and on philosophy, and in addition found lovers" ("Greek Literature, Ancient" 343). Thus, Forman Brown is relying on the ancient concept of homosexuality to provide historical substance while simultaneously refuting the expected criticism that homosexuality in that context often meant man-boy love; *Better Angel* is one of a very few early texts to repudiate this conflation.

lifestyles, he is adamant about "the difference between perversion as a pose . . . and perversion that was deep in the core of you" (236). Despite the unfortunate choice of words, which even the protagonist comments on— "perversion how he loathed the word"—his point is that there are different types of gay men, different types of acts, masks, and performances, and that not all gay men are the same. Brown relies on some of the codes, themes, and terminology that his readers would have been familiar with in order to construct a revolutionary figure in gay male literature, one who manages to find love and happiness and to contradict the stereotypical notions of homosexual men as ill, promiscuous, neurotic, and destined to isolation.

Better Angel employs coded language, motifs, and themes that are in fact commonly present across gay literature. Its exceptionality does not lie in the fact that the character manages to self-identify as gay and to understand himself as "other;" indeed all of the examples discussed have accomplished both of these tasks in some way. Instead, what makes *Better Angel* unique from other examples of early twentieth-century gay literature is its introspection, its complexity, and its willingness to display different types of gay men and gay spaces. Forman Brown also creates for Kurt Gray the possibility of a happy ending, a satisfied life, in a way that had not been so clearly or convincingly achieved in any prior gay American novel, though it is one suggested possibility in *Bertram Cope's Year*. At the end of *Better Angel*, Kurt Gray has experienced a full childhood and youth. He is ready to "marry" his male lover, pursue his career, and live happily ever after.

As Jeffrey Meyers points out in his introduction to *Homosexuality & Literature: 1890-1930* (1987), "the literature of homosexuality begins with the book of Genesis" and since that time, homosexuality has been treated as "both a disease and a crime" (4). Criminal penalties for engaging in homosexual acts have ranged from monetary penalties, to imprisonment and even execution, and the social consequences could be nearly as severe. For these reasons, it has been

necessary for homosexual writers, whether or not they identified themselves by that term, to

develop their themes and transmit their sentiments in ways which their representative

"communities," would understand. It was essential that they did so without being too obvious or

too revealing, as this would draw public criticism and potential social ostracizing or criminal

punishment. Gay male literature in the United States reflects an attention to these concerns, and

the strategies employed by gay authors have been fundamental in creating a gay male American

literary tradition in its own right. As discussed throughout this chapter, some common features

were developed in order to write about this taboo subject. These include such qualities as a

protagonist who self-identifies as homosexual, characters who have or who gain an awareness of

self-as-other, and authors who demonstrate a willingness to communicate, whether relatively

openly, as in *Imre* and *Better Angel*, or more opaquely, as in *For the Pleasure of His Company*

and *Bertram Cope's Year*. In addition, there are often common codes and motifs used to describe

the characters' sexuality, such as the use of lists, the motif of "the mask," and references to

classical Greece. These commonalities make it possible for gay writers to communicate with

their audiences and with other writers, as well as connect with their own histories.

Gay American literature circa 1950 and onward has begun to receive valuable and

warranted critical attention, but these earlier texts developed the language and themes, as well as

created and cultivated the audience, that later texts in the more welcoming decades would draw

upon as the genre progressed and as readership became more widespread. In the next chapter, I

will discuss homosexual texts' portrayals of gay characters on the spectrum of masculinity as

another feature critical to the study of gay male literature in the United States. Just as these texts have dealt with issues of same-sex desire and romance, so have they played a role in crafting

readers' ideas of what "manhood" means for gay men.

CHAPTER 5

RESISTANCE AND ACQUIESCENCE: PROBLEMS OF GENDER & SEXUALITY

"There is no happiness in this so-called sublimation. For your own sake, I hope that you can live without love, for society is not organized with a view to the exceptional individual and makes no allowances for the variation from the conventional type. If you can forswear your own kind, you may not be exactly happy, but you will at least breathe more easily." –*A Scarlet Pansy*, p. 89

One of the most important concerns for gay studies is the relationship between gender

and sexuality. Since the beginning of western civilization, homosexuality has been equated with

femininity. As Louis Crompton notes, "literary descriptions tend to emphasize [homosexuals']

flamboyant theatricality and exaggerated femininity" (41); and, of course, some of the most

famous accounts of literary homosexuality, such as Oscar Wilde's, are accompanied by

descriptions of dandyism and foppishness. Important to a gay literary historiography, then, is an

examination of how gay authors approach the subject of gender and sexuality in their works,

specifically the ways they craft and portray their gay male characters. Examining homosexual

American literature from the first half of the twentieth-century reveals, somewhat surprisingly,

that homosexual writers have approached the gender question from many different perspectives.

It is important to recognize that, while some of these changing views certainly result from

personal and societal perceptions about gender and sexuality at any given point in time, two

important legal changes also occurred during this period which may have affected the way

writers chose to describe their subjects. The first was the Comstock Law of 1873, which

prohibited the free expression of homosexuality in the press until its termination in 1957. A year later, the United States Supreme Court would essentially extend that freedom to writers and

publishers of fiction. Furthermore, playwrights and producers were similarly limited in New

York City by the Wales Padlock Act of 1927, which prohibited homosexual content from being

portrayed on stage. As such, gay texts written and published before and after the abolition of

these prohibitive laws are understandably more or less open about their treatment of sexuality.

Before World War II[1], there was great focus on masculinity as a marker for sexuality.

The earliest example in gay American literature, Prime-Stevenson's *Imre,* delivers an unexpected

argument that is diametrically opposed to the stereotypical one. Its two main characters, Imre and

Oswald, are both homosexual but they are not "feminine." In fact, they are almost obsessively

hyper-masculine. This is a strategic break from commonly perpetuated notions about gay men in

literature, one which demonstrates both Prime-Stevenson's scientific and progressive views

about sexuality as well as his paranoia about gender performance. Just a few decades later,

Robert Scully would publish his own gay novel, *A Scarlet Pansy*, and his treatment of gender is

entirely different. Whereas Prime-Stevenson crafted characters whose masculinity could not be

denied, Scully embraces stereotypes about gay femininity, so much so that recent criticism

suggests the protagonist might more appropriately be considered transgender[2]. Like *Imre,*

---

[1] As Allan Bérubé has noted, perceptions about both homosexuality and gender underwent great changes during the war period. For example, in the military, men could "establish their masculinity by becoming soldiers" and then perform in or enjoy drag performances because of the "wartime relaxation of rigid gender roles" (68).

[2] I use the term "transgender" rather than "transgendered" throughout this chapter in keeping with the contemporary position that transgender individuals believe their sexuality is immutable. This decision is informed by the National Lesbian and Gay Journalists Association (NLGJA), the NPR Ethics Handbook, the National Center for Transgender Equality, and academics such as Professor K.J. Rawson of College of the Holy Cross. I acknowledge, however, that there is disagreement. Gender Rights Advocate Pauline Park, for example, argues that "transgendered" is the correct usage ("GLAAD is Wrong" 2007).

however, *A Scarlet Pansy*, though appearing to offer a liberated viewpoint about gender roles, reinforces certain prejudices as well.

After World War II and the termination of homosexual censorship laws, many writers began to consider gender more genuinely and thoroughly. Sanford Friedman's *Totempole*, for example, describes one character's arduous journey toward coming out and coming of age. Part of that journey includes deep introspection about his own gender, as well as questions about how his gender and sexuality may have been shaped by his environment and the people most instrumental in influencing his personality. *Totempole* is remarkable for engaging with a number of important questions about the nature of gender and sexuality, including how it is developed and whether or not a person can alter his own. A few years later, on the eve of Stonewall, Mart Crowley produced his groundbreaking play, *The Boys in the Band*. Although the play has faced a great deal of criticism for its apparent "self-loathing," it nevertheless incorporates a refreshingly inclusive and diverse cast. Of all of the gay texts before Stonewall, *The Boys in the Band* is arguably the first to offer its audience (or readers) a set of gay characters that ranges from the traditionally masculine to the traditionally feminine and from the stereotypically neurotic to the wholly confident, without demanding that someone die in the end. Ultimately, what we gain by examining gay writers' approaches to gender and sexuality between 1903 and 1968 is a more comprehensive understanding of both what was possible in the literature of this period and also what the common attitudes about homosexual men were at any given time. Most importantly, we are reminded that these concepts, though historically linked, are never static.

The Oscar Wilde trials in 1895 were public and vicious. Despite being "at the height of his career" (Meyers 5) and reaching a level of success and popularity that might under other circumstances protect one from scandal and prosecution, Wilde's particular scandal, homosexual acts with a member of the aristocratic class, could not go unpunished. The immediate lesson for homosexuals following Wilde's public flogging and conviction were two-fold: first, do not get caught engaging in the act of sodomy. This was of course always a concern, but the possibility became even more distressing at this point. Second, and most essential to literary studies, was to avoid being perceived as homosexual. Oscar Wilde was known as a "dandy" whose "'decadent culture' was equated with sexual perversion" (7). His effeminacy, and the aestheticism of *The Picture of Dorian Gray* (1890), came under direct attack as being signifiers of homosexuality and therefore degeneracy. Understanding[3] the effect these trials had on the public is important because it bears a direct relationship to subsequent trends in gay literature, including such practices as publishing gay fiction privately and abroad[4]. Another significant effect was the way that homosexual authors portrayed their gay characters. Edward Prime-Stevenson's novel *Imre* is an excellent example of a writer whose text was responding to both the Wilde incident and to stereotypical opinions about homosexual men at that time.

Prime-Stevenson was well-read in theories about homosexuality that American and European sexologists and psychologists were positing, and he had relationships with some of the most renowned theorists of the time, including a friendship with Richard von Krafft-Ebing, to whom Prime-Stevenson dedicates his own sexological piece, *The Intersexes: A History of Similisexualism as a Problem of Social Life* (1908) (Breen 4). Prime-Stevenson realized that crafting his novel in the form of a case study would be a logical way to present his own counterarguments to conventional assumptions about gay men and gender identity or expression.

---

[3] For an excellent and detailed historiography, see Morris B. Kaplan's *Sodom on the Thames: Sex, Love, and Scandal in Wilde Times* (Cornell 2005).

[4] As discussed in Chapter One.

In so doing, he offers the exact opposite of a traditional case study, which would typically explore the effeminate nature of gay men in order to offer suggestions for the management, treatment, or "cure" of one's homosexuality. Prime-Stevenson chooses to hyper-masculinize his characters in an attempt to, if not disprove those theories, at least offer readers another example of what homosexuality might look like. The goal, ultimately, is to create distance between the "normal" gay man and the "Wilde-type," which Prime-Stevenson's novel implies is indeed an inferior kind of male. Consequently, he creates two interdependent spheres of male gender identity in his novel: the pro-masculine and the homophobic anti-effeminate. These spheres naturally preclude women, leading to a particularly homosexual brand of misogyny.

For Prime-Stevenson, at least within the fictive world of *Imre*, if gay men are to be taken seriously, then they must exhibit, to extreme degrees, characteristics of the masculine male. The relationship between male-male relationships and homophobia is considered by Eve Kosofsky Sedgwick who writes:

> [M]uch of the most useful recent writing about patriarchal structures suggests that "obligatory heterosexuality" is built into male-dominated kinship systems, or that homophobia is a necessary consequence of . . . patriarchal institutions . . . from the vantage point of our own society, at any rate, it has apparently been impossible to imagine a form of patriarchy that was not homophobic. (*Between Men* 3)

Imre is set in arguably the most patriarchal location imaginable, the military. The setting is appropriate to an exploration of masculinity because the military has long been considered both the pinnacle of manliness as well as a situational location for homosexual experiences[5]. As such, Prime-Stevenson creates opportunity to consider gay men's masculinity and sexuality at the

---

[5] See also *Homosexuality and Civilization* (Crompton 2003) and *Colonialism and Homosexuality* (Aldrich 2003), among others.

same time, and to argue that even within the most masculine, patriarchal environment, homosexual men, not just men who engage in same-sex sexual acts when opportune, exist.

Both of the male figures central to the narrative, Imre, subject of the case study, and Oswald, the narrator, maintain the view that homosexual men, as male, should be masculine. The argument aligns with what Gregory Woods describes as "the good homosexual." According to Woods, "the good homosexual was morally and politically conservative. He was sober and dressed soberly; if there were signs of effeminacy in his speech or bearing, he made every reasonable effort to suppress them" (*Homintern* 307). Prime-Stevenson's characters seem almost intentionally crafted to suit these conditions. Imre is, for example, "morally and politically conservative" (50). As a child, he had been a "singularly sensitive, warmhearted boy, indeed too high-strung, too impressionable" (ibid). When he grows up, however, and enters manhood, he begins to adopt his father's moral and conservative, in this case masculine, philosophies. The narrator explains that he gives up the arts and embraces an occupation he hates, the army, because his father's "heart was set on [Imre's] doing what the rest of [them] had done. [He] was the only son left. It had to be" (ibid). Oswald, describing Imre, notes that "he made an excellent officer . . . his sense of personal duty, his pride, his filial affection, his feeling toward his King, all contributed toward the outward semblance that was at least so desirable" (ibid). The phrase "outward semblance" is of the utmost importance, here, as it reminds the reader that these are masculine expectations, established by the father and the community, that Imre feels he must meet, not because he wants to but because gender expressions are supposedly innate. As Mary McIntosh notes, "the existence of a social expectation, of course, commonly helps to produce its own fulfillment" (185). This is true in Imre's career choice and illustrated again soon after, when Oswald exclaims that Imre, "loving not in the least the work, he played his unwelcome part well and manly" (ibid). This passage, given early in the text, is the key to understanding Imre's and

Oswald's perceptions of gender roles. Although they are men who love men, and though Imre, at

least, may be more naturally inclined toward the stereotypically "feminine" pursuits of art[6] and

study, they both nevertheless "play their unwelcome parts." It requires more than simply

fulfilling the role, however; the role must be played "manly," or it would not be effective.

Imre also fulfills the second obligation for the "good," which is to say "manly,"

homosexual, as demonstrated by the way he dresses and by his opinions about jewelry. While

fulfilling his initial appraisal of Imre's appearance in order to establish the fictive case study he

is designing, Oswald writes that Imre "detested all jewelry in the way of masculine adornments,

and wore none: and his civilian clothing was of the plainest" (53). Embedded in this brief

observation of Imre's style are two important points. In the first case, Imre is so self-conscious

about appearing unmasculine that he rejects even "masculine adornments," which would

otherwise be perfectly acceptable. According to James W. Messerschmidt, "gender grows out of

social practices in specific settings and serves to inform such practices in reciprocal relation"

("Masculinities as Structured Action" 207). Imre's "specific setting" is the military and the

"reciprocal relation" for social practices might include exchanging and wearing medals and

ribbons, for example. Imre chooses to abstain from any such expression because his anxiety

about appearing effeminate supersedes his desire for accolades or attention. His clothing choices

when not in uniform also exemplify his need to appear hyper-masculine at all times for fear of

being recognized as homosexual. As David Halperin writes:

---

[6] Art and music have long been related to homosexuality and femininity. As David Bergman
reminds us, Edward Carpenter "argued that the Uranian was twice as often possessed of an
artistic temperament than was the general population" (99). See also Joe Law's excellent essay
"The 'Perniciously Homosexual Art': Music and Homoerotic Desire in *The Picture of Dorian
Gray* and Other *fin-de-siècle* Fiction" (*The Idea of Music*, Routledge, 2004).

> Homosexuality is not just a sexual orientation but a cultural orientation, a dedicated commitment to certain social or aesthetic values, an entire way of being . . . that distinctively gay way of being, moreover, appears to be rooted in a particular queer way of feeling. And that queer way of feeling—that queer subjectivity—expresses itself through a peculiar, dissident way of relating to cultural objects (movies, songs, clothes, books, works of art) and cultural forms in general. (12)

Prime-Stevenson's characters understand that traditional views of homosexuality ascribe certain features relating to style and fashion, among other things, to the gay man. Performing those characteristics, then, makes one identifiable. To counter this "Oscar Wilde effect," Imre rejects anything, including accessories, clothing, and mannerisms, that might challenge his masculinity and thereby reveal his sexuality.

Georges-Michel Sarotte suggests that *Imre* is an "overt glorification of the English narrator's homosexual love affair with" another man (14). It can only function so overtly, however, because of its commitment to "virile homosexuality" (15). Oswald as narrator and observer makes it his priority to acknowledge the many ways that he and Imre demonstrate their masculinity and virility, almost to the point of hyperbole. In the opening pages of the text, for example, Oswald describes Imre's physique in this way:

> His athletic powers were renowned in his regiment. He was among the crack gymnasts, vaulters and swimmers. I have seen him, often, make a standing-leap over an ordinary library table, to land, like a cat, on the other side . . . he could hold out a heavy garden-chair perfectly straight, with one hand; break a stout penholder or lead pencil between his second and third fingers; and bend a thick, brass curtain-rod by his leg-muscles. He frequently swam directly across the wide Duna, making nothing of its cross-currents. (51)

This description might seem fitting for a comic book super hero, so rapturous and venerating is it in nature; and that is the point, after all. The reader is meant to envision a kind of Superman when he reads these descriptions. He is persuaded to reassess his own assumptions about what a homosexual man is and what he is capable of doing physically. What man, the narrator seems to ask, would not look at Imre as an example of virility and manhood? Who cares if he loves another man, as long as that man, too, is acceptably masculine?

Indeed, Imre's love interest, the narrator Oswald, is careful to fulfill that very expectation when he describes himself to Imre and to the reader. For example, he tells Imre that he "was created as a man perfectly male" (96) and that there "was nothing unmanly" (82) about him. The implication, here, is that there *is* something that is "manly" in the first place, and that homosexual men tend not to fulfill the criteria, but *he* does. In his partners, Oswald seeks men who exhibit "manliness, poise, will-power, dignity and strength" (83). Their own preoccupation with masculinity, in themselves and in others, ultimately convinces them "of their perfect mutual love and their ideal lifelong compatibility" (Looby, "The Gay Novel," 419). While the narrator's logical approach to investigating homosexuality and the narrative's happy ending are both welcome variations from the conventional *Sturm und Drang* atmosphere popular in gay fiction, it is important to note, however, that these variations are achieved with a caveat.

Had Prime-Stevenson offered the "masculine" homosexual male as simply one example of the many possibilities of "acceptable" gay men, he would perhaps have avoided the problem of anti-feminine homophobia that appears in direct relation to the hyper-masculinity espoused as the text's ideal. Instead, in elevating his masculine homosexual characters to heroic proportions, the text cannot avoid denigrating effeminacy in homosexual men as a weakness and a threat, which corresponds to heteronormative perceptions of homosexuality more generally. In writing about gender identity and homophobic taboos, Judith Butler argues that "if feminine and masculine dispositions are the result of the effective internalization of that taboo . . . then gender identity appears primarily to be the internalization of a prohibition that proves to be formative of identity. Further, this identity is constructed and maintained by the consistent application of this taboo" (86). For Imre and Oswald, the taboo is femininity, and they have internalized both a fear of and hatred for effeminacy in men because of societal constructs which disallow "real men" to "act like women." These notions are first felt in their youth, relayed retroactively through their respective "coming out" monologues and then maintained throughout their courtship. Despite Prime-Stevenson's probable intentions, these concepts of anti-effeminacy result not only in extolling the masculine and making space for masculine-identifying gay characters, but they also validate homophobic beliefs about gay men who do not act like "real men."

An example of the internalization of anti-effeminate homophobia occurs very early in the text when Oswald is introducing his readers to Imre. The narrator writes that Imre "never seemed to think of his appearance for so much as two minutes together. He never glanced into a mirror . . . he never posed; never fussed as to his toilet, nor worried concerning the ultra-fitting of his clothes, nor studied with anxiety details of his person" (52). The complete disregard for appearance is meant to signify a rejection of supposed feminine vanity, something which, in gay men, had been translated into the practice of drag. Much has been written about cross-dressing and gender performance in same-sex institutions, such as the military and single-sex schools. Morris Kaplan recounts the historical case of "Fanny and Stella[7]," for example, who were victims of the similar backlash against sexual degeneracy to which Oscar Wilde fell victim (Kaplan 62-74). Imre's choice to be indifferent about his appearance implies that he is not at risk of falling prey to this supposedly feminine vanity. Yet, these actions should be identified as more than simple aloofness because of Imre's preoccupation with his manhood.

---

[7] Thomas Ernest Boulton and Frederick William Park, famous cross-dressers and suspected homosexuals who, in 1871, were tried, but not convicted, for "'conspiracy to commit the felony' of sodomy" (Kaplan 23).

In a meeting between Oswald and Imre not long after the above scene, the two discuss another "compromised" (67) officer, a known homosexual, and Oswald jests that he thought Imre was one himself. Not at first understanding the joke, Imre asks, "do you observe anything particularly womanish—abnormal—about me?" (68). Taken together, it is clear that Imre's earlier inactions regarding his appearance are actually premeditated, that he believes effeminacy in men to be abnormal and that any homosexual man who ascribes to the feminine role is a "particular brand of fool" (67). Indeed, a contemporary review of the novel, written by Andre Raffalovich (1907), argues that the book's "virile ideal" includes a "hatred for effeminacy" (187) and that "the superior Uranian" counts among his enemies the "depraved inverts" (ibid). This attitude about gender performance in gay men goes beyond the concept of "passing," wherein some homosexual men simply do not want to be identified as such. It is instead an active dislike of men who "act like women," which is a peculiar brand of homophobia[8] rooted primarily in the fear of exposure.

These fears of effeminacy also lead, unfortunately, to what can be considered a kind of misogyny. At one point, in making a commendable argument, ahead of its time, that Imre's homosexuality was "inborn," the narrator writes that he "had never been a weakling, an effeminate lad, nor cared for the society of the girls about him on the playground or in the house. On the contrary, his sexual and social indifference or aversion to them had been always thoroughly consistent with the virile emotions of that sort" (119). Once again, what Prime-Stevenson's narrator attempts to do is debunk a certain perception about young gay men, or

---

[8] Rictor Norton notes that most gay "histories amount to little more than an account of homophobia in the heterosexual population; often they do not even differentiate between attitudes in general and the attitudes of queers towards themselves – of which the latter is by far the more interesting" (135).

boys, as "girly" and prone to identify and play with young girls instead of other boys. The goal itself is admirable, as it rejects common assumptions about young homosexual males, but the execution creates problems. In this case, the narrator equates manliness and virility with an "aversion" to girls. This sets a dangerous precedent that to be masculine, one must also be anti-woman. The problem then persists into the character's adulthood. Oswald claims that "the man-loving man . . . shudders . . . in something akin to dread and to loathing, though he may succeed in hiding it from wife or mistress, at any near approach of his strong male body to a woman's trivial, weak, feminine one" (85). He goes on to claim that "thousands, thousands, hundreds of thousands, of such human creatures as I am, have not in body, in mind, nor in all the sum of our virility, in all the detail of our outward selves, any openly womanish trait!" (ibid). Thus, what in boyhood was described as an aversion to playing with girls, in adulthood becomes a correlation between the repugnance for women and their "trivial, weak" bodies, and a desire for the opposite in the homosexual self and his desired partner.

Gregory Woods notes that this kind of misogyny dates back to ancient Greece and Japan. Citing Robert Graves, Woods argues that certain myths about Zeus and Ganymede, such as poems written in the sixth-century BC by Theognis of Megara, "helped to institutionalize Greek misogyny" (*A History of Gay Literature* 19). Likewise, in seventeenth-century Japan, a collection titled *The Great Mirror of Male Love* (1687) included stories such as "Who Wears the Incense Graph Dyed in her Heart," which ends thusly: "Would that the love of boys become the common form of love in the world, and that women would die out and Japan become the Isle of Men" (ibid 65). In an attempt to carry forward masculine ideals, then, and argue that "manly love" can go farther than Whitman offers without committing the "failures" of Wilde, consequently shirking certain stereotypes about gay men, Prime-Stevenson commits his narrative to other problematic historical constructs about gender and sexuality.

Edward Prime-Stevenson's motives in creating a counter-narrative to stereotypes about gay effeminacy are laudable in that they are an attempt to both normalize homosexuality and to delegitimize stereotypes about gay men. Neither of these would have been simple tasks in the early-1900s, when viewing homosexuality in terms of criminality and illness was still common practice. Prime-Stevenson, a homosexual man, identified a disturbing and persistent trend in cultural assumptions about gay men and aimed to correct those misconceptions. In his attempt, however, he in fact over-corrects. His characters are hyper-masculine, self-critical, homophobic, and anti-woman. Despite their apparent self-acceptance and their relatively progressive views about romantic and sexual relationships between men, they nevertheless perpetuate the notion that effeminate men, whether homosexual or heterosexual, are an inferior type. Prime-Stevenson receives much-deserved credit for publishing a novel with gay characters that successfully manage to find a long-lasting relationship, one where the two male partners are romantically and physically attracted. It is a happy ending, but this ending comes with a cost. Prime-Stevenson's narrative, despite its attempt to subvert stereotypes about gender and sexuality, inadvertently creates a new problem by suggesting that the "ideal" gay man is of one specific type: the masculine. By hyper-masculinizing the two main characters and by affirming their distaste for effeminacy, raised to the level of homophobia, *Imre* perhaps perpetuates as many problems as it aims to solve. Complicated issues located at the intersection of gender and sexuality in homosexual men are often engaged, with greater or less success, in early gay American literature. Another example of a text which treats the complexities of gender performance in gay men's literature, though from a different perspective, is Robert Scully's *A Scarlet Pansy*.

In stark contrast with the hyper-masculinity and feminine-shaming that defines the treatment of gender and masculinity for homosexual characters in Prime-Stevenson's novel is Robert Scully's high-camp and episodic morality tale, *A Scarlet Pansy*. Scully appears to be a pseudonym, but the author's true identity is as yet unknown. There are two prominent theories, however. The most accepted is that Robert Scully was actually Robert McAlmon[9], a homosexual modernist writer and editor who worked with James Joyce, Ernest Hemingway, and others of the period, and who was successful in his own right. In accepting McAlmon as the author, the novel is typically read as a *roman à clef*, featuring characters based on William Carlos Williams, Marsden Hartley, Sylvia Beach, Gertrude Stein, Alice B. Toklas, and of course Robert McAlmon himself (Pearson par. 5). In the recent publication of a new edition of *A Scarlet Pansy*, however, the editor, Robert J. Corber (2016), argues that it is "highly unlikely" that McAlmon was the author because "his treatment of the queer world contrasts markedly with Scully's" ("Life's a Drag" 15). He argues instead that the author is a physician named Robert Emmet Scully, first identified by Scully's publisher's daughter[10], and that this would explain the protagonist's choice of profession, medicine, as well as the narrative's similarities to *Autobiography of an Androgyne* (1918), which a medical professional at this time would likely have read (14). Regardless of the

---

[9] The case for McAlmon being Scully is made by Jay A. Gertzman ("*A Scarlet Pansy* Goes to War" 2010), Neil Pearson ("*A Scarlet Pansy*: Robert McAlmon's Secret Book" 2016), Counter-Culture Rarities (counterculturerarities.com, 2016), and most significantly, in a critical analysis and biography written by Dr. Hugh Hagius ("*The Mystery of A Scarlet Pansy*: An Underground Gay Novel of the Lost Generation," Unpublished Typescript, 1982).

[10] *A Scarlet Pansy* was originally published by Samuel Roth, who "had acquired a notorious reputation as a 'booklegger' for publishing 'sex pulps' and other forms of erotica" (Corber, "Camping it Up," 12). His daughter, Adelaide Kugel, "recalls that [Scully] was a physician 'who dared not use his name to write about "the love that dare not" in 1932 without losing some of his practice'" ("Life's a Drag" 14).

identity of its author, what is clear is that the novel is, as Jay Gertzman recommends, "a skillful

and mature American novel" (230).

   A Scarlet Pansy's treatment of gender and sexuality is notable for a number of reasons.

One of these is that the text counters the stereotypical melodramatic atmosphere and pessimistic

outlook for gay characters in American fiction by using "camp[11]" to create irony and to subvert

expectations. Camping, an intentional affectation or stylization of mannerisms, speech, gait, etc.,

became very popular in the "thriving American queer/fairy subculture in the 1910s and 1920s"

(Norton 26), which is the setting for *A Scarlet Pansy*. Homosexual men would affect lisps,

feminine-perceived movements of the hand, and a certain kind of walk, often described as

"mincing," in order to make themselves known to each other (Loftin 579). As Norton notes,

through even the next decade, the majority of people, naïve to camp and the subculture it was a

part of, remained oblivious to homosexuality and homosexual culture (ibid). Scully embraces

this style to illustrate how gay men took ownership of their spaces, sought and found sexual

fulfillment, and even took advantage of certain opportunities in business which their affected

style made possible, all while navigating society's more rigid rules and expectations. Perhaps the

most impressive is that its characters, though never fully accepting themselves as "normal" per

se, do embrace their femininity and never find that femininity to be at odds with masculine

appearances. The protagonist, who identifies as "Fay Etrange[12]" and who is referred to by the

---

[11] Craig Loftin writes, "camp writing can legitimately be considered the literary equivalent of effeminate body mannerisms. Both swishing and camp writing appropriated the voice, vocabulary, and linguistic patterns of female impersonators" (586). The camp style of *A Scarlet Pansy* in this way structurally reflects the thematic and symbolic explorations of gender and sexuality that are the novel's primary concern.

[12] "Fay" derived from the French term for "fairy" and "Etrange" from the French term for "strange." All of the characters' names are stylized in this fashion, which is appropriate to a book parodying morality literature where characters are often personifications of virtues; here,

narrator as "she," for example, is often described in terms that are meant to illustrate her masculine physical features. In many cases, especially in the pulp genre, homosexuals are described as wholly feminine, both in appearance and in mannerisms, but Scully's depictions are different, which has led some, such as Robert Corber, to wonder if the novel's main character should be read as transgender[13] rather than gay.

A Scarlet Pansy also reinforces certain cultural norms about gay men's sexual preferences, but it does so while allowing a wider variety of gender performances. Fay, as the main character, is described as traditionally feminine, and thinks of herself that way. Correspondingly, she seems to "fit" gender expectations by virtue of the fact that she is attracted to masculine men and even repelled by those who seem unmasculine. This echoes Prime-Stevenson's work in that it assumes the "correct" sexual object choice for gay men is a "real man[14]," even if the one searching is supposedly not fulfilling those same expectations. Finally, although Scully satisfies some of the more problematic clichés of early twentieth-century gay fiction, such as necessitating the death of the protagonist, he nevertheless creates an opportunity for heroics rather than allowing the death to create melodrama or to reflect causation. When Fay dies, it is not the result of some moral failing, such as addiction or illness, nor is it the result of homophobic violence; instead, she dies saving the man she loves. In this way, A Scarlet Pansy partially subverts one of the primary expectations of the early gay American novel.

---

personification is of sexual significance (Miss Fuchs, Miss Kuntz, Miss Godown, etc.), in lieu of such characters as "Charity" or "Hope".

[13] Others, such as Jay Gertzman, identify her as simply a "cross-dresser" (230).

[14] This is of course a constructed "type" of character meant to indicate some level of "manhood" that does not exist but is perpetuated by both gay and straight culture, as will be explored later in this section.

In contrast to Corber's argument that Fay Etrange and possibly her compatriots are meant to be read as transgender, Matt Sussman argues that "Fay's gender—along with the genders of other female characters—is only nominally female; no doubt a safeguard against moral watchdogs not carefully attuned to the signifying practices of 'fairies' who commonly addressed each other with female pronouns" ("My Strange Affair," 2006, n.p.). While it is true that the author was likely concerned with issues of censorship[15], it is unreasonable to suggest that Scully's decision to gender all of the biologically male characters as female was simply an act of literary obfuscation, nor does it necessarily indicate that Fay is what we would today describe as transgender, though that is certainly an interesting possibility. Regardless, the dissonance between masculine physical descriptors and the use of feminine pronouns throughout creates interesting questions regarding the culture's perceptions about gender and sexuality at the time, perceptions that Scully seems to be challenging. For example, Fay's homosexuality is usually signaled by references to her voice, her feminine[16] personality type, and her choice of clothes and cosmetics, yet she is often described as physically masculine.

In the first pages of the novel, Fay is given a female name and referred to by feminine pronouns. Yet, the narrator hints that she is in fact biologically male. In describing her childhood, for example, the narrator relays that "her school fellows always went to her for advice" and that her "father demanded much of Fay's time for work in the fields or about the barns" (33). The narrator calls attention to her "school fellows," not simply her "friends," and

---

[15] The publisher, Samuel Roth, had been "arrested nine times, convicted six, and spent a total of nine years in jail, mostly for obscenity and literary piracy" (Pearson par. 7).

[16] By which I mean, the stereotypically constructed feminine, as when the narrator describes Fay as one who "belonged to the emotional type" (31). The relationship to reality is not relevant, as we are meant to infer the *narrator's* perceptions of gender.

notes that, although she has a brother and two sisters, she is the one required to work in the field, which causes her to "develop sturdily" (ibid). The discord between feminine pronouns and masculine relationships and duties makes it clear at least that Fay is not a "typical" girl. This is reinforced consistently, though subtly, as the narrative progresses, as when she moves to Baltimore and takes a room with a landlady who boards "young men" (37) and when the narrator notes, following Fay's first sexual encounter in the city, that "she was beginning to realize that she was different from the majority of her sex" (40). We can add to this the fact that "Fay's voice made her conspicuous . . . she had not yet learned to control it . . . it was a revealing voice" (56) which is the signal that "normal" men use to identify her as "one of them," a homosexual (57). In this way, the narrative continues to reinforce the very perceptions about which the narrator and characters of *Imre* were most concerned, that there is an assumed relationship between being homosexual and being feminine, and that it is the perceived feminine aspects in gay men which make them "conspicuous."

In his brief commentary on the novel, Roger Austen argues that "Scully knew that his readers would remember the insufferably virtuous Elsie Dinsmore[17] types from their childhood reading and would be delighted with this inverted spoof about a country innocent turning into a flaming sexpot" (*Playing the Game* 63). Indeed, Scully's novel undoubtedly parodies traditional morality tales, yet characterizing it as simply a spoof for spoof's sake overlooks the very serious questions about gender and sexuality that it does raise. That we can ask of Fay, is she a cross-dresser or is she transgender, is significant when considering the book was published in the

---

[17] A popular children's book series (published between 1867 and 1905) written by Martha Finley. According to BreakPoint, "the books are based on the life of the fictional Elsie, whom they describe as being a "graceful, accomplished, and beautiful young woman who raises the standard of godly womanhood to new heights" (Campbell par. 2).

early-1930s and set at least a decade earlier. Either avenue encourages us to ask questions about masculinity and femininity in homosexual men at this time, including how gay men felt about their own identities as well as how others perceived them. Fay struggles to accept her sexuality, but she is much less self-conscious about her gender performance. This is clear in the way that many of her sexual encounters are described as taking place in the shadows (45, 49) and in the way Fay feels about herself afterward, as "debased and defiled" with a desire to "rid herself of a loathsome practice" (50); but in contrast to these sexual anxieties is her acceptance of her femininity, or gender identity[18] as it were. When Fay's brother Bill attacks her for "lisping" and demands she "change that damned voice," Fay responds that "she could not change herself . . . God made us all" (64-65). In other words, though she struggles throughout her life with the fact of her sexuality, she does not struggle to accept that her personhood, including her "womanly" voice and mannerisms, simply is what it is. The extraordinary thing about Fay, then, is that she can wear a "wig and drag" (169) at night, but keep "pace with Irish Mac and Black John" in her job as a coal mine laborer during the day. Put another way, her sexuality is not defined by her gender identity, nor does her identification as female preclude her from traditionally masculine work. This complexity distinguishes Scully's novel from other texts of the period and it contradicts the hyper-masculine anxieties expressed in the majority of those texts.

---

[18] This term is a contemporary one, but for the sake of the argument I am making here, I believe it can function without being anachronistic. Fay's experience is unique in early-American gay literature: she is not simply being described as feminine in order to make the point (through code and innuendo) that she is gay. Instead, she herself is expressing comfort with her gender non-conformity *while* engaging in homosexual experiences. These two, gender performance and sexual orientation, should not be conflated and therefore I use the specific terms available in order to mark the difference.

It is clear that *A Scarlet Pansy* is different from some of the other early gay novels, such as Prime-Stevenson's *Imre*, in that it allows its characters to function as both masculine and feminine, without contradiction. On the other hand, one way that *A Scarlet Pansy* treats gender and sexuality issues similarly to other early gay texts[19] is in the male protagonist's preference for masculine sex partners. Idealizing the masculine type is common in gay fiction, but it is particularly significant when considering texts published in the early-1930s. As George Chauncey notes, this was a period that gay men "looked back fondly on . . . as a time of relative calm" (358). Homosexuality and heterosexuality were beginning to be understood as separate identities defined by an individual's sexual and romantic object choice, and spaces like bars and restaurants that catered specifically to homosexuals were becoming common in places like New York City. As such, just as gay men were beginning to identify themselves as men (not inverted women[20]) who were attracted to other men, subsequently embracing their own masculinity, they also began to recognize that there was no inherent hypocrisy in a man loving another man, even if both men performed the masculine gender type (358-359). *A Scarlet Pansy*, written and published during this time, subtly reflects some of these shifting perceptions about gender and sexuality; but Scully nevertheless sets the narrative pre-World War I, at a time when it seemed necessary for homosexual men to perform the feminine role and to seek out sexual partners who

---

[19] The majority of texts in my work, including *Imre*, *Bertram Cope's Year*, and *Better Angel*, for example, as well as *The Boys in the Band*, to be discussed later in this chapter, are highly critical of effeminacy in their male homosexual characters.

[20] "Let us recall," writes David M. Halperin, "that homosexuality, as a distinctive classification of sexual behavior, sexual desire, and sexual subjectivity, was originally precipitated out of the experience and concept of gender inversion. The first psychiatric definitions of deviant sexual orientation . . . were not definitions of homosexuality but of sex-role reversal or transgenderism" (43).

were masculine *and* straight-identifying. Leila J. Rupp notes that "this is how sexologists who first developed the concept of homosexuality explained people with same-sex desires: they were feminine men attracted to masculine men and masculine women attracted to feminine women" (20-21). The homosexual men and women depicted in *A Scarlet Pansy* follow this pattern exclusively. As such, Fay's desired sexual object choices are always described as being (or performing) the masculine role, in binary opposition to her own.

Fay discovers her preference for masculine men gradually. Just as her "coming out" process is taken in steps throughout the narrative, as she grows up and experiences more of the world, particularly the larger cities, so too are her sexual preferences and fetishes refined. Fay's "first love experience" happens shortly after moving to Baltimore. Her friend, Sandy, a bookish and awkward young man, brings Fay to his room under the guise of helping her learn business. When he attempts to make lover to her, Fay realizes that "physically the man was repulsive to her," but she cannot articulate why. The narrator, however, provides some clue to the reader in Sandy's personality (intelligent, self-conscious, and awkward: in other words, "soft") and in the fact that he is couched between Fay's introductions to other, more masculine men, including Mr. Strong (her landlady's lover) and Mr. Rush (her boss), as well as Irish Mac and Black John with whom she competes physically. In addition, her lovemaking with Sandy is interrupted by the gym instructor, whom Fay notices more conspicuously and whose attention causes her to react bashfully and with "a deep blush" (39).

This initial experience, awkward and incomplete as it is, allows the reader to begin to understand Fay's preferences before she can articulate them for herself. A second experience soon follows, which makes the situation even clearer. In the rising action to their sexual episode, the narrator makes explicit an important distinction in their features: Fay's "sturdy, muscular hardworked brown hand was grasped in his effeminately white, soft, weak paw" (45). Fay at first "thrilled to this touch," but when she is drawn "away to the shadow" and "completely defiled" by Fisher, her feelings change dramatically. She realizes subconsciously, and the narrator makes obvious, that it is not just the sexual act she regrets, but the fact that she participated in it with such an effeminate man[21]. Following this affair, Fay "awoke to realize that she must adjust herself to a new conception of her personality" (47). In reflecting on the experience and acknowledging her sexuality, she also begins to understand her desire for masculine partners. From this point on, as James Levin notes, "a sharp division into masculine and feminine stereotypes is the order of the day" (44).

Her successive encounters, of which there are many, solidify her preferences in ever-increasingly concrete terms. For example, her first relationship that is described in terms of "love" and "friendship," rather than as a shadowy encounter, is with Theodore Wemys Cocke. The man is described as "dark, intense, quick in his decisions and actions" (67); in other words, the exact opposite of Mr. Fisher. Their names, too, Cocke and Fisher, rather crudely reflect their level of masculinity. Fisher is wet, limp, and cold, whereas Cocke is suave, worldly, and virile. Indeed, Cocke had three affairs "developing at the same time" (ibid). When Fay and Cocke consummate their love, there is still a level of anxiety on Fay's part, "but this time she was calmer in the face of self-realization" (71). The favorable descriptions and the dissipation of anxiety about having sex with another man signify that Cocke, as a more masculine partner, comes closer to fulfilling Fay's sexual desires.

---

[21] Similar regrets are portrayed in *Giovanni's Room* and *Twilight Men*, for example. When the male lovers begin to seem, or act, more "feminine," their partners begin to reject them and sometimes even react violently to their partner's change.

This trend continues throughout the narrative, Fay becoming more vocal and aware of her preference for "he-man" masculine partners and feeling less insecure about her sexual relationships with them, until the end of the narrative when she meets Lieutenant Frank. The narrator repeatedly makes a point of describing the Lieutenant as "clean," a term not used for any of Fay's former partners. He is also called "beautiful" and "sweet" (214-215). Perhaps most significant in revealing the idealizing of masculinity, however, is the fact that this man is a soldier during war time, and they are in the midst of combat. The hyper-masculinity of the situation is obvious, but the narrator also notes, importantly, that "relations of all sorts, so close to the front, were accepted in those times without comment and without the urge to pry" (217). It would appear, then, that Fay should be most at ease with her desire for Lieutenant Frank, considering he admits to liking her, too, and that the environment provides opportunity for their desires. Instead, however, Fay commits to making this relationship, the ideal one, pure. Having sex with the Lieutenant would "tarnish" (ibid) their love.

Their relationship accomplishes two important tasks: first, within the narrative, it completes Fay's self-realization. Despite what appeared to be a gradual self-acceptance, her final decision indicates that she feels she must reject her sexual desires if she is to avoid "perverting" her romantic attachment. The second task is a reflection of what was happening with masculinity in American culture at this time. As Michael Bronski notes, the "conflation of physical strength, traditional gender roles, heterosexuality, and patriotic manliness solidified a concept of manhood that increasingly seemed to be under attack. Threats included the increasing visibility of the homosexual . . . in the midst of all this, the country itself was at war" (*A Queer History* 138). Scully's narrator makes it clear that homosexual encounters were accepted in the military at war time with the assumption that they were situational and therefore divorced from romantic notions that would threaten heteronormative constructs. Sex was fine, if it was just sex. Fay's and the

Lieutenant's relationship could not be consummated, therefore, because they were both engaged

in performing "patriotic manliness" or acting in the gendered-male role. The assumption about

masculine and feminine roles in same-sex relationships that the narrator makes rather delicately

throughout the course of the novel becomes stark in these final pages, and in Fay's last, ideal

relationship with another man. Whereas Prime-Stevenson found no conflict in allowing two

masculine-identifying men to pursue a sexual and romantic relationship, Scully deems that

suggestion impossible.

    A Scarlet Pansy deserves critical attention, even acclaim, for many reasons, not the least

of which is its open portrayal of the life of a gay man and his (her) attempts to navigate the

public and private spheres. Scully creates in his protagonist a gay man who, in the private sphere,

identifies and performs the feminine gender (perpetuating the inversion myth), but who also

succeeds in the traditionally masculine-identified public spheres of academia and business. In

this way, *A Scarlet Pansy* at least nudges forward the conversation about queer people, their

contributions to society, and their capacity for doing good work. However, to champion the

novel as an uncharacteristically positive[22] portrayal of homosexuality is problematic for two

reasons. First, it mistakenly credits the narrative for allowing its gay protagonist to find

happiness in fulfilling an "ideal" love, a same-sex partner whom she loved, and who "thought he

loved her," too (31). Second, the gay character, heroically or not, must die. Jay Gertzman notes

that the narrator, in "the last page of *A Scarlet Pansy* . . . begins as he ends, as a mature,

---

[22] *Counter-Culture Rarities* calls it "an extraordinary depiction" (par. 2); Neil Pearson claims that Fay "finds true love" and is a "hero" (par. 4-5); Sussman argues that *A Scarlet Pansy* is "a gay classic" of "exceptional fabulousness" ("My Strange Affair," 2006, n.p.).

admiring, yet laconic observer of ultimate realities beyond surfaces, and beyond his militant

nation's gender absolutes" (238). To this, Corber adds that the novel "celebrat[es] rather than

condemn[s] the outlaw sexual culture invented by queer men and women" ("Camping it Up" 8),

and Matt Sussman goes so far as to argue that "*Pansy* offers a remarkably nonjudgmental and

surprisingly frank depiction of the lives of urban gay men in the thirties" ("My Strange Affair,"

2006, n.p.). I do not disagree that the narrative is frank, even courageous, in its depiction of gay

life, but to claim that it is "nonjudgmental" or "celebratory" misses the point.

At the end of her life, Fay can only find "true love" in the Whitman-esque style of manly

friendship[23]. The narrator implies that Fay's last love is a pure one, the *right kind* of love,

because it is never consummated. Thus, to understand the complex relationship that *A Scarlet*

Pansy's narrator has with homosexuality, one must acknowledge that, despite the camp style

designed to add levity to the narrator's quest to understand her own gender identity and her

sexual desires, it nevertheless perpetuates two damaging stereotypes: physical love between men

is morally wrong and an "out" gay man cannot expect to live a long or successful life. Despite its

failings, *A Scarlet Pansy* deserves a place in the tradition of gay literary discourse. It is a

uniquely crafted modernist novel that adds to the cultural conversation about homosexuality in

the first half of the twentieth-century, particularly in its portrayal of gay and lesbian

relationships, of gender non-conformity, and of queer spaces. Robert Scully's novel is a

fascinating example of the gay novel before World War II and the subsequent "crisis of

---

[23] Writing about Rechy's *City of Night*, Stanton Hoffman argues that "the 'gay world' not only is the only place where the individual homosexual is made to feel he can exist, but also is the result of his guilt over his choice of a way of life, the result of his acceptance of the stereotypes of a culture and an obsessive consciousness of effeminacy and masculinity" (196). This is clear in Fay's guilt about her sexual encounters, by her identifying the "ideal" as a love between men that abstains from sexual activity, and by the persistent tension between masculine appearance and feminine identity that she must navigate throughout the narrative.

masculinity" in the United States. Gay literature written after this period continues to explore

issues of gender and sexuality, often with cultural implications and heightened levels of anxiety.

Totempole holds a unique position in the history of gay American literature. Friedman's

novel follows the tumultuous 1950s and early-1960s, which saw a great wave in gay and lesbian

pulp publication and readership. In addition, authors such as James Baldwin, Gore Vidal, and

Truman Capote began to write for, and reach, more traditional audiences by publishing their gay

literary fiction with major publishing houses. Much has been written about this period[24],

including a number of works specifically about Gore Vidal's The City and the Pillar (Dutton

1948) and Truman Capote's Other Voices, Other Rooms (Random House 1948), both of which

are considered groundbreaking works of gay American fiction. James Baldwin's Go Tell It on

the Mountain (A.A. Knopf 1953) also deals with same-sex attraction and, of course, Giovanni's

Room (Dial 1956), discussed in the second chapter, is another example of an American novel

written by a major literary figure that deals openly with homosexuality[25]. Since this period and

its most prominent representative literary artifacts have been more generously accounted for in

scholarship and criticism, I have chosen to focus the second half of this chapter on significant but

---

[24] See, for example: The Queer Sixties (Routledge 1999), Queer Pulp (Chronicle Books 2001), Pulp Friction (St. Martin's Griffin 2003), The Golden Age of Gay Fiction (MLR Press 2009), and Queer 1950s (Palgrave 2012).

[25] See, for example: Stephen J. Whitfield's "Sex and the Single Decade" (2000), Ihab Hassan's "The Character of Post-War Fiction in America" (1962), Louie Crew & Rictor Norton's "The Homophobic Imagination" (1974), Jeff Solomon's "Capote and the Trillings: Homophobia and Literary Culture: At Midcentury" (2008), Thomas Fahy's "Violating the Black Body: Sexual Violence in Truman Capote's Other Voices, Other Rooms" (2013), Yasmin DeGout's "Dividing the Mind: Contradictory Portraits of Homoerotic Love in Giovanni's Room" (1992), and James R. Giles's "Religious Alienation and "Homosexual Consciousness" in City of Night and Go Tell It on the Mountain" (1974).

under-appreciated texts published in the later-1960s. Both examples were published on the cusp

of the momentous social and political changes signified by the 1969 Stonewall Riots.

Sanford Friedman's *Totempole* was first published by Dutton in 1965. Despite mixed

criticism, it was re-released as a mass-market paperback the following year and, according to

Peter Cameron, received multiple reprints followed by new editions in 1984 (North Point Press)

and 2014 (New York Review Books) (413). Contemporary writers who praised the book

included James Dickey, Anthony Burgess, and Gore Vidal. In his blurb, Dickey calls *Totempole*

"an extraordinary book, vivid and utterly convincing," while Burgess adds it "was a dangerous

book to write" and that its "impact as a document of great honesty will, without doubt, be

considerable." Gore Vidal agrees that it is an "extraordinarily courageous and highly moral

work" ("Totempole" *NYRB.com*). Some reviewers were equally generous. In his 1965

commentary, Granville Hicks indicates that *Totempole* "seems to be a wholly honest" coming-

of-age novel that "treats the homosexual theme . . . with great candor and no lubricity" (21).

Other contemporary critics, however, were much less enamored by the book and its open

treatment of homosexuality. In the *Times Literary Supplement,* John Barnard claims *Totempole* is

a "bad novel with a 'brave' message" (332). He adds that the protagonist, Stephen Wolfe, is "a

dull creation" and that the book itself "comes nowhere near to deserving the high praise that has

been given to it" (ibid). Similarly, writing for *The Hudson Review*, Paul Levine remarks that

Sanford Friedman's novel is "frank, tedious, and sentimental" (592). Significantly, he adds: "I

don't know if the limitations are inherent in the material, the treatment, or my imagination, but

homosexual love scenes are invariably talky and mawkish, terribly serious and terribly dull"

(592). This last statement, in its honest attempt to consider the reviewer's heterosexuality in

regards to a reader's ability to appreciate an overtly homosexual novel, with descriptive sex scenes, is important. If one compares Friedman's novel to the popular melodramatic pulps that preceded it, then it is not difficult to understand why some, such as Barnard and Levine, might describe *Totempole* as "dull." Peter Cameron remarks, accurately, that "when *Totempole* was first published, a homosexual novel was still expected to end badly. Homosexuality had to be presented as a doomed and damning affliction from which the only recourse was drug addiction, alcoholism, suicide, or a miraculous conversion" (416). There were of course exceptions; nevertheless, the pulp genre and the very few literary examples printed by major publishing houses tended to fulfill audiences' expectations for melodrama and hopelessness.

Totempole offers the exact opposite, much to the chagrin of some critics and readers. Webster Schott, for example, believes Friedman missed an opportunity to demonstrate "the homosexual's anguish in a world unprepared to accept his equivalent of heterosexual love" (BR26). Clearly, the more realistic portrayal of homosexuality and same sex-love demonstrated by the romance of Stephen and his Korean partner Sun-Bo is a new approach that was, to many, unsatisfying because it did not fulfill the genre's customarily tragic prospects. The reviewers' reactions are the key to understanding changes taking place in gay men's literature after the middle twentieth-century. Sanford Friedman makes no attempt to sensationalize the homosexual experience or to excite readers with salacious innuendo and depictions of the gay characters as emotionally damaged, mentally deficient, and prone to violence or suicide. Instead, informed by post-Kinsey and Freudian[26] theories of gender and sexuality, he draws on experimentalism and fascination with individual struggle that is at the heart of American Modernism, as well as the

---

[26] Reviewers seemed generally dissatisfied with the critical attention to sexuality, lamenting that it compromises the artistic narrative elements. Granville Hicks found it to be "a little too much like a case study" (21) and Paul Levine described it as a "clinical account" (591).

anti-prudery and sexually inquisitive nature of the Beat Generation, in order to craft a coming of age narrative that acts, as its title implies, as a "totem pole." Each section of the novel is named after an animal, and each animal represents a different phase in Stephen Wolfe's identity development. At issue throughout are questions of gender and sexuality in the homosexual male, particularly in relation to childhood, to situational environments, and as a question of racial privilege and power or submission.

In the first half of the novel, young Stephen Wolfe learns through interactions with his parents, nanny, and camp counselors, what it means to be a boy and a sexual being. Inherent in these formative identity[27] experiences are the "nature versus nurture" questions: do homosexuality and gender performance occur naturally, or are they influenced by early childhood environment? What does it mean to be perceived by others as sexually deviant? In addition, questions about the supposed relationship between gender and sexuality are explored. Such open treatment of these questions is unheard of in gay literature to this point. Peter Cameron rightly calls Friedman's attempt a "literary coup" because it engages with the protagonist's interior and exterior worlds (413). The reader's impressions of Stephen Wolfe are shaped alongside his own self-awareness, which is then shaped in relation to or in comparison with the primary adult figures in his life. As David Bergman notes, "gay selfhood is constantly being lost in the opacity of the parental gaze" (45). It is clear in the first pages of the novel that young Stephen Wolfe's sexuality is being scrutinized, if not shaped, by his parents, and that each of them plays a particular role in revealing to the reader what is "different" about the protagonist. In the opening scene, for example, Stephen, a toddler, is being questioned by his mother. Harriet

---

[27] Another aspect of Stephen Wolfe's identity is his religion, Judaism. In *Gaiety Transfigured*, David Bergman makes a compelling case for the importance of reading *Totempole* not just as a gay text, but as a gay Jewish text (204).

Wolfe wants to know why her son has taken off his pajama bottoms, and the reader learns it is

because the boy's father, Saul, makes a habit of going without pajama bottoms himself. The

expectation being established, here, is that the young boy is emulating his father and that this is

an example of masculine identity-development in progress. Yet, Friedman immediately disrupts

the reader's expectations by contrasting this emulation with a scene that demonstrates Stephen's

unconscious erotic fascination with his father's penis:

> "Horsie," he said, staring at the bald mound of dadda's kneecap. Bald, like dadda's head.
> Bald foot, bald knee, bald popo, bald head . . . but then a billion furs, like momma's black
> fox in the other closet . . . Leg furs, thigh furs, ding-dong furs . . . bushy black ding dong
> furs . . .
>
> "I want you to promise me you won't go near the horsies by yourself anymore."
>
> "Horsie," Stephen said, staring, stretching all of him to reach, to touch, to pet dadda's
> ding-dong.
>
> "Damn it! Don't do that! Can't you see I'm shaving!" (13)

To most readers, gay and straight alike, the implication of this scene is clear: something about

this boy is not as it should be. Harriet and Saul place the blame for their son's as yet

unarticulated "difference" on each other. Harriet tells Saul that the boy was "imitating" (15) him,

and Saul responds by claiming "he wouldn't be doing things like that" if Harriet had not "dressed

him like a girl when he was little" (16). The narrator is relying on a conventional question of

nature versus nurture to highlight the parents' "sweats of tension and conflict" (Schott BR26). Is

the boy born gay? Is he different because he is regularly exposed to his father's penis and thus

becomes too intently fascinated by the elder male's manhood? Is his sexuality influenced by his

mother's choice to clothe him like a girl? The line between gender and sexuality is tightly wound

in the construction of Stephen's relationship with his parents, but, surprisingly, the narrator

leaves the parents to debate it without conveying any position of his own, as if he knows something they do not: the answer is none of the above. As David Bergman so aptly notes, "no one can point the gay child toward a model of who he is" (45).

Stephen's potential "difference" is often expressed in relation to such descriptions of or questions about gender. For instance, Stephen is described as an imaginative artist[28] with "quite a reputation for his sand creations" (28). Significantly, in conveying Stephen's creative successes with sand castles, the narrator forms a dialogue between Stephen and his nanny, Clarry, who attempts to explain why the ocean tide rises and wipes away his creations every night. As she describes it:

> There's a war goin' on between them two—between the ocean and the land. Has been since the beginnin' of creation. That old ocean's on the warpath 'cause it come first and the land come after. It jealous now 'cause the land so much larger. Jealous 'cause the land has got itself collected—sittin' cool and pretty—while the ocean, it always on the go, restless and rampagin'. Sort of like the difference between a man and woman . . . the natural, born-in difference between a man and a woman. (29)

The war she describes between land and sea, man and woman, is a metaphor for the war Stephen has within himself throughout the narrative and is reflected externally in the way others describe him. His Aunt Ida, for example, thinks he is "indescribable[29]" and "a doll" (30) while his father's friend, whose nude body Stephen stares at in the communal showers, calls him "peculiar" (36). In addition, he keeps a marine garden and thinks of himself as a "blend" of the sea and sand represented in that garden, reinforcing the notion that he feels partly male, partly female. All of this uncertainty leads Saul to believe that Stephen must be masculinized before it is too late. He sends the boy to camp a year before he is eligible because "he's been around . . . women too long" (61).

---

[28] Having an "artistic temperament" is a common euphemism used to express homosexuality.

[29] She uses the German word *unbeschreiblich*.

Gregory Woods notes that, for obvious reasons, "twentieth-century homosexual writers have been foremost among those who have analyzed and described boyhood" (321). The majority of *Totempole* describes Stephen Wolfe's youth, with just the last few sections devoted to his college and military experiences. Woods rightly adds that "if boyhood itself is going to be of interest to a gay novelist, it follows that gay novels are going to concern themselves with the various kinds of loving relationship which may develop between boys" (323). This is certainly the case in *Totempole*. Camp is a place for boys and the expectation is that, Stephen, surrounded by boys and men who are engaged in "masculine" undertakings such as hiking, cooking by fire, and working with tools, will learn how to be manlier[30]. As Schott observes, however, "at camp, fascist organization, robust counselors, and lakes of opportunity turn Stephen further toward inversion" (BR26). Stephen develops a special relationship with one teenage counselor in particular, Uncle Hank, whom the narrator describes as "powerful," "good-looking," and "savage" (99). Hank is also the man in charge of the totem pole, an obviously phallic symbol which becomes, not coincidentally, the inspiration for both the structure of the novel and its title. Their relationship is what Saul was perhaps hoping for: a virile young man, masculine in appearance and with manly interests, to mentor young Stephen, who is more interested in nature and drama.

It becomes clear, however, that Stephen is more interested in Hank as a romantic figure than a masculine role model. Stephen expresses his love for Hank on the last day of camp and

---

[30] Michael Kimmel also explains that G. Stanley Hall, one of the most influential adolescent sociologists of the early-twentieth century, championed single-sex environments such as segregated schools, the YMCA, and the Boy Scouts of America. Hall believed these were masculinity-building institutions that prevented boys from becoming gay by rescuing them from "the feminizing tendencies of girls" (107).

wonders why they can't "share each other's world" (115-116). It is also clear that the single-sex

environment does not change the fact that Stephen would prefer to daydream about birds and

perform plays than to engage in the more traditional "boy's games" of camp. His personality and

interests are so innate that his counselors eventually stop trying to get him involved and instead

leave him to his own pursuits. He is "a triumph" (97) in his first minstrel show, which leads him

to being cast as a Russian heroine the following year. This is significant because, as David M.

Halperin indicates, "for a man to occupy the stage and to claim it for himself is to cast doubt on

his masculine credentials" (243). This is made explicit when the counselors compare Stephen to

Sarah Bernhardt, a famous female actress. In addition, Stephen's success in the female role is not

because he caricatures femininity but because he fully embraces it as natural[31]:

> In Stephen's case, it was different. He didn't achieve his effects by exploiting or even
> parodying the humorous aspect of the female sex. He never overstuffed his bosom, never
> pitched his voice too high or exaggerated the swing of his hips. He was too serious, too
> accomplished, too authoritative an actor for that—besides, it simply would not have
> occurred to him. (110)

This rationale for Stephen's success, combined with the narrator's descriptions of Stephen as a

"striking beauty" with exotic eyes and delicate lips (110-111), helps to confirm the impression

that Stephen, though never described as blatantly effeminate, certainly embraces what would be

considered the "feminine" elements of his personality. While he faces some slight teasing from

his camp counselors as well as moderately critical attention from his parents, his "feminine"

interests are far less censured than the gender-nonconforming gay characters of the 1950s and

earlier. Internally, however, Stephen struggles to rectify his desire for men with ideas about

---

[31] It is helpful to compare this to a similar scene in *Bertram Cope's Year*, published thirty years
earlier. When Arthur Lemoyne plays his female role "too well," he is ostracized to the point of
leaving his job and the city. Friedman's perceptions of, or at least arguments about, gender
expression are quite different.

"natural" masculine gender performance, such as being the assertive or dominant partner in

sexual situations. Webster Schott argues that "no real story remains to be told by the time

Stephen reaches Korea. Everything was settled 100 pages earlier" (BR26). This assessment is not

only inaccurate but it also ignores the most crucial event in the narrative: Stephen questioning his

gender and sexuality, then learning to accept himself. Without Korea, Stephen would not have

had the opportunity to question socially codified perspectives of gender roles and come to his

own conclusions about their relevance to him.

When *Kirkus* reviewed the book in 1965, they seemed to take issue with the fact of its

homosexuality generally. First, the reviewer snidely remarks on the supposedly disconcerting

quantity of homosexual novels being published at that time, and then argues that "the

homosexual novel . . . elicits a problematical receptivity at best" ("Totempole," *Kirkus*, 1965). In

closing, the reviewer articulates what he finds most "problematic" about this particular

homosexual novel:

> The earlier chapters are relevant and revelatory by implication . . . they occasioned the
> initial excitement in this book which is the leading title on the publisher's list; they feel
> that it is very powerful. But is power necessarily to be equated with candor? when does
> the graphic trespass on the pornographic? and while Stephen overcomes all constraint
> through Sun-Bo, what of the reader? The procedural detail may occasion a certain
> queasiness in even the most enlightened. (ibid)

To put it plainly, the reviewer was uncomfortable with inclusion of unobscured narrations of sex

scenes including two men. Roger Austen, on the other hand, writes that "although Friedman's

theme of an American finding love in the arms of a foreigner is not new, he does succeed in

bringing a certain freshness and sharpness" to it (211). The success of the "mature" and

consummated gay relationship, then, seems to depend on whether or not the reader is prepared to

accept it as both natural and necessary. Furthermore, that Stephen achieves his sexual awakening in a military setting is important for two reasons: first, it reinforces the counter-notion that all-male environments will necessarily perpetuate masculinity in those engaged there, and second, it raises questions about equality in same sex relationships.

In the first case, the military environment allows the narrator to continue to plumb the depths of Stephen's sexual persona by contrasting his outsider status as a private, sensitive person with his presence in a public, hypermasculine environment. During World War II, perceptions of male-male environments as locations for masculinizing young men began to be doubted and, instead, questions pertaining to a "causal relationship between martial culture and perversion" began to arise (Canaday 69). Stephen takes his place as a member of the company's personnel, alongside the effeminate Kirk and the "soft-spoken" (314) warrant officer, Mr. Robbins. That Stephen is placed in personnel is suggestive. As David K. Johnson notes, "clerical jobs . . . attracted gay men" because of the "feminized work culture" therein (44-45). Friedman relies on a common belief about male secretarial government workers to imply that Stephen has been placed in the personnel office due to his homosexuality, which makes him better suited for "feminine" work. Comparisons between Stephen and the rest of the company are drawn throughout the remainder of the text. For example, his fellow soldiers comment on his "pathological modesty" and nickname him "Garbo" after the famous actress Greta Garbo, which recalls his experience at camp (319). In addition, while the other men are comfortable taking showers together and masturbating openly in their beds at night, Stephen chooses to abstain, so self-conscious is he about his sexuality and the fact that public circumstances might expose him to the rest of the men. Indeed, while Stephen falls asleep to the sounds of his comrades, he dreams that he is in a bar being asked for his "pervert pass" (323). He wakes to the sounds of a rat chewing into his bed covering and, rather than deal with the situation, he panics. It is up to another soldier to capture the rat and kill it while Stephen watches "squeamishly" (326). This first condition, being a soldier at war, allows the narrator to compare and contrast Stephen with other men in a single-sex environment. Whereas some earlier texts take advantage of such a setting in order to hyper-masculinize or hyper-feminize their gay characters, Friedman continues to present his protagonist as a different type of gay man, one who is neither too explicitly male or female. This ambiguity, first projected in Stephen's childhood, becomes even clearer in his relationship with Dr. Sun Bo Pak, the Korean prisoner of war with whom he falls in love.

A second formative experience for Stephen that arises as a result of his presence in the Korean War camp, is his relationship with Sun Bo, an anti-Communist North Korean refugee. Their relationship, slow in developing, ultimately results in the self-awareness and acceptance that Stephen's experiences have been building toward throughout the entire narrative, and they rely on a different interpretation of masculinity in male-male sexual relationships. As Maurice Wallace notes, "historic masculine identity" is generally constructed "by realizing the homosocial/homosexual enactments of dread and desire" (388). Stephen struggles to reconcile the dread of forfeiting his own masculinity with the desire he feels for another man. He believes that submitting to another male means playing the female role and therefore sacrificing his manhood. This self-consciousness is hinted early in their relationship, when Sun Bo asks Stephen to dance and Stephen struggles to understand whether he is "expected to lead or to follow" (363). At first unwilling to yield his manhood to another male, Stephen demands to lead. As they dance, Stephen contemplates "predetermined" (363) male and female roles, convinced that he could never adopt the "woman's role" for anyone, nor does he imagine that Sun Bo could do so for him because the Korean had previously been married to a woman (364). Stephen adds, "he couldn't suddenly reverse himself, couldn't suddenly become feminine and passive" (ibid).

These fears reflect deeply stereotypical conflations of gender and sexuality. Lee Edelman

helpfully adds that "in the dominant culture's ideological definition of same and different,

private and public, passive and active . . . male homosexuality in general . . . and its synecdoche,

gay male anal sex in particular, bear the stigma" of such binaries (104).

Stephen's anxiety is due to this very rigid interpretation of what it means to be a gay

male, and what it would mean for him to give up that position by submitting sexually to another

man. As Mary McIntosh notes in "The Homosexual Role" (1968), beliefs about gay men that

"affect the self-conception of anyone who sees himself as homosexual" include "the expectation

that he will be effeminate in manner, personality, or preferred sexual activity" (185). These are

the stereotypes with which Stephen Wolfe is grappling and that he will ultimately reject. In

another gay text, his anxiety would have led to extreme rejection of the sexual situation or

rejection of the self, but Friedman allows his character to develop through introspection and

patient experimentation with his lover. Sun Bo at first plays the receptive role in their love-

making but, eventually, Stephen does the same for Sun Bo. This moment is groundbreaking in

gay fiction because, as the narrator describes, Stephen rejects the traditional interpretations of

receptive anal sex as emasculating or submissive. Instead, his experience is almost cathartic:

> Stephen bit the pillow to keep from crying out. But even as he did, he understood at last that it was not a matter of submission or surrender but of self-assertion—of actively laying claim to Sun Bo, wanting him, demanding him—and his teeth released the pillow, as he took Sun Bo into himself, shouting out triumphantly, "Yes! yes! yes!" (403)

Connotations of sexual possession might at first raise some concerns, particularly considering

Sun Bo is technically a prisoner and Stephen his "master." However, following Stephen's logic,

he allowed Sun Bo to claim him first, when Sun Bo was the receptive partner, particularly

because Sun Bo instigated their early sexual encounters. In this way, Friedman's character suggests a changing perception about gender and sexuality in male-male relationships. Instead of ceding one's masculinity to another, the narrator suggests that two men in a romantic sexual relationship can define their own roles rather than necessitating loss and gain, power and submission.

As Peter Cameron indicates, *Totempole* is an "honest and unapologetic depiction of a homosexual child, a homosexual adolescent, and a homosexual man" (417). Sanford Friedman's frank descriptions of a pensive but non-neurotic young man's coming of age and coming out process is the first of its kind in the tradition of gay men's literature in the United States[32]. While Friedman knowingly engages with certain genre conventions, such as questions of nature versus nurture, notions of anti-effeminacy in males, and self-consciousness and gender anxiety in gay men, the novel is unique in the realistic approach it takes to the subject of homosexuality and the freedom it allows its protagonist to think deeply and critically about himself and his relationships. At no point in the narrative does Stephen Wolfe feel doomed because of his sexuality, though he does panic somewhat about his masturbatory habits as a child. This led many contemporary reviewers to feel disappointed about its less-than-sensational subject matter. What they missed, however, willingly or not, is just how revolutionary *Totempole* is. Friedman's gay narrative is unapologetically direct and unabashedly positive. Just as Stephen Wolfe is "borne back to the Pacific Coast" (411) of San Francisco in the final moments of the text, Friedman tows the reader forward toward a new era of openly gay fiction, one that offers more than stock characters, binary constructs of gender and sexuality, and predetermined, gloomy endings. Indeed, Stephen Wolfe returning to San Francisco after discovering and accepting

---

[32] Prohibitions such as the Comstock Law had made it very difficult, indeed a crime, to publish openly homosexual material before 1958.

himself recalls the earlier tradition of gay characters, such as Stoddard's Paul Clitheroe, leaving the United States in order to do the same. Nothing better demonstrates the changes taking place in the country and the literature than this transformative ending. Other writers, like Mart Crowley, would follow suit and continue to question what it meant to be gay and male in the United States in the 1960s.

As Terry Helbing argues in his important introduction to gay theatre[33], "most often, gay theatre history is a literary history—playwrights, whatever their sexual preference, have included homosexual characters or subject matter in their works" (35). Although the history of drama and theatre is distinct from the history of the novel, it is important to recognize the influence of the genre on gay American literature, especially when discussing a concept such as performance, which is as fundamental to gay literary studies as it is to theatre studies. Mart Crowley's play *The Boys in the Band* was first performed in 1968. It was wildly popular upon its release, running more than 1,000 performances and eventually being adapted to film. Despite its commercial success, scholars consistently note that the play "has infuriated [gay] audiences" (Schiavi 76) for decades. This is due, ironically, to the fact that the play "has a candour [sic] that never before its staging belonged to any other American mainstream production on gay themes and characters" (Costa 26). Gay audiences and critics have felt that what is most freely expressed in its candor, however, turns out to be stereotypical and generally negative. These charges miss some of the play's subtleties and also ignore the wildly tumultuous moment in which it was written and performed.

---

[33] In *Gay Plays, Gay Theatre, Gay History* (*TDR* 19810), Helbing traces gay drama from classical Greece to the contemporary period. Though a brief overview, it is nevertheless an important one.

Crowley's play was not by any means the first gay play, but it was written and performed during a time of revolution, just one year after gay protests in Los Angeles[34] and one year before the infamous Stonewall Riots in New York City. Georges-Michel Sarotte argues that "Crowley was able to speak openly and frankly" (33) about homosexuals, because of the recent successes of plays like *Hair* (1968), which made it "possible to say anything and to show anything on the American stage" (ibid). What must also be understood is that changes in the law made these performances possible, or at least legal, in the first place. In 1967, a decade after the elimination of the Comstock Law made it possible for writers and publishers to disseminate printed works with homosexual content without fear of fines or imprisonment, New York's Padlock Act was revoked. The Padlock Act had outlawed "any play 'depicting or dealing with the subject of sex degeneracy, or sex perversion'" (Chauncey 313). Crowley's play, then, is situated at a pivotal moment in history when open portrayals of homosexuality had just been made legal on stage and in print, and when both gay activism and the rejection of tragic gay characters were on the rise.

While the action of the drama takes place entirely in a private setting, one character's apartment, the general public, many of whom would have been unfamiliar with intimate gay spaces, is allowed to gaze into that world. What they witness, somewhat problematically indeed, is the way that gay men perform gender and sexuality. In the first place, Crowley's characters engage in camping as a convention of gay lifestyle and as a way of communicating with each other. They express and demonstrate their anxieties about gender and sexual performance as dependent upon their location in a public or private sphere, which is to say, whether or not they have a friendly audience. In addition, Crowley's characters represent a range of gender

---

[34] For a helpful description of the event at The Black Cat in Los Angeles, see Lilian Faderman and Stuart Timmons's *Gay L.A.* (Basic Books 2006).

difference so that, despite the generally self-deprecatory tone of the play, readers and audiences witness a spectrum of gender and sexual performances, including polar depictions of effeminacy and masculinity in gay men.

An important feature of gay community and identity, as noted earlier in my discussion of *A Scarlet Pansy*, is the concept of camp. David and Harold Galef (1991) helpfully explain that "an important element of camp is its group function" (18) and that "for a homosexual to parade in an exaggerated female mode . . . is to use exposure as a weapon, to reveal one's hidden sexuality by discharging the attendant anxiety onto the audience" (17). Crowley applies camp as a strategy to communicate familiar ideas about homosexuality to an audience that might be more or less "in the know." He rightly considers that, at this point in time, a small number of the audience might fully comprehend the joke inherent in his characters' camping, but the majority of the public would see the style as a marker of gay men's sexuality because it perpetuates their preconceived and stereotypical notions about effeminacy in homosexual males. As Louie Crew and Victor Norton suggest, "homosexual authors [who wrote] for an audience that largely consist[ed] of hostile heterosexuals" had to "somehow accommodate their work to the expectations of that audience" (274). This is especially true for Mart Crowley, a gay writer whose characters would be appearing not only in print, but performing live on stage and more openly than had ever been allowed in the United States to that point. The "group function," then, is applicable to both "the boys" in the play and the actors and audience members inside the theatre.

A prime example of Crowley's accommodating instinct is the level of camping that occurs throughout *The Boys in the Band*, despite the fact that "perhaps the only people toward whom camp is favorably disposed are those complicit in the act" (Galef and Galef 18). Most significant in the characters' camp performances is the idea that, as Susan Sontag posits in her seminal piece on the subject, "camp is the triumph of the epicene style . . . the convertibility of 'man' and 'woman,' 'person' and 'thing'" (280). Simply put, the "boys" engage in camp by adopting ironic femininity, such as calling each other "screaming queens" (7), curtsying to new acquaintances, and using female pronouns to talk about themselves and each other. What is fascinating about their camping is the suggestion that this is a "natural" form of interaction for gay men. The theatre audience is allowed to see it, but the expectation is that this is a privileged viewing, one which supposedly "reveals" the homosexual world to them without requiring them to participate in it. It is no surprise, then, that largely heterosexual audiences would find the play so compelling. Audience members see Michael singing and posing like a popular movie starlet and find their perceptions of the interior gay world validated. Homosexual audiences, on the other hand, were uncomfortable with the fact that *The Boys in the Band* exposed certain conventions of their private world, ones which were meant to be subversive, and that its implied argument is that camping somehow translates to truth[35]. As Galef and Galef remark, "a private joke shared by everyone is no longer funny" (21). As soon as the audience, largely heterosexual, is offered entry to gay men's private sphere, camping itself becomes dangerous and disconcerting.

This progression of "safe camp" to "disrupted camp" is best demonstrated by the tension created by Alan's presence at the party. Alan is Michael's former college roommate, a

---

[35] Judith Butler notes a problem with this kind of assertion. If camping is imitation, then it must be imitation of some heterosexual reality that homosexuals can only copy in their attempt to perform gender in same-sex environments. Butler asks us to "reconsider . . . the homophobic charge that queens and butches and femmes are imitations of the heterosexual real" and, instead, consider that homosexuality is the origin and heterosexuality the copy ("Imitation" 313). In other words, as Susan Sontag argues, camping may be for the most part entirely honest (282-283).

heterosexual who signifies within the play the audience that is external to it, the observer-interloper. Before Alan arrives, Michael and Donald engage in subtle camp. Their interactions with each other seem genuine and unguarded. Michael imitates Judy Garland, singing and dancing, and Donald tells him that the only thing "more boring than a queen doing a Judy Garland imitation [is] a queen doing a Bette Davis imitation" (10). They also discuss, sarcastically, their experiences with psychoanalysis, their relationships with their parents, and their laughable "first times." The conversation is meant to appear more serious than it is, although neither Michael nor Donald makes it obvious that they are being facetious. As Sontag notes, honesty and naivety are essential for true camp (283) because "camp is art that proposes itself seriously, but cannot be taken altogether *too* seriously" (284). In this situation, Michael and Donald seriously wonder if they are neurotic, if their parents caused their sexual deviance, and if their coming out processes were somehow "wrong." Throughout the sober conversation, though, the two take repeated jibes at the other, such as references to being spoiled with expensive clothes, their obsession with movies and movie stars, and, of course, inside jokes loaded with sexual innuendo and expletives. At one point, for example, when Donald appears to be making a serious point, Michael responds: "You know what you are, Michael? You're a *real* person." To this, Michael can only reply, "thank you and fuck you" (16). Ultimately, though the content of their discussion seems serious, the delivery of it and the interaction itself are far from sincere.

A change in the nature of their conversation is signaled, however, by the arrival of Michael's former roommate. Just as the camp atmosphere is gathering steam, the doorbell rings. Because they believe that Alan has arrived, Michael begins to warn Donald about how to act. Donald, understanding the rules for camp performance, cuts him off: "Michael, don't insult me by giving me any lecture on acceptable social behavior. I promise to sit with my legs spread apart and keep my voice in a deep register" (19). Michael, taking a last opportunity to remain in character, offers his gratitude by saying, "Donald, you are a real *card-carrying cunt*" (ibid). The implication is that their camp performance must stop here because Alan, being a heterosexual man, will either not understand the nature of the game or, perhaps more troubling, he might understand it all too clearly. Their performance will expose them. In this way, camp is set up as a strictly homosexual practice. Crowley takes this assertion further, however, and suggests that camp is perceived to be not only a homosexual practice but primarily an effeminate one.

Francisco Costa addresses this concern when he writes, "heteronormativity is not undermined solely by camp, but also by an ambiguity in the construction of masculinity that questions if that masculinity is synonym of an [sic] heteronormative sexuality, or just a performance that hides a dissident sexuality" (37). In this way, I would argue, the idea of "masculinity" itself is just another kind of camp, a different style of performance, but one which is no less true or false than queer community camp. Indeed, camp is easily identified by non-complicit audiences not because it is a divergent gender performance and therefore easily distinguished from "reality" but because it is aware of itself in a way that traditional binary gender performances, validated by a heteronormative *status quo*, are not. In *The Boys in the Band*, this is illustrated by heterosexual Alan's supposedly innocent attraction to Hank, the most masculine-performing of the queer party-goers. Upon entering the party, Hank is the only man whom Alan formally greets. They shake hands and begin to talk about sports, their marriages, and their kids, while the rest of the party, especially Emory, returns to its "normal" routine, which is to say, camping. Alan does not at first realize and then has trouble accepting the fact that Hank, who seems heterosexual because he seems masculine, could be in a romantic and sexual relationship with another man, Larry.

In the midst of such an overly melodramatic gay drama, Crowley introduces, here, a

subtle subversion. Michael Bronski, in agreement with most critics, rightly claims that "Crowley

made sure that heterosexual critics and audiences saw what they really believed: gay men who

were unhappy and willfully cruel to one another" (*Culture Clash* 131). Alan and Hank's meeting,

however, is highly significant because, through their interactions, Crowley positions masculine

gender identity or performance as non-exclusive to heterosexual males. In other words,

audiences "expecting" certain depictions of homosexual men are simultaneously rewarded by the

play's atmosphere of camp and challenged by the presence of a masculine gay male who is

comfortably located within that supposedly effeminate performative sphere. Alan is

uncomfortable by the camp performances not because he is masculine in a feminine environment

but because he is heterosexual in a homosexual environment. Hank understands the ironic

etiquette involved, but Alan does not, and when the rules are pressed upon him, he reacts

violently:

> Alan. If you're ever in Washington—I'd like you to meet my wife.
> Hank. Good.
> Larry. That'd be fun, wouldn't it, Hank?
> Emory. Yeah they'd love to meet him—*her*. I have such a problem with pronouns.
> Alan. How many esses are there in the word pronoun?
> Emory. How'd you like to kiss my ass---that's got two or more *essessss* in it!
> Alan. How'd you like to blow me!
> Emory. What's the matter with your *wife*, she got lock-jaw?
> Alan. Faggot, Fairy, pansy . . . queer, cocksucker! I'll kill you, you goddamn little
> mincing, swish! You goddamn freak! FREAK! FREAK!

Some have read this moment as Alan's reaction against homosexuality generally, but of

additional significance is the fact that this is the moment when camp is injected into the

masculine bubble that Alan and Hank had been creating for themselves. Subconsciously, at least,

Alan must know that everyone at the party is homosexual. There are no women present and when Alan first arrived, he walked in on the group dancing together. Yet, by latching onto the one guest who seems more masculine than the others, Alan can engage in his own performance, ignoring the reality of the situation around him until it threatens the position he wishes to maintain.

Judith Butler, elaborating on the concept of compulsory heterosexuality, writes, "it may be that the very categories of sex, of sexual identity, of gender are produced or maintained in the effects of this compulsory performance, effects which are disingenuously renamed as causes" ("Imitation" 318). Rather than homosexuality causing effeminacy, then, one might believe that a lack of *performing* the masculine gender might make one prone to homosexuality[36]. As such, Alan's terrible fear of the camp happening around him, and the reason that he ignores it for as long as he can, may not be because he fears homosexuality per se but because he fears that accepting the performance and engaging in it might "turn" him gay. Alan and Hank's interactions reflect an important consideration about camp and the implications it has on the observer, as well as popular beliefs that people might "catch" homosexuality the way they might catch a cold.

Another significant feature of the play, often overlooked, is that it includes a number of gay male characters who perform gender differently. In some cases, Crowley offers his audience stereotypical depictions of the homosexual man as neurotic, petty, and selfish. Valid critiques have been raised about this perceived failing. However, other criticisms seem to imply that effeminate male characters, like Emory, perpetuate negative stereotypes simply because they are effeminate. As Costa notes, "Emory's effeminacy is . . . insufferable to post-Stonewall gay audiences, who do not want to see homosexuality associated to effeminacy" (39). Certainly, the

---

[36] How many fathers have told their sons that "boys don't cry," for example?

erroneous belief that all gay men are effeminate is a problem that has been perpetuated in literature, but this particular argument ignores the fact that *The Boys in the Band* is a play that depicts an entire group of friends with distinct personalities and no single predominant kind of gender performance. As Charles Kaiser recounts in *The Gay Metropolis* (1997), *The Boys in the Band* was "revolutionary because of its honesty and its openness" (187). Mart Crowley was determined to write and produce a play that was "a homosexual play" specifically, and not one where "homosexuality was [a] big surprise in the third act" (ibid). He achieves this honesty by composing characters who sometimes fulfill stereotypes alongside characters who completely subvert them. This honest diversity is an effort on Crowley's part to "re-create the tenor of gay life as he knew it" (Loughery 294).

Characters who fulfill stereotypical expectations and thus enrage gay audiences tired of being typecast include the exaggeratedly effeminate Emory; the neurotic Donald; the promiscuous Larry; and the self-loathing Michael, who still, a decade later, has not gotten over a crush on his straight college roommate. Alternatively, however, are characters like Hank, who prefers monogamy to licentiousness and whose masculinity confuses the only straight character in the play; Bernard, a masculine and presumably wealthy black man; and "the Cowboy" who is introduced as a homosexual outsider, one who does not "speak the language." The Cowboy does not understand any of the film references, for example, which are part of the queer discourse in which the rest of the partygoers engage, and he comes across as masculine but rather stupid, as opposed to the stereotypically effeminate but intellectual gay man[37]. The contrasting types,

---

[37] For a thoughtful examination of the perceived relationship between homosexuality and intellectualism, see Carlos L. Dews and Carolyn Leste Law's "Anti-Intellectualism, Homophobia, and the Working-Class Gay/Lesbian Academic" (*The Radical Teacher* 1998).

including the opposition of Emory's femininity with Hank's masculinity, but also the various

performances in-between these poles, is what makes the play both relevant today and significant

as a milestone text.

Surely, then, the effeminate male character cannot be considered a negative type simply

because he exists, especially given the range of characters that Crowley incorporates. Bradley

Boney makes an important argument about this trend in "the politics of representation" (38):

> Effeminacy has been the traditional and 'derogatory' marker for gay male characters in
> modern drama. In general, the authors of these studies have viewed effeminate male
> characters in contemporary theatre as 'negative stereotypes' because such characters
> position gay men outside 'normal' masculinity (and hence sexuality). These authors
> rightfully argue for an expansion of the gay representational field to honestly reflect the
> diversity of the gay community. This does not, however, require the annihilation of the
> sissy boy, something too often implicit in the expansionist argument. (ibid)

Boney's point could not be more critical to placing *The Boys in the Band* accurately within the

tradition of gay American literature. Crowley, in fact, is one of the first who gets this right[38].

In the 1960s, Victor Seidler writes, "there was a widespread sense that people had to

experience something for themselves before they could genuinely know it" (34). For

heterosexuals, the theatre was one place where they felt they could experience the homosexual

world and thus begin to understand it. Although some, like Francisco Costa, believe that

"queerness" in *The Boys in the Band* is represented through "internalized homophobia and

femininity" (39), I argue the play deserves credit for its range of characters with independent

gender identities who are, except perhaps for Michael, unafraid to perform gender and sexual

expression that is natural *to them*, at least in private. There are valid concerns about the way

---

[38] Compared to early texts like *Imre* or *A Scarlet Pansy* which focus almost exclusively on either
end of the spectrum and to texts like *Totempole* which offer a much more realistic and measured
depiction of gender identity but which do not offer such diversity of characters.

homosexuals are portrayed as cruel and self-loathing in this play, but that is only one way of

viewing the play. Limiting judgment to a single track of critique disregards much of what is

remarkable about *The Boys in the Band*. It is undeniable that the play's "popularity in and

beyond New York brought a new level of visibility to gay theater and to homosexuality in

general" (Bernstein 204), and that despite its flaws, *The Boys in the Band* marks an important

moment in gay American literary history. It afforded a wide and diverse audience, gay and

straight alike, the opportunity to witness gay attitudes about self and community for the first

time, and it remains a critical text in the study of gay American literature because it is situated so

conspicuously at the intersection of "a historic rupture" (D'Emilio 107) defined by two periods,

one in which homosexuality "could not speak its name" and one in which homosexuals began

unequivocally to proclaim their presence.

While much has been written about the "crisis of masculinity" in America during and

after World War II and the threatening homosexual "connection to masculinity" (Adams 134),

there is still much work to be done in investigating the many questions about and iterations of

gender and sexuality in gay men's literature before and after this historical moment. The first

half of the twentieth-century offers surprisingly diverse perspectives on gender and sexuality in

gay men's literature. In an essay about transgender issues and feminism, Laura Kacere writes,

"the problem isn't femininity or masculinity. It is compulsory femininity and masculinity tied to

a value system that devalues all things feminine" (par. 43). This very problem arises when

analyzing gender and sexual performance in gay fiction's same-sex relationships. The effeminate

homosexual has long been an accepted cliché in literature, one who is typically intended to be

treated with derision; yet, where did that stereotype come from? How has it affected the

reception of gay characters in literature and thus gay men in society? What caused writers to embrace, reject, adapt, or respond to that stereotype in different ways and at different times? In addressing these questions as they pertain to gay literary studies, I do not attempt to provide concrete arguments about which writers are "right" or "wrong" in the way they develop their gay characters. Instead, the investigation itself results in fascinating and important discoveries about how gay American writers have sometimes effectively subverted those dominant norms and how they have sometimes failed. Where Prime-Stevenson successfully disrupts the clichéd homosexual type, he inadvertently projects other homophobic notions about the "wrong kind" of gay men. Where Robert Scully celebrates the feminine, he concedes to stereotypical expectations about the social possibilities, or lack thereof, for gay characters. After mid-century, writers like Sanford Friedman and Mart Crowley begin to explore the complexities of gender and sexuality by offering, as in the first case, a gay character whose internal development is visible to the reader and, in the second, a cast of characters that represent a range for the "ways of being" a gay man. Each of the texts in this chapter adds to the discourse about gender and sexuality in gay American literature and offers unique avenues for considering men's performative choices against the cultural normative of a given time

CONCLUSION

As an investigation based on literary history, this research makes no attempt to offer empirically defined or classified "answers" to the major questions posed within it, including "what is the gay American tradition?" Indeed, the title of this work and its chapters are designed to express my exploratory approach to the question through a number of scopes of inquiry. In addition, the research is informed by feminist standpoint theory. I ask four primary questions about the gay American tradition, described in each chapter, by engaging with problems that matter to me and by researching and writing with my own potential biases in mind. It was also not my intention to provide queer readings of heterosexual or *potentially* homosexual texts; a number of scholars have already done this successfully and the purpose of this book, as a gay literary historiography, is to focus on openly homosexual writers who published openly homosexual texts in challenging times. This is a field of inquiry that has been routinely minimized in favor of queer readings for more popular or critically established American texts. Essentially, through a literary historiography that aims to "fill in the gaps," I combine queer theory's goal of questioning power, value, and normativity in the questions I ask, in the texts I apply to these questions, and in the tradition this process describes, with the postmodernist's openness to individual perspective and resistance to certainty.

My approach recalls Graham L. Hammill's belief that "queerness isn't about the ego; it's about history" (69). I aim to advance gay American literary history by investigating some of the ways that "the queer, subversive, or antinormative implications of [these] works arise" and by considering how these homosexual authors and their texts are treated and "altered in and through history" (Radel 768). Why did authors who were well respected in their time, including Charles Warren Stoddard, Parker Tyler and Henri Ford, Henry Blake Fuller, and Robert McAlmon (Robert Scully) essentially disappear from scholarship and readership while critical and popular engagement with their heterosexual contemporaries, such as Herman Melville, Mark Twain, Ernest Hemingway, and F. Scott Fitzgerald persisted even to the point of canonization? What is a gay American tradition? Which texts best illustrate the various elements of this tradition? Which texts deserve to be re-introduced to the "gay canon?" How can we break said gay canon once we have unwittingly constructed it[1]? These questions must necessarily be fluid, challenged, and interrogated if scholarship is to respect the unique quality of this marginalized tradition and its most influential critical lenses.

It is not the case, however, that I resist positing an argument. On the contrary, my argument has been consistent throughout, even as I approach it through different interrogative viewpoints. The gay American tradition is difficult to define and is appropriately impossible to articulate conclusively; nevertheless, one fact remains: there is a gay American literary tradition and this

---

[1] Indeed, I would argue that this gay canon must be broken. In 1998, when Robert Drake's *The Gay Canon* was published, gay writers, readers, and scholars surely celebrated. At last, we have a canon of our own! Yet, I suggest two problems with such a text: first, the idea of a "canon" suggests that only a prescribed set of texts is valuable or representative, which limits our engagement with and appreciation for a great variety of gay texts that continue to be overlooked. Second, we discover that this canon includes heterosexual men and women writers alongside the potentially homosexual and self-identified gay writers. It is important to move away from this sweeping approach, now, and embrace the numerous and eclectic examples of gay texts written by gay writers that do in fact exist.

tradition is richer and more complex than has been generally acknowledged. To paraphrase Walt Whitman, the gay American tradition is large and it contains multitudes. In completing this project and presenting my scholarship, my hope is that I have added to the discourse on gay literary studies in a way that encourages scholarly and pedagogical curiosity. We can continue to investigate critical moments in gay history, such as the Stonewall Riots, the AIDS crisis, and the marriage and family equality movements, without limiting ourselves to those events. I believe it is critical that we become less concerned about being "right" about gay literary studies ("Do I contradict myself? Very well, then") and less concerned about determining which are the "correct" gay texts, and instead continue to investigate, write about, and teach the diverse and expansive threads that shape this historically rich tradition.

Gay American literature from about 1950 onward has begun to receive valuable and warranted critical attention, yet the early gay literature, equally worthy of study, remains disappointingly neglected. In this book, I have attempted to begin to address this oversight by identifying and interrogating four specific questions about the tradition and describing how gay authors created or engaged with those questions. These four questions are: How did early-twentieth century gay American authors manage to publish openly gay texts?; how did the most popular gay genre treat homosexuality and influence cultural perceptions about gay men, for better or worse?; how did gay authors use language, history, and intertextuality to foster community and to speak to relevant audiences while simultaneously avoiding censors?; and finally, how did gay literature before Stonewall tackle the complicated issues of gender and sexuality in texts focused on same-sex-desiring characters?

It is clear that distance, or "convenient displacement," as I call it, allowed American audiences a certain degree of comfort while engaging with the culturally forbidden subject of homosexuality because of the barrier that distancing created between fictive worlds and readers' own. This strategy created opportunity for homosexual authors to publish and disseminate their gay texts. Although the period is often overlooked, early gay American literature was nevertheless an active field and these texts influenced generations of writers to follow, writers who would receive popular and critical attention. More widely read and discussed were the gay pulp novels, many of which were printed numerous times due to continually successful sales. The gay pulp novels, however, were often sensational and melodramatic, and thus created misconceptions about homosexual men and culture. The success of this genre of fiction resulted in the perpetuating of negative stereotypes about homosexual men and gay spaces so overwhelmingly that even the later literary texts would borrow from it; hence, the pervasive narrative technique of eliminating a gay character by murder or suicide.

Regardless of genre or style, one element that gay texts in the American tradition share is a certain intertextuality that generates a conversation between gay writers and their readers. Homosexual writers needed to develop their themes and communicate their thoughts in ways that their representative "communities" would understand but could keep private. Authors who were too obvious about their subject matter risked being ostracized or even imprisoned, given the attitudes about homosexuality at the time and the anti-obscenity laws of the period. Therefore, gay writers relied on sets of codes in language and themes, as well as rhetorical strategies such as listing prominent gay historical figures or referencing classical mythology, to develop contemporary narratives about same-sex desire and actions. These strategies were essential to developing the gay male literary tradition in the United States and helped establish the foundation upon which later writers would build.

Lastly, one of the most significant and complicated issues in gay studies is the relationship between gender and sexuality. For a number of reasons relating to culture, power, and patriarchy, homosexuality, including acts and identities, has been associated with femininity. A necessary focus for this this gay literary historiography of the early-twentieth century, then, was to explore how gay writers dealt with the subject of gender and sexuality when their main characters were homosexual before homosexuality could be broadly discussed and when it was so widely misunderstood. One important consideration became the distinction between pre- and post-World War II literature, including the elimination of anti-obscenity laws that had previously restricted what could be written and how it could be written. Contrary to expectations, though, the pre-War texts offer great diversity regarding gender and sexual expression while some of the post-War texts have been criticized as being too prescriptive. When taken together, however, we discover that even before the mid-century gay renaissance, homosexual writers in the United States were offering distinctive and provocative perspectives about gay men's performative choices and the cultural norms of their representative periods.

While these four inquiries have helped me to describe the gay American literary tradition and to consider both how that tradition developed and how it persisted, I acknowledge that there remains much work to be done. American literature itself is not a single, independent entity, nor should any of its representative traditions be treated as statically demarcated and therefore closed to continued discussion, interrogation, and counter-suggestion. Reflecting on literary studies' ever-evolving engagement with "critical assumptions," Mark Lilly notes, "the traditionalists' implied claim to have discovered some transcendent criteria, good for all time, is . . . profoundly unhistorical" (xv). This project has been necessarily narrow in scope. Some might argue that focusing exclusively on gay male literature is a limitation. I respect that interpretation and agree that similar studies for lesbian literature, bisexual literature, and transgender literature in the United States must receive critical attention as well; but I further argue that a commitment to the unique realities of gay, lesbian, bisexual, and transgender literature and history must be reaffirmed.

Recently, especially since the late-1980s, gender and sexual minority groups have consolidated their resources for social and political reasons. This is an understandable phenomenon and has been an effective strategy; however, treating "LGBTQ+" history as if these unique groups have always been united in this way is dangerous and disingenuous[2]. The early gay and lesbian movements in the United States were distinct[3]; separate representative organizations were created by and for gay men and by and for lesbian women respectively. While their goals were often necessarily aligned, their methods and priorities were not always shared[4]. Later, transgender studies would develop through the lenses of intersexuality and transsexuality[5]. Much more recently, bisexuality studies began to receive the scholarly attention it deserves, as demonstrated by the publication of Steven Angelides' seminal work, *A History of Bisexuality* (U Chicago, 2001). Given their distinct histories, these segments of the "umbrella"

---

[2] Dangerous because it denies the long history of each of these types of people, allowing for arguments that, for example, would define transgender issues as only a contemporary problem (e.g. the current "bathroom bill" debates) or marriage equality as "too recent" an idea to risk legal codification.

[3] The Mattachine Society and the Daughters of Bilitis, for example, were distinct organizational entities that did not function as cooperative partners.

[4] See, for example, Leila J. Rupp and Susan K. Freeman's *Understanding and Teaching U.S. Lesbian, Gay, Bisexual, and Transgender History* (U Wisconsin, 2014), George Chauncey's *Gay New York* (Basic Books, 1994), Lillian Faderman and Stuart Timmons's *Gay L.A.* (Basic Books, 2006), and Vern L. Bullough's *Before Stonewall* (Harrington Park Press, 2002).

[5] See Joanne Meyerowitz's important historiography *How Sex Changed* (Harvard, 1980).

that makes up LGBT literary studies must be attended to specifically and thoroughly. Future scholarship can advance LGBT literary studies by concentrating, for example, on bisexual literary history and transgender literary history, as these are critically under-represented. This lack of scholarship and subsequent academic attention (in literature pedagogies, for example) adds to continued misunderstandings about transgender and bisexual people. Excavation and criticism of transgender and bisexual literature should place these texts into conversation with their own histories and into the larger discourses of American literature and LGBT studies.

There are also a number of ways in which this work, specifically, can continue to inspire critical inquiry about gay male literature in the United States while also considering contributions from other perspectives. One example is to consider the influence that women who write gay male narratives have had on gay literature. In considering this question, two important texts come to mind: Blair Niles's *Strange Brother* (1931) and Patricia Nell Warren's *The Front Runner* (1974). Compared to gay texts published by gay male authors, these two examples were received more generously in both the commercial and critical spheres[6]. One reason for this might relate to my first chapter and the concept of "displacement." Is it possible that imaginative works about homosexuality are (or were) more acceptable to reading audiences when written by women because the "fiction" of them was more explicit[7]? After all, a woman writing about gay men cannot be drawing upon the same kind of autobiographical experiences as gay male writers were. Researching this phenomenon might add much to our understanding of gay literary publication

---

[6] The same was true for Virginia Woolf's *Orlando* (1928), which suggests a broader possibility in western literature generally.

[7] It should be noted that Blair Niles drew upon her own experiences as a journalist in Harlem during the 1920s to write *Strange Brother*; however, she is nevertheless writing someone else's story.

history and criticism and point to new understandings about gay fiction, including, for example, why a majority of works in the contemporary young adult and gay erotica genres are written by women.

In short, the study of gay American literature should focus on the prioritization of gay texts by openly or self-identified homosexual writers and on the exploration of questions that reveal both how gay authors have navigated the challenges of publishing their narratives in periods that were more or less hospitable and what gay writers have determined is critical to gay literary discourse in the United States. In addition, gay American literary studies must be concerned with an appropriate balance of scope to avoid being too broad or too narrow. If we cast our net too widely, we risk including texts that can be understood as gay only through a specific, strategic critical lens. This negates the purpose of gay literary historiography as it adds unneeded conjecture to an investigation that has the potential to be treated at least somewhat tangibly. On the other hand, if we severely limit our scope of inquiry, focusing only on contemporary literature, for example, then we risk losing a culturally rich history and a deeper understanding of this already elusive, oversimplified, and underappreciated tradition in American literary studies.

BIBLIOGRAPHY

Abrams, Steve. "Forman Brown, the Yale Puppeteers." *The Puppetry Journal* 62.2 (2010): 26.

Adams, Jon Robert. "The Great General Was a Has-Been: Homoerotic Re-Definitions of Masculinity in 1950s Conformist Culture." *Harrington Gay Men's Fiction Quarterly* 6.3 (2004): 117-135.

Aldrich, Robert. *Colonialism and Homosexuality*. New York: Routledge, 2003.

Aldrich, Robert and Garry Wotherspoon. *Who's Who in Gay and Lesbian History: From Antiquity to World War II*. New York: Routledge, 2001.

Amory, Richard. "Richard Amory Discovers a 29-Cent Jackson Novel." *Vector* 8.4 (Apr 1972): 31-32.

Angelides, Steven. *A History of Bisexuality*. Chicago: University of Chicago Press, 2001.

Anesko, Michael. "The Evasive Art of Henry Blake Fuller." *ATQ* 21.2 (2007): 111-126.

Austen, Roger, and John William Crowley. *Genteel Pagan: The Double Life of Charles Warren Stoddard*. Amherst: U of Massachusetts, 1991.

Austen, Roger. *Playing the Game: The Homosexual Novel in America*. Indianapolis: Bobbs-Merrill, 1977.

Bailey, Blake. *Farther and Wilder: The Lost Weekends and Literary Dreams of Charles Jackson*. New York: A.A. Knopf, 2013.

Baldwin, James. *Giovanni's Room*. 1956. London: Penguin, 2001.

Barnard, John Michael. "Other New Novels." *Times Literary Supplement*, 14 April 1966, p. 332.

Bergman, David. "The Cultural Work of Sixties Gay Pulp Fiction." *The Queer Sixties*. Ed. Patricia Juliana Smith. New York: Routledge, 1999. 26-41.

Bergman, David. *Gaiety Transfigured: Gay Self-Representation in American Literature*. Madison, WI: University of Wisconsin Press, 1991.

Bernstein, Robin. "Staging Lesbian and Gay New York." *The Cambridge Companion to the Literature of New York City*. Ed. Bryan Waterman and Cyrus R.K. Patell. New York: Cambridge University Press, 2010. 201-217

Bérubé, Allan. *Coming Out Under Fire: The History of Gay Men and Women in World War II*. 1990. Chapel Hill, NC: University of North Carolina Press, 2010.

Boney, Bradley. "The Lavender Brick Road: Paul Bonin-Rodriguez and the Sissy Bo(d)y." *Theatre Journal* 48.1 (Mar 1996): 35-57.

Boston Evening Review. "Unsigned Review of Henry Blake Fuller's *Bertram Cope's Year*." *Bertram Cope's Year*. Ed. Joseph A. Dimuro. New York: Broadview, 2010. 277.

Breen, Margaret S. "Homosexual Identity, Translation, and Prime-Stevenson's *Imre* and *The Intersexes*." *CLCWeb: Comparative Literature and Culture* 14.1 (2012): <http://dx.doi.org/10.7771/1481-4374.1786>

Bronski, Michael. *A Queer History of the United States*. Boston: Beacon Press, 2011.

Bronski, Michael. *Culture Clash: The Making of a Gay Sensibility*. Boston: South End Press, 1984.

Bronski, Michael. Introduction. *The Fall of Valor,* by Charles Jackson, 2016, Valancourt, v-ix.

Bronski, Michael. *Pulp Friction: Uncovering the Golden Age of Gay Male Pulps*. New York: St. Martin's Griffin, 2003.

Brown, Forman (Richard Meeker). *Better Angel*. 1933. Boston: Alyson Publications, 1990.

Bullough, Vern L, ed. *Before Stonewall: Activists for Gay and Lesbian Rights in Historical Context*. Binghamton, NY: 2002.

Butler, Judith. *Gender Trouble*. 1990. New York: Routledge, 2006.

Butler, Judith. "Imitation and Gender Insubordination." *The Lesbian and Gay Studies Reader*. Ed. Henry Abelove, Michele Aina Barele, and David M. Halperin. New York: Routledge, 1993.

Cady, Joseph. "American Literature: Gay Male, 1900-1969." *The Gay and Lesbian Literary Heritage: A Reader's Companion to the Writers and their Works, from Antiquity to the Present*. Ed. Claude J. Summers. New York: Henry Holt, 1995. 30-39.

Cameron, Peter. "Afterword." *Totempole* by Sanford Friedman. 1965. New York: New York Review Books, 2013. 413-419.

Campbell, Karen Allen. "An Era that needed to End: Vision Forum is No Longer Publishing *Elsie Dinsmore*." *BreakPoint.org*, 31 May 2013, http://www.breakpoint.org/component/blog/entry/12/22395.

Canaday, Margot. *The Straight State: Sexuality and Citizenship in Twentieth-century America.* Princeton, NJ: Princeton UP, 2009.

Carey, Christopher. *Trials from Classical Athens*. 1997. New York: Routledge, 2012.

Chauncey, George. *Gay New York: Gender, Urban Culture, and the Makings of the Gay Male World, 1890-1940*. New York: Basic Books, 1994.

Connelly, Mark. *Deadly Closets: The Fiction of Charles Jackson*. New York: University Press of America, 2001.

Corber, Robert J. "Camping it Up: *A Scarlet Pansy*'s Queering of Gender and Sexual Identities." *A Scarlet Pansy* by Robert Scully. Ed. Robert J. Corber. New York: Fordham UP, 2016. 5-14.

Corber, Robert J. Introduction. *A Scarlet Pansy*, by Robert Scully, 1932, New York: Fordham UP, 2016, 1-23.

Corber, Robert J. "Life's a Drag, Dearie: Reclaiming Bert Savoy's Queer Legacy." *A Scarlet Pansy* by Robert Scully. Ed. Robert J. Corber. New York: Fordham UP, 2016. 14-18.

Costa, Francisco. "Faggot, Fairy, Pansy . . . Queer': Gay/Queer Confrontations in Mart Crowley's *The Boys in the Band*." *Revista de Estudios Norteamericanos* 17 (2013): 25-37.

Crew, Louise, and Rictor Norton. "The Homophobic Imagination: An Editorial." *College English* 36.3 (Nov 1974): 272-290.

Crompton, Louis. "Greek Literature, Ancient." *The Gay and Lesbian Literary Heritage: A Reader's Companion to the Writers and their Works, from Antiquity to the Present*. Ed. Claude J. Summers. New York: Henry Holt, 1995. 342-348.

Crompton, Louis. *Homosexuality & Civilization*. Cambridge: The Belknap Press, 2003.

Crowley, John W. "Charles Jackson's *Fall of Valor* Revaluated." *Sewanee Review* 114.2 (March 2006): 259-277.

Crowley, Mart. *The Boys in the Band: a Play in Two Acts*. S. French, 1996.

De la Croix, St. Sukie. *Chicago Whispers: A History of LGBT Chicago Before Stonewall*. Madison: University of Wisconsin Press, 2012.

D'Emilio, John. *Making Trouble: Essays on Gay History, Politics, and the University*. New York: Routledge, 1992.

DeGout, Yasmin Y. "Dividing the Mind: Contradictory Portraits of Homoerotic Love in *Giovanni's Room.*" *African American Review* 26.3 (1992): 425-435.

Dimuro, Joseph. "The Salient Angle: Revising the Queer Case of Henry Blake Fuller's *Bertram Cope's Year.*" *Textual Cultures: Texts, Contexts, Interpretation* 2.1 (2007): 136-154.

Doenecke, Justus D. "Viereck, George Sylvester." *American National Biography Online*. New York: Oxford University Press, 2000.

Drake, Robert. *The Gay Canon: Great Books Every Gay Man Should Read*. New York: Anchor Books, 1998.

Edelman, Lee. *Homographesis: Essays in Gay Literary and Cultural Theory*. New York: Routledge, 1994.

Edsall, Nicholas C. *Toward Stonewall: Homosexuality and Society in the Modern World*. 2003. Charlottesville, VA: University of Virginia Press, 2006.

Ellis, Havelock, and John Addington Symonds. *Sexual Inversion*. London: Wilson and Macmillan, 1897.

Faderman, Lillian, and Stuart Timmons. *Gay L.A: A History of Sexual Outlaws, Power Politics, and Lipstick Lesbians*. New York: Basic Books, 2006.

Fiedler, Leslie A. "A Homosexual Dilemma." *Critical Essays on James Baldwin*. Ed. Fred L. Standley and Nancy V. Burt. Boston: Hall, 1988. 146-49.

Field, Douglas. *All Those Strangers: The Art and Lives of James Baldwin*. Oxford: Oxford University Press, 2015.

Fone, Byrne R.S. *The Columbia Anthology of Gay Literature: Readings from Western Antiquity to the Present Day*. New York: Columbia UP, 1998.

Fone, Byrne R.S. *Hidden Heritage: History and the Gay Imagination*. New York: Irvington, 1981.

Ford, Charles Henri, and Parker Tyler. *The Young and the Evil*. 1933. New York: Masquerade Books, 1996.

Foucault, Michel. *The History of Sexuality, Volume 1: An Introduction*. Trans. Robert Hurley. 1978. New York: Vintage, 1990.

Friedman, Sanford. *Totempole*. New York: Dutton, 1965.

Fuller, Henry Blake. *Bertram Cope's Year*. 1919. New York: Broadview, 2010.

Galef, David, and Harold Galef. "What Was Camp." *Studies in Popular Culture* 13.2 (1991): 11-25.

Geddis, Catherine. "Ghost and Horror Fiction." *The Gay and Lesbian Literary Heritage: A Reader's Companion to the Writers and their Works, from Antiquity to the Present*. Ed Claude J. Summers. New York: Henry Holt, 1995. 324-326.

Gertz, Elmer. *Odyssey of A Barbarian: The Biography of George Sylvester Viereck*. Buffalo, NY: Prometheus Books, 1978.

Gertzman, Jay A. "*A Scarlet Pansy* Goes to War: Subversion, Schlock, and an Early Gay Classic." *The Journal of American Culture* 33.3 (2010): 230-239.

Gibson, Michelle A., Jonathan Alexander, and Deborah T. Meem. *Finding Out: An Introduction to LGBT Studies*. Los Angeles: Sage, 2014.

Gifford, James. *Glances Backward: An Anthology of American Homosexual Writing, 1830-1920*. Orchard Park, NY: Broadview, 2007.

Gifford, James. "Introduction." *Imre: A Memorandum*, by Edward I. Prime-Stevenson. 1906. Ed. James Gifford. New York: Broadview, 2003. 13-26.

Gifford, James. "Left to Themselves: The Subversive Boys Books of Edward Prime-Stevenson (1858-1942)." *Journal of American and Comparative Cultures* 24.3-4 (2001): 113-116.

Gumery, Keith. "Repression, Inversion and Modernity: A Freudian Reading of Henry Blake Fuller's *Bertram Cope's Year*." *Journal of Modern Literature* 25.3/4 (2002): 40-57.

Gunn, Drewey Wayne. *The Golden Age of Gay Fiction*. Albion, NY: MLR Press, 2009.

Halperin, David M. *How to Be Gay*. Cambridge, MA: Harvard University Press, 2012.

Hammill, Grahm L. *Sexuality and Form*: *Caravaggio, Marlowe, and Bacon*. Chicago: University of Chicago Press, 20015.

Helbing, Terry. "Gay Plays, Gay Theatre, Gay Performance." *The Drama Review* 25.1 (1981): 35-46.

Henderson, Mae G. "James Baldwin: Expatriation, Homosexual Panic, and Man's Estate." Callaloo 23.1 (Winter, 2000): 313-327

Herzog, Dagmar. *Sexuality in Europe: A Twentieth-Century History*. New York: Cambridge UP, 2011.

Hicks, Granville. "The Many Faces of Failure." *Saturday Review*, 21 Aug. 1965, p. 21.

Hoffman, Stanton. "The Cities of Night: John Rechy's *City of Night* and the American Literature of Homosexuality." *Chicago Review* 17.2/3 (1964): 195-206.

Isola, Mark John. "The Fluviographic Poetics of Charles Warren Stoddard: An Emergence of a Modern Gay Male American Textuality." Dissertation, Tufts University, 2007. UMI 3244621.

Jackson, Charles. *The Fall of Valor*. 1946. New York: Arbor House, 1986.

Jackson, Florence. "Current Books Reviewed: *For the Pleasure of His Company: An Affair of the Misty City*." *The Overland Monthly* 42.2 (1903): 365-366.

Johnson, David K. *The Lavender Scare: The Cold War Persecution of Gays and Lesbians in the Federal Government*. 2004. Chicago: University of Chicago Press, 2006.

Johnson, Niel M. "George Sylvester Viereck: Poet and Propagandist." *Books at Iowa* 9 (1968): 22-36.

Jones, Norman W. *Gay and Lesbian Historical Fiction: Sexual Mystery and Post-Secular Narrative*. New York: Macmillan, 2007.

Kacere, Laura. "Why the Feminist Movement Must Be Trans-Inclusive." *Everyday Feminism*, 24 Feb. 2014, http://everydayfeminism.com/2014/02/trans-inclusive-feminist-movement.

Kaiser, Charles. *The Gay Metropolis: 1940-1996*. New York: Houghton Mifflin, 1997.

Kaplan, Morris B. *Sodom on the Thames: Sex, Love, and Scandal in Wilde Times*. New York: Cornell University Press, 2005.

Katz, Daniel. *American Modernism's Expatriate Scene: The Labour of Translation*. George Square, Edinburgh: Edinburgh University Press, 2007.

Keller, Phyllis. "George Sylvester Viereck: The Psychology of a German-American Militant." *The Journal of Interdisciplinary History* 2.1 (Summer, 1971): 59-108.

Keller, Phyllis. *States of Belonging: German-American Intellectuals and The First World War*. Cambridge: Harvard University Press, 1979.

Kennedy, Hubert. Introduction. *Better Angel*, by Forman Brown. 1933. Boston: Alyson Publications, 1990. n.p.

Kimmel, Michael. "Guyland: Gendering the Transition to Adulthood." *Exploring Masculinities: Identity, Inequality, Continuity, and Change*. Ed. C.J. Pascoe and Tristan Bridges. New York: Oxford University Press, 2016. 107-120.

Kunitz, Stanley. "Stoddard, Charles Warren." *American Authors, 1600-1900*. New York: H.W. Wilson Company, 1938.

Law, Joe. "The 'Perniciously Homosexual Art': Music and Homoerotic Desire in *The Picture of Dorian Gray* and Other *fin-de-siècle* Fiction." *The Idea of Music in Victorian Fiction*. Ed. Sophie Fuller and Nicky Losseff. 2004. New York: Routledge, 2016. 173-196.

Levin, James. *The Gay Novel: The Male Homosexual Image in America*. New York: Irvington Publishers, 1983.

Levine, Paul. "Some Middle-Aged Fiction." *The Hudson Review*, 18.4 (Winter 1965-1966): 587-594.

Lilly, Mark. *Gay Men's Literature in the Twentieth Century*. London: Macmillan, 1993.

Livesey, Matthew J. "From this Moment On: The Homosexual Origins of the Gay Novel in America." Dissertation, University of Wisconsin-Madison, 1997. OCM 37797607.

Loftin, Craig M. "Unacceptable Mannerisms: Gender Anxieties, Homosexual Activism, and Swish in the United States, 1945-1965. *Journal of Social History* 40.3 (Spring 2007): 577-596.

Looby, Christopher. "The Gay Novel in the United States 1900-1950." *A Companion to the Modern American Novel 1900-1950*. Ed John T. Matthews. Oxford: Wiley-Blackwell, 2009. 414-436.

Looby, Christopher. "The Literariness of Sexuality: Or, How to Do the (Literary) History of (American) Sexuality. *American Literary History* 25.4 (2013): 841-854.

Looby, Christopher. "Sexuality's Aesthetic Dimensions: Kant and the *Autobiography of an Androgyne*." *American Literature's Aesthetic* Dimensions. Ed. Cindy Weinstein and Christopher Looby. New York: Columbia UP, 2012. 156-177.

Loughery, John. *The Other Side of Silence, Men's Lives and Gay Identities: A Twentieth-Century History*. New York, Henry Holt, 1998.

Makowski, John F. "Bisexual Orpheus: Pederasty and Parody in Ovid." *The Classical Journal* 92.1 (1996): 25–38.

Martin, Robert K. *The Homosexual Tradition in American Literature*. Austin, TX: U of Texas P, 1979. Print.

McElroy, Walter. "Anatomy of Conscience." *The New Masses,* Dec 1946, p. 20.

McGinty, Brian. "Charles Warren Stoddard: The Pleasure of His Company." *California Historical Quarterly* 52.2 (1973): 153-169.

McIntosh, Mary. "The Homosexual Role." *Social Problems* 16.2 (Autumn 1968): 182-192.

McRuer, Robert. *The Queer Renaissance: Contemporary American Literature and the Reinvention of Lesbian and Gay Identities.* New York: New York University Press, 1997.

Mencken, H.L. "The Flood of Fiction" *The Smart Set* 61 (1920): 141.

Messerschmidt, James W. "Masculinities as Structured Action." *Exploring Masculinities: Identity, Inequality, Continuity, and Change.* Ed. C.J. Pascoe and Tristan Bridges. New York: Oxford University Press, 2016. 207-219.

Meyers, Jeffrey. *Homosexuality & Literature: 1890-1930.* 1977. Atlantic Highlands, NJ: The Athlone Press, 1987.

Mitchell, Mark, and David Leavitt. *Pages Passed from Hand to Hand: The Hidden Tradition of Homosexual Literature in English from 1748 to 1914.* New York: Mariner Books, 1997.

Muñoz, José Esteban. "Feeling Brown, Feeling Down." *The Routledge Queer Studies Reader.* Ed. Donald E. Hall and Annamarie Jagose. New York: Routledge, 2013. 412-421.

Murphy, Peter Francis. *Fictions of Masculinity: Crossing Cultures, Crossing Sexualities.* New York: New York UP, 1994

Nealon, Christopher. *Foundlings: Lesbian and Gay Historical Emotion before Stonewall.* Durham, NC: Duke UP, 2001.

Nelson, Emmanuel S. "James Baldwin's Vision of Otherness and Community." *Critical Essays on James Baldwin.* Ed. Fred L. Standley and Nancy V. Burt. Boston: G.K. Hall & Co, 1988. 27-31.

Norton, Rictor. *The Myth of the Modern Homosexual: Queer History and the Search for Cultural Unity.* London: Cassell, 1997.

Park, Pauline. "GLAAD is Wrong on 'Transgender' vs. 'Transgendered.'" *Pauline Park: Gender Rights Advocate.* 8 April 2007. http://www.paulinepark.com/2011/03/glaad-is-wrong-on-transgender-vs-transgendered

Payne, William Morton. "Recent Fiction." *The Dial,* 1 Oct. 1903, pp. 154-156.

Pearson, Neil. "*A Scarlet Pansy*: Robert McAlmon's Secret Book." *Neil Pearson Rare Books*, 2016. http://www.neilpearsonrarebooks.com/books-and-articles/a-scarlet-pansy-robert-mcalmons-secret-book

Person, Leland S. "Middlesex: What Men Like in Men." *American Literary History* 17.4 (Winter 2005): 753-764.

Phillips, Thomas Hal. *The Bitterweed Path*. 1949. Chapel Hill: U North Carolina Press, 1996.

Preston, Keith. "'North of Chicago,' 'The Periscope.'" *Bertram Cope's Year*. Ed Joseph A. Dimuro. New York: Broadview, 2010. 281.

Prime-Stevenson, Edward I. *Imre: A Memorandum*. 1906. Ed. James Gifford. New York: Broadview, 2003.

Rabinowitz, Paula. *American Pulp: How Paperbacks Brought Modernism to Main Street*. Princeton, NJ: Princeton UP, 2014.

Radel, Nicholas F. "(E)Racing Edmund White: Queer Reading, Race, and Sexuality in *A Boy's Own Story*." *Modern Fiction Studies* 54.4 (Winter 2008): 766-790.

Raffalovich, Andre. "Review of Imre: A Memorandum," by Xavier Mayne. *Imre* by Edward Prime-Stevenson. 1906. Ed. James Gifford. New York: Broadview, 2003. 186-188.

Rascoe, Burton. "Review of Henry Blake Fuller's *Bertram Cope's Year*. *Bertram Cope's Year*. Ed. Joseph A. Dimuro. New York: Broadview, 2010: 276-277.

Raul, K.B. *Naked to the Night*. 1964. New York: Paperback Library, 1965.

Redman, Ben Ray. "A Cross Section of Current Fiction. *The American Mercury*, Feb 1947: 240-246.

"Robert Scully [Robert McAlmon] – *Scarlet Pansy*." *The Boo-Hooray Top 100 Counter-Culture Rarities*, 2016. http://www.counterculturerarities.com/boohooray-top-100/robert-scully-robert-mcalmon-scarlet-pansy

Rupp, Leila J. "Outlining the Past: U.S. Queer History in Global Perspective." *U.S. Lesbian, Gay, Bisexual, and Transgender History*. Ed Leila J. Rupp and Susan K. Freeman. Madison, WI: University of Wisconsin Press, 2014. 17-30.

Sarotte, Georges-Michel. *Like a Brother, Like a Lover: Male Homosexuality in the American Novel and Theatre from Herman Melville to James Baldwin*. 1976. New York: Doubleday, 1978.

Schavi, Michael R. "Teaching the 'Boys': Mart Crowley in the Millennial Classroom." *Modern Language Studies* 31.2 (2001): 75-90.

Schott, Webster. "Stephen Wolfe's Pilgrimage: *Totempole*." *New York Times*, 29 Aug. 1965, p. BR26.

Scully, Robert. *A Scarlet Pansy*. 1933. New York: Fordham University Press, 2016.

Sedgwick, Eve Kosofsky. *Between Men: English Literature and Male Homosocial Desire*. New York: Columbia UP, 1985.

Sedgwick, Eve Kosofsky. *Epistemology of the Closet*. 1990. Los Angeles: University of California Press, 2008.

See, Sam. "Making Modernism New: Queer Mythology in *The Young and Evil*." *ELH* 76.4 (Winter 2009): 1073-1105.

Seidler, Victor J. *Rediscovering Masculinity: Reason, Language, and Sexuality*. New York: Routledge, 1989.

Slide, Anthony. *Lost Gay Novels: A Reference Guide to Fifty Works from the First Half of the Twentieth Century*. New York: Harrington Park Press, 2013.

Smith, Harrison. "The Seed of Evil." *The Saturday Review*, Oct 1946: 12.

Sontag, Susan. "Notes on Camp." *Against Interpretation and Other Essays*. 1961. New York: Dell Publishing, 1966. 275-292.

Stein, Marc. *Rethinking the Gay and Lesbian Movement*. New York: Routledge, 2012.

Steward, James M. "Introduction." *Quatrefoil*. 1950. James Barr. Boston: Alyson, 1982. ix-xii.

Stoddard, Charles Warren. *For the Pleasure of His Company: An Affair of the Misty City*. San Francisco: Gay Sunshine Press, 1987.

Stryker, Susan. *Queer Pulp: Perverted Passions from the Golden Age of the Paperback*. San Francisco: Chronicle Books, 2001.

Sugrue, Thomas. "In Current Fiction: Louisiana Plantation." *New York Times*, 10 Sep 1950, p. 216.

Summers, Claude J. *The Gay and Lesbian Literary Heritage: A Reader's Companion to the Writers and their Works, from Antiquity to the Present*. New York: Henry Holt, 1995.

Sussman, Matt. "My Strange Affair with Fay Etrange." *Queerty.com,* 11 Oct 2006, https://www.queerty.com/words-on-homo-words-the-scarlet-pansy-2-20061011

Tarnoff, Ben. *The Bohemians: Mark Twain and the San Francisco Writers who Reinvented American Literature.* New York: Penguin, 2014.

Taylor, Bayard. *Joseph and His Friend: A Story of Pennsylvania.* New York: G.P. Putnam & Sons, 1870.

Tellier, Andre. *Twilight Men.* 1931. New York: Pyramid Books, 1957.

Tomlinson, Robert. "'Payin' One's Dues': Expatriation as Personal Experience and Paradigm in the Works of James Baldwin." *African American Review* 33.1 (1999): 135-148. Web.

"Totempole." *Kirkus Reviews*, 30 Aug. 1965, https://www.kirkusreviews.com/book-reviews/sanford-friedman/totempole/

"Totempole." *NYRB.com*, 2 Sept. 2014, https://www.nyrb.com/products/totempole.

Trilling, Dianma. "Fiction in Review." *The Nation*, Oct 1946, pp. 450-452.

Van Vechten, Carl. "Review of Henry Blake Fuller's *Bertram Cope's Year*." *Bertram Cope's Year*. Ed. Joseph A. Dimuro. New York: Broadview, 2010. 282-283.

Viereck, George Sylvester. *Men into Beasts.* New York: Fawcett Publication, 1952.

Wallace, Maurice. "Libidinal Intelligence: Shocks and Recognitions." *Novel Gazing: Queer Readings in Fiction.* Ed. Eve Kosofsky Sedgwick. Durham, NC: Duke University Press, 1997. 379-400.

Wasiolek, Edward. "The Sexual Drama of Nick and Gatsby." *The International Fiction Review* 19.1 (1992): 14-22.

Watson, Steven. Introduction. *The Young and Evil. The Young and the Evil.* 1933. New York: Masquerade Books, 1996. n.p.

Wilper, James. "Sexology, Homosexual History, and Walt Whitman: the 'Uranian' Identity in *Imre: A Memorandum.*" *Critical Survey* 22.3 (2010): 52-68. Web.

Wolmer, Bruce, and Charles Henri Ford. "Charles Henri Ford." *BOMB* 18 (Winter 1987): 54-57.

Woods, Gregory. *A History of Gay Literature: The Male Tradition.* New Haven, CT: Yale University Press, 1998.

Woods, Gregory. "Absurd! Ridiculous! Disgusting! Paradox in Poetry by Gay Men." *Lesbian and Gay Writing*. Ed. Mark Lilly. London: Macmillan, 1990: 175-198.

Woods, Gregory. *Homintern: How Gay Culture Liberated the Modern World*. New Haven, CT: Yale University Press, 2016.

Yingling, Thomas. "Reviewed Work(s): *For the Pleasure of His Company* by Charles Warren Stoddard: *Cruising the South Seas* by Charles Warren Stoddard and Winston Leyland." *American Literary Realism, 1870-1910* 21.3 (1989): 91-93.

Young, Ian. "The Paperback Explosion: How Gay Paperbacks Changed America." *The Golden Age of Gay Fiction*. Ed. Drewey Wayne Gunn. Albion, NY: MLR Press, 2009: 3-12.

Made in the USA
San Bernardino, CA
28 July 2019